Vulnerable Groups in Health and Social Care

Vulnerable Groups in Health and Social Care

Mary Larkin

Los Angeles | London | New Delhi
Singapore | Washington DC

First published 2009
Reprinted 2011

SAGE Publications Ltd
1 Oliver's Yard
55 City Road
London EC1Y 1SP

SAGE Publications Inc.
2455 Teller Road
Thousand Oaks, California 91320

SAGE Publications India Pvt Ltd
B 1/I 1 Mohan Cooperative Industrial Area
Mathura Road
New Delhi 110 044

SAGE Publications Asia-Pacific Pte Ltd
33 Pekin Street #02-01
Far East Square
Singapore 048763

Library of Congress Control Number: 2008932893

British Library Cataloguing in Publication data

A catalogue record for this book is available from the British Library

ISBN 978-1-4129-4823-4
ISBN 978-1-4129-4824-1 (pbk)

Typeset by C&M Digitals (P) Ltd, Chennai, India
Printed in Great Britain by the MPG Books Group
Printed on paper from sustainable resources.

For Shaun, Ruth and Matt

Contents

List of Illustrations

FIGURES

TABLES

Introducing Vulnerable Groups

OVERVIEW

- The meaning of 'vulnerable' and 'vulnerability'
- The definition of 'vulnerable groups' used in this book
- The concepts of social exclusion and citizenship and their implications for policies directed at vulnerable groups
- Outline of the content and format of the book
- Suggestions for further exploration of issues addressed in the chapter

THE CONCEPT OF 'VULNERABLE'

Although the word 'vulnerable' is now widely used in health and social care, its precise definition remains elusive. This is partly because of its universality and dynamism in that everyone becomes or feels vulnerable to a greater or lesser extent at different times in their lives (Rogers, 1997; Pritchard, 2001). There are also many other reasons. These include the fact that it has a variety of meanings, such as that a person is in danger, at risk, under threat, susceptible to problems, helpless, and in need of protection and/support (Rogers, 1997; Sloboda, 1999; Spiers, 2000; Mawby, 2004; Grundy, 2006; Simpson, 2006). Its meaning also varies according to the context in which it is used. For instance, the Department of Health regards an adult as being 'vulnerable' when he/she is 'unable to take care of him or herself' (DOH, 2000, Section 2.3). In contrast, within youth justice the concept has more of a gatekeeping purpose and refers to those who have an enhanced risk of suicide, self-harm or harming others (Smith, 2007). The overlap between the concept 'vulnerable' and other categories such as victim, troubled, troublesome is problematic (Goldson, 2002). In addition, there are different types of vulnerability; innate/person vulnerability is unique to the person concerned. Terms such as structural/contextual/environmental vulnerability are used to indicate when the particular circumstances in which a person is situated render them vulnerable (Rogers, 1997; Goldson, 2002). A distinction has also been made between emic and etic vulnerability; the former refers to the experience of being vulnerable whereas the latter involves the identification of demographic factors that lead to some groups being at a higher risk of health and social problems (Spiers, 2000).

A definition of 'vulnerable' is further complicated by the way vulnerability can be shaped by many interacting influences such as individual perceptions, and situational, social, historical, political and cultural factors (Rogers, 1997; Spiers, 2000; Pritchard, 2001; Goldson, 2002; Dixon-Woods et al., 2005).

VULNERABLE GROUPS

Thus the concept of 'vulnerable' is relative and open to interpretation. As a consequence, the term 'vulnerable group' is similarly contestable. There is little explicit definition of 'vulnerable groups' in the literature, and, when this does occur, the groups vary. For instance, Rogers (1997) defines those groups in society who are more likely to be vulnerable to ill health as the 'very young and very old people, women, racial minorities, those who have little social support, those with little education, those who earn a low income and those who are unemployed' (Rogers, 1997: 66). In contrast, Spiers (2000) says that vulnerable groups in healthcare include 'the elderly, children, the poor, people with chronic illnesses and people from minority cultures, foetuses and members of captive populations, such as prisoners and refugees' (Spiers, 2000: 716). Researchers focus on particular vulnerable groups for the purposes of their own study. An example is Dixon-Wood et al's (2005) work on access to healthcare by vulnerable groups. This study focused on socio-economically disadvantaged (less wealthy) people, people from a black and minority ethnic background, children and older people. Similarly, Sanatana (2002) in her study of inequalities in access to healthcare in Portugal adopts a less specific approach; she argues that the most vulnerable groups in Portuguese society are 'those affected by poverty, deprivation and social exclusion' (Sanatana, 2002: 33).

Analysis of other sources, such as policy documents, shows that the definition of a 'vulnerable group' varies according to context. For instance, with reference to homelessness, Shelter identifies older people, people with mental health problems, drug users, female sex workers and gypsies and travellers as being 'vulnerable groups' (Shelter, 2007a). For the purposes of the Safeguarding Vulnerable Groups Bill (2006) the criteria used to define a vulnerable adult are being in receipt of health and social care, living in sheltered housing, requiring assistance in the conduct of their affairs, in prison or in contact with the probation service, detained under Immigration Act powers, and involved in certain activities targeted at vulnerable adults, such as some forms of education and training (House of Commons, 2006).

In addition, the concept of a 'vulnerable group' varies between theoretical perspectives; **feminism** would argue a consequence of patriarchy is that women are a more vulnerable group in society than men. A Marxist perspective according to **Marxist theory** would attribute the vulnerability of workers in low-paid jobs to ill health and work-related deaths to capitalist employment practices. Any attempt to define a 'vulnerable group' is further complicated by the fact that group members have multiple identities, lack homogeneity and membership of any group may be transient (Rogers, 1997; Goldson, 2002; White, 2002). For example a young homeless person can be unemployed and be experiencing mental health problems. He/she may also be temporarily homeless because he/she has just left care.

DEFINITION OF 'VULNERABLE GROUPS' USED IN THIS BOOK

These discussions therefore show that the definition of a 'vulnerable group' is flexible, refers to a wide range of people, and depends on the context in which it is used with many definitions only being applicable to areas of research and specific issues. Moreover, the concept is problematic and there is no universally accepted definition of a 'vulnerable group'. Consequently, a definition was developed that both engaged with the different aspects of the concept highlighted above and clearly related to the purpose of this book.

Over the past ten years, New Labour has produced a raft of policies that specifically use the words 'vulnerable groups' and are aimed at groups who are deemed to be 'vulnerable' in contemporary United Kingdom society. A recent example of such legislation is the Safeguarding Vulnerable Groups Bill (2006) that has already been mentioned. An analysis of these policies shows that a variety of criteria have been used in the construction of groups as being 'vulnerable'. These are based on the ways in which they are marginalized, socially excluded, have limited opportunities and income, and suffer abuse (physical, sexual, psychological and financial), hardship, prejudice and discrimination. Such groups include lone parents, people with disabilities, older people, children, ethnic minority groups, those living with a mental illness, the homeless, and asylum seekers and refugees.

The determination to address the needs of these groups is particularly illustrated by the focus on eliminating **social exclusion.** This has been defined as 'a shorthand term for what can happen when people or areas suffer from a combination of linked problems such as unemployment, poor skills, low incomes, poor housing, high crime environments, bad health and family breakdown' (Social Exclusion Unit, 2002). Social exclusion occurs because of the way that these problems are linked, mutually reinforce each other and are clustered in particular areas/neighbourhoods, which can lead to the creation of 'a vicious cycle in people's lives' (Social Exclusion Unit, 2004a: 7) unless there is effective intervention. It is also linked to multiple disadvantages that individuals face at birth and has been shown to persist from one generation to another. Several causes and consequences of social exclusion have been identified. These are 'poverty and low income; unemployment, poor educational attainment; poor mental and physical health; family breakdown and poor parenting; poor housing and homelessness; discrimination; crime; and living in a disadvantaged area' (Social Exclusion Unit, 2004a: 7).

The concept of social exclusion has displaced terms such as 'deprivation' and 'inequality' and is now 'firmly entrenched' (Levitas, 2006: 123) in both British and European Union policy. New Labour embraced it vigorously soon after its election to its first term in government in 1997; it promised 'inclusive politics' and set up the Social Exclusion Unit. This aimed to prevent the exclusion of vulnerable groups (such as those mentioned above) from full participation in society, ensure that mainstream services are delivered for everyone, and reintegrate people who had fallen through the net. The emphasis has been on addressing both the structural causes and individual causes of social exclusion. An example of the former is deprivation that has been transmitted across generations, and factors that have led to individuals not taking advantage of the opportunities available to them are an example of the latter (Deacon, 2002).

Many policies have ensued from this political determination to eliminate social exclusion. Among the most notable are the **welfare-to-work** policies. The philosophy behind these is that the answer to poverty and social exclusion lies in work not welfare, and that as many people as possible should move from benefits into work. This is summarised in the much-quoted statement 'Work for those who can, support for those who can't' (Blair, 1998: 3). One of the initiatives that embodies this approach is the New Deal strategy, which aims to give those who are on out-of-work benefits the help and support that they need to get into paid employment. There are several packages aimed a different groups, such as those over 50, disabled people and lone parents. Everyone on a New Deal programme is allocated a personal advisor who is their point of contact throughout the programme. The personal advisor takes the time to understand each applicant, explains their options and helps them to find a suitable job. These New Deal packages will be addressed as and when their target groups are discussed in this book.

Since the General Election in 2001 social exclusion has been even more at the heart of government. The posts of Minister for Social Exclusion and

Parliamentary Secretary for Social Exclusion have been created. The drive to help disadvantaged groups who have unique and complex needs gathered momentum in 2004, with more policies to address the needs of those groups that are 'harder to reach and last to benefit from policies' (Social Exclusion Unit, 2004b: 6) and experience 'deep exclusion' (Levitas et al., 2007). Indeed, the Social Exclusion Unit was closed down in 2006 and its work transferred to a taskforce in the Cabinet Office. This task-force is responsible for ensuring that government departments focus on the '2.5 per cent of every generation ... stuck in a lifetime of disadvan-tage' (Cabinet Office, 2006: 3) who are the most severely vulnerable and have been immune to previous social exclusion initiatives. It evaluates and revises polices with the aim of embedding social exclusion work more deeply in relevant departments, such as health, education and communities (Deacon, 2002; Social Exclusion Taskforce, 2007).

Another concept that has simultaneously attained significance within political discourse is **citizenship**. New Labour's construction of this con-cept has had a direct influence on its approach to the social inclusion of vulnerable groups (Craig, 2004; Kidger, 2004; Lunt, 2006; Rummery, 2006). In order to explain the effects of this influence, it is necessary to briefly discuss citizenship and its interpretation by New Labour.

Although it has existed within political thought in the Western world from the eighteenth century, its popularity has waxed and waned. It has re-emerged in political and academic discourses in Europe, Canada, and the United States since the late twentieth century. Not only is it complex and multidimensional, but there are also many contested versions of citizenship, and what it means to be a citizen. The main dimensions of the contemporary approach to citizenship can be summarised as follows: all those who are full members of society have equal status. The conferment of this status on indi-viduals is referred to as citizenship, and from it ensues feelings of self-worth, national belonging and identity. It also locates individuals in a series of legal and social relationships with other individuals and with the state. These rela-tionships involve both equal rights and obligations. In terms of relationships between individuals, individual citizens are seen as being affectively con-nected with others with whom they share citizenship. This connectivity gen-erates mutual concern and solidarity, which in turn entail rights and obligations between fellow citizens. With respect to the relationship between individual citizens and the state, the status of citizenship means that indi-viduals have certain rights; they are accorded a nationality and can make legitimate claims on the state (Lister, 1997, 1998; Lewis, 2004). Marshall (1992), whose work formed the basis of a theory of citizenship in postwar Britain, held that this relationship between the individual and the state entails three types of rights: *civil citizenship* refers to the right to individual freedom, such as the freedom of speech, thought, faith and the right to justice. *Political citizenship* is the right to exercise political power, whether this is as a member of the public or as an elected member of a body that has political power. The third element is *social citizenship*. This ranges from the right to economic security and welfare to the right to be able to participate in 'civilised society according to the standards prevailing in society' (Marshall, 1992: 8). In return for these rights from the state, individuals have certain obligations and duties in that they are expected to behave in ways that promote good citizenship. Examples of these are duties to obey the law, ensure that your children are educated, pay taxes and undertake jury service when required (Lister, 1997, 1998; Powell, 2000; Deacon, 2002; Lewis, 2004).

As indicated above, the whole issue of citizenship is controversial, and even though it has political currency once more, criticisms still abound. For instance, it has been argued that it is exclusionary in relation to age, gender, sexual orientation, class, ethnicity and disability. Its unstable nature and the fluidity of its boundaries have also been highlighted (Lister, 1997, 1998; Lewis, 2004). Nonetheless, the main political parties have incorporated it into their discourses; Conservatism adopted some aspects of citizenship in the 1980s and 1990s and themes such as self-reliant citizenship featured in their policies. However, in general the emphasis was more on citizens' rights as opposed to obligations, as illustrated by the Citizen's Charter (1991). Indeed, Lister (1998) argues that the Conservative conception of rights was both market-orientated and consumerist, reflecting the depoliticised and individualistic nature of the relationship between the state and the individual at that time. This sort of view was echoed in many academic and political circles with concerns about 'dutiless rights' being expressed.

When New Labour came to power in 1997, it not only embraced but also transformed the concept; it has been much more explicit in its advocacy of citizenship and has emphasised individuals' obligations. A key theme has been that there is a contract or partnership between the state and individuals with mutual obligations on each side. As part of their rights to the citizenship that the state is obliged to grant them, individuals are expected to ensure social order and cohesion by showing personal responsibility and fulfilling their social obligations as citizens. This includes their duties to each other as citizens, being responsible parents and community members, and undertaking paid work. Different types of citizenship to represent the range of obligations we have as citizens have also emerged within political and academic discourses. Examples are environmental citizenship to indicate our responsibility to protect our environment, and active citizenship which refers to our responsibility to give some of our private time to participating in community activity, such as voluntary work (Deacon, 2002; Lister, 1998, 2003; Parker, 1998; Lewis, 2004).

New Labour's approach to social exclusion reflects this interpretation of citizenship; the right to full participation and inclusion in society and the associated enjoyment of the status of citizenship is not automatic but conditional on fulfilling certain obligations. Consequently, preconditions have been attached to many of the routes offered out of social exclusion.

This reframing of social issues, such as vulnerable groups, in terms of inclusion and within the language of citizenship is not exclusive to this country; it has been a 'major trend in western nation states' (Invernezzi and Williams, 2008: x) over the last decade. However, there are many debates about the effectiveness of the obligations and preconditions in New Labour's policies to address essential aspects of social exclusion. These will be addressed in the chapters on the specific vulnerable groups concerned in more detail; recurring criticisms centre around New Labour's increasing shift towards an employment-based citizenship and the primacy it has placed on paid work as a precondition for addressing the social exclusion of vulnerable groups. Consequently, the concept of citizenship will be returned to on many occasions during the course of the book.

   To conclude this discussion of an appropriate definition of 'vulnerable groups', this book will focus on the groups identified above as having been constructed as 'vulnerable'. Therefore, the 'vulnerable groups' who are the subject of this book are those groups who are and have been politically constructed as 'vulnerable' through government policies.

USING THIS BOOK

The very nature of the concept of vulnerable means that those in the aforementioned 'vulnerable groups' are more likely to have multiple, rather than discrete sets of vulnerabilities. For instance, childhood is not the only cause of a child's vulnerability; ethnicity, belonging to a lone-parent family and the mental illness of a parent can also be significant factors. As this book aims to enable the reader to identify and understand the health and social care needs of selected 'vulnerable groups' in society, each chapter will focus on the key issues for one particular group from a broadly social science perspective. While repetition will be avoided, examples of overlapping vulnerabilities will be acknowledged where appropriate. Although these groups now have a high profile in health and social care courses, relevant, contemporary information and material about them is time-consuming to research because it is currently only available from numerous disparate sources and organisations. Therefore the chapters in this book will also draw on the wide range of literature about each of the groups and the reference list should be a resource in itself. The groups are as follows:

- lone parents;
- people with disabilities;
- older people;
- children;
- ethnic minority groups;
- the mentally ill;
- the homeless;
- asylum seekers and refugees.

In order to provide the reader with a clear and comprehensive overview of health and social care issues for each group, the chapters will address a range of relevant models, concepts and theoretical perspectives and cover three main areas; one main area is the key concepts, definitions and statistical data required to gain an understanding of the group that is the subject of the chapter. Another is those needs and experiences of the group under discussion that contribute to their vulnerability. The third main area is the trends in policy responses to the groups. Reference will be made to specific policies to illustrate these trends. The same terminology may not be used to denote these three main areas and they will not necessarily be addressed in the same order in each chapter. The data and policy references will be as up to date as possible at the time of going to press.

The intention is that the chapters can be read independently, although it is suggested that readers familiarise themselves with the overall approach taken in the book as set out in this introductory chapter before starting any of the other chapters. While the emphasis will be on the contemporary United Kingdom, material presented and discussed will be located in its historical, European and wider international context as and when appropriate. A brief outline of the content of each chapter is set out below.

Chapter 1 – Lone parents

This chapter will discuss the increase in lone parents, the nature of their experiences and the causes of their vulnerability. The policies aimed at lone parents will be outlined and evaluated.

Chapter 2 – People with disabilities

The arguments that disability is socially constructed will be discussed at the beginning of the chapter. The problems experienced by those in this vulnerable group will then be explored, followed by an analysis of recent approaches to addressing their needs.

Chapter 3 – Older people

The length of this chapter reflects the growing body of literature about this vulnerable group; after examining the concept of an 'ageing society', this chapter moves on to examine the experiences of ageing and old age. Both recent and planned initiatives aimed at reducing the vulnerabilities of older people are also considered in relation to the evidence presented.

Chapter 4 – Children

This chapter starts by looking at the changes in the construction of childhood and the growing national and international concerns about children's vulnerability. It then discusses and assesses some of the many policy initiatives that have been produced as a result of these concerns.

Chapter 5 – Ethnic minority groups

The extent of the inequalities still experienced by many of those in this vulnerable group in our society is a major theme in this chapter. Definitions of race, ethnicity and ethnic minority groups are discussed before the chapter looks at the evidence of these inequalities and their relationship to racial divisions. Existing policies and approaches are then evaluated in the light of current research.

Chapter 6 – The mentally ill

The various explanations and theoretical perspectives about mental illness are explored at the beginning of this chapter. Discussion of the nature of the vulnerability and the extent of the social exclusion of those living with a mental illness is followed by a critical evaluation of the initiatives that have been introduced to increase the inclusion of this group in society.

Chapter 7 – The homeless

The many different types and causes of homelessness are explained in the first part of this chapter. It then moves on to consider what life is like without a home. The second half of the chapter discusses the nature of support available to the homeless, the implications of recent policy changes and possible directions for future initiatives.

Chapter 8 – Asylum seekers and refugees

The concepts of 'asylum seeker' and 'refugee' are clarified at the beginning of this chapter. The exploration of the extent of the vulnerability of asylum seekers and refugees both upon arrival and when living in this country that follows shows how this can lead to their marginalisation and social exclusion. The impact and effectiveness of past and current policies are also considered.

Chapter 9 – Concluding comments: the future for vulnerable groups in health and social care

This final chapter gives a brief overview of the main arguments in the book in relation to the concepts of vulnerability, social exclusion and citizenship. It then makes some recommendations about future approaches to addressing the social exclusion of vulnerable groups.

This concentration on the three main themes outlined above will also give students the breadth of information about these groups that they require. Those students who wish to deepen their knowledge will be able to independently explore the extensive range of literature cited in each chapter. In addition, there will be suggestions about points for further discussion and study (see below).

CHAPTER FEATURES

The aim will be to make the text as readable and interactive as possible. Features will include:

- An overview of the main topics to be addressed at the beginning of each chapter.
- Key concepts will be highlighted in the text on their first appearance and clearly outlined in the glossary at the end of the book. The glossary is designed to provide relevant understandings for those with differing levels of social science knowledge. It can also serve for reference purposes.
- Activities based on extracts from primary sources (for example, case studies, historical documents, newspaper articles, policy documents and statistical data). Where appropriate, post-activity comments to help the reader reflect on his/her work on the activities are set out at the end of chapters. Some can also be enlisted and/or adapted by lecturers and tutors for workshops and classroom discussions. The presentation of these activities is designed to reinforce and support students' learning as opposed to being essential to the main text in each chapter. They are easily identified as they are presented in boxes and can be omitted by those students who do not require them and they feature:
  - o links with other chapters highlighted;
  - o tables, diagrams and graphs;
  - o discussion points for either individual study or teaching purposes;
  - o suggestions for further study and reading, plus web resources.

FURTHER STUDY

A visit to the Social Exclusion Taskforce website is useful if you want to gain a deeper understanding of its philosophy and current initiatives to address the needs of vulnerable groups in health and social care. For further insights into citizenship, it's worth reading Marshall's seminal (1992) essay 'Citizenship and social class' and Chapter 1 in Lewis (2004). Lister's work provides interesting criticisms of this concept, particularly New Labour's use of this and its exclusionary powers (Lister, 1997, 1998, 2003).

Chapter 1
Lone Parents

OVERVIEW

- The increase in lone-parent families
- Defining lone parent familes
- Lone parents' life experiences
- Lone parents as a political issue
- The political ideologies of the New Right and New Labour
- The New Right and lone parents
- New Labour and lone parents
- Evaluation of recent policies
- Conclusions
- Suggestions for further study

INTRODUCTION

Even before the recent focus on vulnerable groups, lone parents were frequently discussed in the media and in political circles, particularly in connection with concerns about changes in traditional family structures and how these may threaten social stability and cohesion. They have also found themselves at the centre of certain controversies, for example, about mothering, the rights of fathers, benefit dependency and the allocation of council housing. Some lone parents, such as teenage mothers, have been stigmatised more than others.

The number of lone parents has tripled since the 1970s and there are now 1.8 million lone-parent families in Britain. This represents one-quarter of all families, who care for a total of 3 million children. Britain has the highest proportion of lone-parent households in Europe (Chambaz, 2001; National Statistics, 2007a). The extent of lone parents' vulnerability has featured in many policy documents on social exclusion, most notably those on the promotion of paid work and the eradication of poverty. This chapter will explore some of the key issues in relation to the social and political concerns about lone parents. These are their experiences, the costs of supporting them and the different approaches reflected in the political initiatives directed at them. As 90 per cent of lone parents are women, the focus in the discussions will mainly be on lone mothers. However, lone fathers will be addressed to illustrate particular points as appropriate.

DEFINING LONE-PARENT FAMILIES

For official and statistical purposes a **lone-parent family** is usually defined as a divorced, separated, single or widowed mother or father living without a spouse (and not cohabiting) with his or her never-married dependent child or children. The reality is that definitional precision is elusive. One reason is that, as already indicated, there are many different routes into lone parenthood. These are divorce, separation, having a child as a teenager or during adulthood without having a partner or being married, and the death of a partner or spouse. Another variable is that, although nine out of ten lone parents are female, lone parents do include both men and women. The final complicating factor is that lone parenthood can be transitional. A summary of the changes in family structure that have occurred in recent decades is required in order to fully explain this factor. One such change is that there has been a move away from traditional **nuclear** and **extended families** and an increase in lone parents and **reconstituted families**. The latter constitute household units that include a step-parent as a consequence of divorce, separation and remarriage. This type of family is created when a new partnership is formed by a mother and/or father who already have dependent children. Since most children remain with their mother following divorce or separation, most stepfamilies have a stepfather rather than a stepmother. The fluid boundary between these two types of family means that being a lone parent is often a temporary, albeit recurring, stage in parenthood; Ermisch and Francesconi (2000) found that, although about 40 per cent of mothers will spend some time as a lone parent, the duration of lone parenthood is often short, with one-half remaining lone parents for 4.6 years or less. A reason for this is that about three-quarters of these lone parents will form a stepfamily. However, over one-quarter of stepfamilies dissolve within one year, leading to lone parenthood once more (Stewart and Vaitilingham, 2004). Indeed Levitas et al. (2006) argue that some lone parents do not 'think of themselves as such' because they 'may have a variety of different (and shifting) relationships with partners or ex-partners living elsewhere' (Levitas et al., 2006: 408).

THE EXPERIENCES OF LONE PARENTS

ACTIVITY 1.1

The following case studies of lone parents illustrate some of the more negative experiences that lone parents share. Note the experiences that are highlighted as you read. Some suggestions are set out at the end of the chapter. These and other experiences are discussed in more detail in the main text below.

Kirsty's story

Kirsty's own mother developed severe mental health problems during adolescence and she still struggles with her health problems. Her relationships with her four children's fathers were all transient and on a co-habiting basis only. Indeed, Kirsty never knew her own father. During her childhood, when she was not living in temporary accommodation with her mother and other siblings, she was in care.

Kirsty is now 21 and had her first child at 16. She left school before completing her GCSEs and gave birth to her second child at 18. Her children's father left over two years ago and contact is intermittent.

When she became a mother, Kirsty decided that her priorities were being with her children and doing her best for them. She has tried to make a home for the children in the council flat that she was given. However, it is very cold and damp and in need of extensive redecoration. Although she manages her benefit money very carefully, the family diet is limited, with chips and peas often on the menu as the main meal and Kirsty missing meals herself. She has a persistent cough and the youngest child is frequently admitted to hospital with respiratory problems. Visiting her mother involves an hour's bus journey. Her nearest friend is two bus rides away, and when they can afford to get together, they do support each other and

(Continued)

share in activities with the children. Both reported that they and their prams were often watched suspiciously in department stores by security guards when they were trying on clothes during shopping trips.

Annabelle's story

Annabelle has three children and struggled for years to save her marriage. However, her husband was frequently unfaithful and often drank to excess. This drinking meant that he was regularly unemployed, and she ended the relationship when she found that he had squandered their savings on socialising and their house was repossessed.

She is a fully qualified physiotherapist and immediately returned to work after they separated After three years, she managed to buy the council house that she and the children were allocated. Her husband refused to contribute financially to the family and successfully resisted all attempts by the Child Support Agency to track him down. Managing the mortgage and all the other financial outgoings was a huge strain on her. In addition, one of the children suffers from severe asthma and often has to miss school. Despite the fact that several friends were always willing to help and provide her with an, albeit limited, social life, she began to feel very depressed and unable to cope. She took the decision to move back to her home town to be near her parents and sister.

Unfortunately, the difference in house prices between the two areas has meant that since moving she has struggled even more financially. Furthermore, she could only afford a ground floor flat with a shared garden. The children have become more fractious because of the limited space they have at home and the move to new schools. The eldest one in particular seems to feel the changes in their lives most, and has developed behaviour problems which her school are also concerned about. Her parents have recently announced that they cannot cope with the children and her sister has taken up full-time employment.

She has not had the time to develop friendships with other mothers and therefore does not have the sort of social support from friends that she had benefited from in the town where she used to live. Moreover, her social life is now non-existent. Her health has deteriorated and she feels that she has no choice but to take the antidepressants that her GP has offered to help her cope with her everyday life.

As demonstrated in the first section of the chapter, there are considerable variations between lone parents. Nonetheless, both British and international research has shown that lone parents have many negative, often interconnected, experiences in common. These are discussed below.

Poverty

With the exception of Scandinavian countries, lone parents in Europe – whether single, separated or divorced – have been consistently shown to have higher poverty rates than average. Indeed lone parents, particularly teenage lone parents, are more likely to be poor than any other type of family and up to 52% of children in lone-parent families were classified as 'poor'. This is either because lone parents work part-time or are in low-waged jobs supplemented by benefits, or because they are out of work and claim income support. Lone mothers are most likely to be poor, as they are less likely to be in employment than lone fathers. (Chambaz, 2001; Sanatana, 2002; Stewart and Vaitilingham, 2004; Gardiner and Millar, 2006; Levitas, 2006).

Poorer diets

One of the consequences of the high rates of poverty among lone-parent families is that their diets seem to be poorer. Dowler and Calvert (1995) showed that about a fifth of the lone parents in their study had low nutrition intakes and were more likely to have unhealthy diets. This was despite efforts to be creative and careful when it came to budgeting and shopping for food. Those that had the poorest diets tended to deprive themselves of good food in order to protect their children from the worst nutritional consequences of poverty. Interestingly, ethnicity is an important factor: those who followed diets that are typical of black British or Afro-Caribbean families tended to eat more nutritionally than those eating meals that are typical of white families.

Social isolation

Lone mothers and lone fathers are both more likely to feel excluded from social participation than parents who live in couples. There are several possible reasons for this, for instance, they may be unable to take part in social activities. Although this was mainly attributed to lack of money, time did also curtail lone-parent participation in socialising (Meadows and Grant, 2005). In addition to no longer being able to take part in social activities with their peers, teenage mothers cited the fact that they may be housed a long way from their existing support networks and experience unsupportive relationships with the father of the child as other reasons for feeling socially isolated (Kidger, 2004).

Although they may feel socially isolated, with the exception of teenage lone mothers, lone mothers tend to have good **social networks** and **social support** systems; they have more contact with family and friends than most other members of the population. However, this support tends to be emotional and financial rather than practical (Dench, 2006; Levitas, 2006).

Health

Lone parents, but lone mothers more so than lone fathers, and children in lone-parent families are more likely to have poorer physical and pyschological health in Britain and other European Union countries (Whitehead et al., 2000; Butterworth, 2004; Levitas, 2006). Popay and Jones (1990) argue that this is because lone fathers tend to to have older children and are more likely to get help from others. However, other studies have contradicted these findings about the differences in health between lone mothers and lone fathers. For instance, Weitoft et al. (2004) found that lone fathers (along with childless men, with or without partners) are at a higher risk of injury, addiction, all-cause mortality, and ischaemic heart disease than other groups.

Several studies have linked the poorer health of lone parents to their higher poverty rates (Sanatana, 2002). However, factors other than poverty in lone-parents' lives have been identified; the stress of being the sole parent, a lack of control over their lives and the relative lack of social support can all contribute to poorer physical and mental health (Berkman and Syme, 1979; Berkman et al., 2000; Whitehead et al., 2000; National Statistics, 2007a). Others studies have found that lone parents are more likely to be at risk of ill health because of their health-related behaviour. For instance, smoking rates among lone parents are higher than among parents living together (Rajkonen et al., 2005).

Stigma

Teenage mothers have received the most negative political and media attention *but* only 3 per cent of lone parents are teenagers – the average age of a lone parent is 35. Studies have identified other more specific areas in which teenage lone mothers are likely to be stigmatised; Breheny and Stephens (2007) found that health professionals (such as doctors, midwives and nurses) constructed teenage mothers as problematic, and this **stigma** had negative implications for the quality of their healthcare.

Educational attainment

Although young lone parenthood has been found to limit a person's chances of completing their education and gaining a well-paid job, recent studies have started to present evidence to the contrary. These studies have shown that, with the right support, many teenage parents do re-engage with education, and progress well in terms of gaining qualifications and enhancing their ability to compete effectively in the labour market (Brown and Hosie, 2005; Dench, 2006). Such findings have been linked to some of the research about the positive impacts of parenthood on teenagers' lives identified in the literature. These include the way it gives disadvantaged teenagers a sense of identity and fulfillment (Whitehead et al., 2000; Breheny and Stephens, 2007).

Children of lone parents

Children in lone-parent familes have a greater risk of lower educational achievement, ill health, unemployment, becoming homeless and getting involved in crime (Ram and Hou, 2003). Once again, these problems have been linked to the low incomes of lone-parent families (Sanatana, 2002). In contrast, Adamson (2007) recently found no relationship between overall child well-being and lone parenthood.

Housing

Lone parents have worse housing than other types of parents; they are more likely to experience problems with their accommodation, such as lack of space inside and outside, damp, rot, mould, lack of light and a poor state of decoration. They account for nearly half (43 per cent) of all those in temporary accommodation, whereas couples with dependent children account for only 26 per cent, and represent the biggest group living in temporary accommodation. They are also heavily dependent on rented housing and on rented social housing in particular; Table 1.1 shows that half of lone-parent households with dependent children in Great Britain live in rented social sector housing compared with one in seven households containing a couple with dependent children. This dependence on rented housing can limit their choice as to where they live, which can mean that they are also far from friends and other family members (Millar and Rowlingson, 2001; Levitas, 2006; Department of Communities and Local Government, 2007a; National Statistics, 2007a).

Interconnections between lone parents' experiences illustrated in these discussions include the way that their general lack of income can lead to a limited social life, poorer health and lower-quality housing than other families. Findings about the impact of lone parenthood on life experiences have also led to debates in the literature about their relationship

Table 1.1   Household composition, percentages by tenure, Great Britain, 2005

	Owned outright	Owned with mortgage	Privately rented	Rented from social sector
One person				
Under pensionable age	18	39	20	22
Over pensionable age	58	4	6	33
One-family households				
Couple:				
No children	46	35	9	10
Dependent children	8	70	8	14
Non-dependent children only	35	52	2	10
Lone parent				
Dependent children	6	29	14	52
Non-dependent children only	42	29	6	33
Other households	20	22	44	14
All households	30	38	12	20

Source: Adapted from National Statistics, 2007a

to the concept of **underclass**. This is because some of their characteristics, such as low income, poor housing and benefit dependency, correlate with the characteristics of other groups regarded as being part of the underclass. Although those who have made associations between this vulnerable group and the underclass have been criticised because it carries strong connotations of blame, any comparison with this concept signifies a recognition of the extent of lone parents' vulnerability (Morris, 1998).

POLICIES AIMED AT LONE PARENTS

Both Conservative and New Labour governments' have targeted lone parents. This section will outline their political ideologies and show how these were/are reflected in their policies.

Although the increase in those identified as lone parents, the number of children and recognition of the vulnerability of both the parents and children involved has attracted the attention of policy-makers, the costs of supporting lone-parent families have received the most attention. These became a big political issue in the 1990s when it became apparent that expenditure on benefit claims for lone parents in the 1990s was double that of the 1980s and it was increasing; in 1995 lone parents cost the welfare state £9.1 billion in benefit claims and £10 billion in 1997. As reducing public expenditure has been a priority for both Conservative and New Labour governments, such rising costs became a cause for concern. However, the political ideologies that influenced each government have meant that their approaches to lone parents have differed.

Conservative government policy in the 1980s and 1990s was influenced by the political ideology of the New Right. Although there are discontinuities within this ideology, there were some common themes. Key tenets of this ideology were its emphasis on a smaller role for the state, greater emphasis on the rights of the individual and individual choice, greater role for markets, with the removal of impediments for the operation of the free market. This was combined with strong beliefs in individual responsibility, the social and moral order, 'traditional family life' and appropriate sexuality. In relation to welfare, the welfare anti-statism and emphasis on **individualism** and **consumerism** that ensued essentially meant that there was a move away from the collective provision of welfare by the 'nanny state' that was reliant upon excessive taxation towards more privatised and market-style provision, cost reductions, financial accountability, and encouragement of the voluntary sector. There was also an emphasis on individual responsibility. This was known as 'new public management' (Baggott, 1998; Carabine, 2001).

When a Labour government came to power in 1997, it called both itself and its approach New Labour. This was distinctive from previous Labour governments and is also referred to as the 'Third Way'. It is influenced by communitarian ideology, which has also been influential in other parts of the Western world, such as in the United States. There is much diversity within this ideology and it is the 'responsive communitarianism' that has emerged since the 1980s that has been incorporated into New Labour thinking. This has strong moral and ethical elements, is opposed to the individualism of the New Right, and stresses common interests and common values arising from communal bonds. While it does emphasise the responsibilities of the state and the rights of individuals, it also emphasises the social responsibilities of individual citizens, families and communities. Indeed families are viewed as essential in the transmission of moral values to and support of their members. Communities are seen as vital units of social organisation with shared moral values, and as a means for ensuring social cohesion (Johnson, 2000; Powell, 2000; Deacon, 2002).

The adoption of communitarianism by New Labour governments has had several implications for welfare provision. One is that New Labour is against purely individualistic conceptions of welfare. Therefore, a dominant theme has been the obligations as well as the rights of welfare recipients, with welfare benefits being conditional on the demonstration of individual and social responsibility. Inherent in this are moralistic and judgmental themes, and an overall aim of shaping individual values and characters to produce an increased sense of individual responsibility and social concern. In order to pursue a welfare agenda that embodies communitarianism in this way, it has been necessary for New Labour to persuade voters that everyone will benefit and that policies serve social and communal needs.

However, ambiguities in New Labour's appeal to communitarianism have been identified; Chamberlynne and King (2000) argue that there are conservative elements in New Labour's approach, for instance their firm belief in the value of conventional families. Nonetheless, New Labour has produced a plethora of welfare polices that illustrate its distinctive approach. Examples include cross-departmental initiatives focusing on social exclusion and welfare-to-work (as discussed in the Introduction).

ACTIVITY 1.2

Read through the outlines of the New Right and New Labour ideologies above again. How do you think each would have manifested itself in terms of its approach to lone parents? List your main ideas and compare them to the discussion of the New Right and New Labour policies and attitudes towards this group.

The New Right and lone parents

The New Right's individualistic approach to social problems, its emphasis on 'traditional family life' and normalised ideas about appropriate sexuality manifested itself in a negative attitude to lone parents. The increase in their numbers was seen as being 'indicative of a growing underclass presaging moral and social breakdown' (Levitas, 2006: 406).

Its antipathy to welfare dependency meant that it tried to reduce their dependency on the state and reduce the costs of lone parents. The benefit structure was seen to be both financing and encouraging lone parenthood, which contributed to a 'culture of dependency'. Lister (1998) argues that the New Right's views on traditional family life led them to construct lone mothers' primary obligation as being to care for their children as opposed to undertaking paid work. Thus, instead of encouraging lone mothers to enter the labour market, changes were made to the benefit system so that there were incentives to be less reliant on income support by introducing packages that combined child support, wages and benefits that were linked to being in paid employment. In addition, attempts were made to reduce the cost of single parents by making the absent parent (whether married or not to the other) pay in respect to their biological children. To this effect, the Child Support Act was passed in 1991 and the Child Support Agency introduced in 1993 to ensure that absent parents supported their children financially (Lister, 1998).

Although they only constituted a small percentage of all lone parents, teenage mothers were demonised in particular. For instance, some sections of the media portrayed them as immoral scroungers living off the state. In 1988 Margaret Thatcher spoke of the apparent problem of young single girls who were deliberately getting pregnant in order to jump the housing queue. These ideas were forcibly endorsed at a Conservative party conference when a series of swinge-ing attacks on young, single, unmarried mothers were made. Although some argued that they were scapegoated, such views did influence policies and the message came through loud and clear that welfare benefits and housing should only be made available to 'respectable' married women (Lewis, 1997; Lister, 1998; Carabine, 2001).

However, young, single, unmarried mothers are not a new phenome-non and they have featured in policies for nearly two centuries; the 1834 Poor Law addressed the concerns about increasing illegitimacy and related increased demands for poor relief. Unmarried mothers were neg-atively portrayed as being immoral and seen to be less deserving than other people who were poor and they were only given poor relief through the workhouse (Lewis, 1997). So why did they become such a big issue?

Lewis (1997) offers an explanation; she argues that this particular group of lone parents has gradually became more visible in the late twentieth century. She says that until recently such lone mothers were hidden away. In the early part of the twentieth century, women could be sent to an institution if they became pregnant outside wed-lock as pregnancy in unmarried women was regarded by many as such a profound mark of deviance that it could only be explained by mental instability. In the middle of the century, young, single, pregnant women may not have run the risk of incarceration but often went to a 'mother and baby home' for the birth. The mother's family would then bring up the child without making public the circumstances of its birth. Another reason put forward as to why single, unmarried moth-ers have remained invisible is that in the 1960s teenage girls who became pregnant often resorted to a backstreet abortion, while others gave their child up for adoption (often under parental pressure). Lewis maintains that it is only since the 1970s that single, unmarried mothers have become more visible as they started to live more autonomously in the community (often in social housing) and draw state benefits. This is when more attention became focused on them.

New Labour and lone parents

Like the New Right, New Labour has viewed lone parents as problem-atic, mainly because of the increasing costs of supporting them from public expenditure and their dependency on welfare benefits. However, New Labour rejected the New Right's stigmatisation of lone parents and has also focused much more on the social exclusion and poverty of this vulnerable group.

In the 1990s, the United Kingdom had one of the lowest percentages of lone parents in paid work in the OECD and the poverty rates for lone parents were also one of the highest. Cross-national evidence indicated that lone parents were less prone to poverty when in paid employment (Lister, 2002). As mentioned in the introductory chapter, New Labour sees paid employment as the route out of poverty. Thus it was argued that the solution to these problems lay in encouraging more lone parents to work and a target of getting 70 per cent of lone parents into work by 2010 was set (Bell et al., 2005). The New Deal for Lone Parents was introduced (see the Introduction for an outline of the New Deal strategy). Although the obligation for lone parents to work is almost universal in other welfare states (Lister, 1998, 2002), this is a *voluntary* programme specifically designed to help lone parents into work. Nonetheless, in 2007 more pressure was put on lone parents to work through the limitation of their benefits by expecting them to apply for paid employment when their youngest child reached 12 and not 16, which had been the previous cut-off age.

The personal advisors appointed to the New Deal for Lone Parents not only take those interested through the steps to find, apply for and start a job but also offer practical advice and help in finding childcare and training. In addition, advisors are able to tell lone parents how their benefits will be affected once they start work, help them apply for any in-work benefits or tax credits, and meet expenses (including fares and registered childcare costs) incurred when attending any meetings, job interviews or training arranged.

Other initiatives to assist lone parents combine employment with parenting have focused on help with supplying more good-quality, convenient and affordable childcare (such as the National Childcare Strategy); offering taxation subsidies (the Working Families Tax Credit); and removing any barriers to work that lone parents face (for instance, a legal framework for the provision of leave for family emergencies is provided by the Employment Relations Act 1999).

Efforts have also been made to discourage people from becoming lone parents; New Labour's communitarism means that the economic rationality embodied in the approach above is interwoven with social morality. This has led to the political promulgation of the views that children are better off with two parents rather than one, and that marriage is better than co-habitation as married couples are more likely to stay together (Carabine, 2001). Even though New Labour has not demonised teenage mothers as the New Right did, it has targeted them specifically. This has been mainly because of the evidence that teenage motherhood is more likely to lead to reduced opportunities for both the mother and her child(ren) than other types of lone parenthood. Thus, tackling their social exclusion has been part of the drive to break the 'cycle of disadvantage' whereby deprivation in one generation is passed down to the next. The Social Exclusion Unit produced a strategy in 1999 to reduce the number of conceptions among those under 18 and hence to reduce the number of young, single mothers (Social Exclusion Unit, 1999).

More recently they have been identified as still being one of the most excluded groups who require additional support. Proposals include revising the original strategy, focusing on those areas where teenage pregnancy rates have not fallen, an expanded media campaign and better access to contraceptives (Cabinet Office, 2006).

EVALUATION OF RECENT POLICIES

ACTIVITY 1.3

Read the following extract:

The Work and Pensions Secretary, John Hutton, signalled his willingness to consider more stringent requirements for lone parents to look for work as part of a package of measures to encourage them back into employment and to alleviate child poverty ... Jane Ahrends, spokeswoman for the group One Parent Families, said that two-thirds of single parents who had children aged between 11 and 16 years were already working. "The majority usually amongst those who are not working have very good reason for not doing so; a third of divorces happen when children are in that age category, so that it may well be that single parents decide that their priority must be to stabilise family life and to be at home with their children ... while most single parents want to work when the time is right for them, there are very high barriers for them, particularly in the absence of affordable childcare."
(Hutton, 2007)

What issues does this extract highlight about recent attempts to address the social exclusion of lone parents? See how your thoughts compare with the points made in this section. Some ideas to help get you thinking can be found at the end of the chapter.

The discussions above showed that there were two main themes in the more recent policies about lone parents – namely the focus has been on increasing their employment rates and discouraging lone parenthood. Although the former is exclusive to New Labour's policies, both New Right and New Labour governments have introduced initiatives to address the latter. The evidence about the effectiveness of this two-pronged approach is considered below.

Lone parents and employment

The workforce participation rate for lone parents increased from 44 per cent in 1997 to 57.1 per cent in 2007 (Levitas, 2006; Office for National Statistics, 2007). Lone parents themselves have identified the many advantages of paid work. These include improved self-esteem, wider social contacts, increased sense of personal identity, break from childcare, and greater stimulation. However, despite these positive outcomes and all the efforts to encourage lone parents into work, the workforce participation rate for lone parents is still the lowest in Europe. There is no evidence to suggest that the characteristics of lone parents vary between European countries and in countries such as Sweden and Denmark up to 80 per cent of lone parents work (Millar and Rowlingson, 2001; Hutton, 2007).

As mentioned in the Introduction, the importance that New Labour has attached to paid work as a route out of social exclusion for vulnerable groups and its shift to employment-based citizenship has been a constant theme in the criticisms of its policies. This criticism has also been made about the emphasis on workforce participation for lone parents as it ignores other impediments and barriers to the social inclusion of this group.

Some of these are associated with practicalities, such as a lack of skills, job history, the fact that some types of work are limited because lone parents want to be near home and to have hours to fit in with children (lone parents prefer 'normal hours' because of the difficulty in getting childcare for unsocial/shift hours, and prefer term-time contracts only), and the need for flexibility to respond to exceptional childcare situations (Millar and Rowlingson, 2001). Interestingly, childcare costs are rarely cited as a major difficulty to overcome in order to enter and/or remain in paid work. There do seem to be moves to address some of these difficulties. For instance, New Labour has promised that by 2010 there will be a 'childcare place for all children aged between three and fourteen from 8am to 6pm each weekday, including school holidays' (Hutton, 2007).

Other obstacles that exist and have been specifically identified include the fact that, as sole carers and providers, lone parents can experience conflicts between work and family duties; Bell et al. (2005) found that effectively coordinating work, childcare, running a home and their children's education could be very complex and that lone parents often suffered from role strain. In addition, many lone mothers want to look after their children themselves at least when they are of pre-school age, and are not motivated by economic rationality (Millar and Rowlingson, 2001; Lister, 2002; Bell et al., 2005; Meadows and Grant, 2005).

Research has shown that there are psychological barriers to work-force participation for lone parents. There is a need to address other more personal obstacles to their inclusion such as the development of self-esteem and confidence, and a feeling of agency. It is argued that more small-scale initiatives based at community level are required, such as support groups, voluntary work and college courses to help develop their transferable skills. These include, for instance, increasing levels of social contact, confidence, regaining some element of control over their lives, an ability to deal with fluctuating situations and the setting of personal goals. All of these have been shown to help lone parents feel that they are prepared for work and can facilitate their integration into the labour market (Kidger, 2004; Meadows and Grant, 2005).

There are also structural barriers. Using teenage lone parents as an example, the highest rates of teenage pregnancy are in the poorest areas (with high unemployment) and among the most vulnerable young people, including those who have been in care and excluded from school. Ethnicity is another example; lone parenthood is far more common among black Caribbean families than any other groups. It is therefore argued that New Labour's policies are not addressing the underlying causes of the social exclusion of lone parents, such as poverty, unemployment and ethnicity. Indeed, there is evidence to suggest that policy reforms only account for about 50 per cent of the increase in lone-parent employment and that there has only been a slight overall improvement in lone parents' income. Furthermore, research has shown that those who have gone back to work were already committed to starting work in the short term or were those who would have done so in any case (Millar and Rowlingson, 2001; Department for Education and Skills, 2006; Levitas, 2006).

This evaluation clearly indicates that focusing on getting lone parents into employment as a means of addressing their social exclusion cannot be effective on its own. In addition, it suggests that a broader approach needs to be taken that acknowledges the heterogeneity of lone parents and the multidimensional nature of their social exclusion that has been identified. The SureStart Plus initiative, which aimed to improve the social and emotional well-being of teenage parents and their children, is an example of an approach that addresses some of the wider, non-financial issues associated with the social exclusion of specific groups of lone parents (Kidger, 2004). Increased support for such programmes may be one way forward. Unless the criticisms of existing policies are effectively addressed through the development of different approaches, Britain will remain behind its European counterparts in the drive to ensure that more lone parents are in paid employment.

Discouragement of lone parenthood

Both the New Right and New Labour political discourses have placed a strong emphasis on the value of stable family life and the credo that 'two parents are better than one'. Under New Labour in particular, there has been a range of family-friendly policies such as the introduction of parental leave (Pascall, 1997; Civitas, 2002; Driver and Martell, 2002). Critics have argued that tensions within such policies meant that the New Right actually contributed to family breakdown (Pascall, 1997) and that the current tax and benefit system discourages marriage for lower-income families (Civitas, 2002). Nonetheless, such rhetoric and policy initiatives can at the very least be interpreted as political support for more traditional family structures and the discouragement of lone parenthood.

With reference to discouraging teenage lone parenthood, there have been efforts to provide teenagers with appropriate information about contraception and to convey the realities of being pregnant and bringing up a child alone. There have also been attempts to address the contradictory nature of British culture which declares for both male and female teenagers that 'sex is compulsory but contraception is illegal' (Social Exclusion Unit, 1999: 7). However, although the birth-rate to teenage girls has declined in Britain since the 1970s, it is still the highest in Europe and the second highest in the world (Daguerre and Nativel, 2006; Firth, 2007a). It is argued that more efforts are needed to address the underlying causes of teenage lone parenthood. For instance, the fact that teenage parents often have low expectations about their future employment prospects and 'see no reason not to get pregnant' (Social Exclusion Unit, 1999: 7). Another underlying cause is that they are also more likely to come from a disadvantaged background and be the children of teenage parents themselves (Social Exclusion Unit, 1999; Millar and Rowlingson, 2001).

CONCLUSIONS

In this overview of lone parents, their experiences and policy initiatives, we have seen that there is still a long way to go in order to address the key issues around lone parenthood. Further research into the effects of past and current initiatives both in this and other countries could yield insights into ways of progressing. As discussed at the beginning of this chapter, more and more adults and children are facing the potential disadvantages of being in a lone-parent family at some stage in their lives. According to recent figures, there will be further increases in some types of lone parenthood. For instance, the number of live births outside marriage continues to rise. It has also been predicted that if current divorce rates continue, 45 per cent of all marriages will end in divorce and that almost half of all divorces will take place before married couples reach their tenth wedding anniversary. In view of the fact that divorce in the early years of marriage is more likely to involve young children, there will be an upward trend in divorced lone-parent families (National Statistics, 2008). It is therefore imperative that effective solutions are identified if this 'vulnerable group' is to achieve true social inclusion and enjoy full citizenship both now and in the future.

DISCUSSION POINTS

What definition of a lone-parent family do you think should be adopted?

Explore the concept of underclass further. Do you think the comparison between this concept and lone parents is justified?

Compare and contrast the approaches adopted by the New Right and New Labour to lone parents.

FURTHER STUDY

See Ermisch and Francesconi (2000) and Ram and Hou (2003) for more discussion about the changing nature of families and increasing numbers of people who may spend some time in their lives in a lone-parent family. For more information about lone parents in relation to poverty and social exclusion, see the chapter by Levitas et al. (2006), which presents an analysis of recent data from the Poverty and Social Exclusion Survey of Britain (PSE). Several of the sources below offer a cross-national perspective on lone parents. These include the work done by Lewis (1997), Lunt (2006), Millar and Rowlingson (2001), Sanatana (2002) and Whitehead et al. (2000). Detailed evaluations of recent policies can be found in the articles by Kidger (2004) and Lister (2002).

Key readings

Ermisch, J. and Francesconi, M. (2000). 'The increasing complexity of family relationships: lifetime experience of lone motherhood and stepfamilies in Great Britain.' *European Journal of Population*, **16** (3) 235–249

(Continued)

Levitas, R., Head, E. and Finch, N. (2006). 'Lone parents, poverty and social exclusion' in Pantazis, C., Gordon, D. and Levitas, R. (eds) *Poverty and social exclusion in Britain: the millennium survey.* Bristol: Policy Press

Lister, R. (2002). 'The dilemmas of pendulum politics: balancing paid work, care and citizenship.' **31** (4) 520–532

POST-ACTIVITY COMMENTS

ACTIVITY 1.1

What sort of experiences did you identify? Some suggestions are:

- living on a low income;
- lack of social contacts and social support;
- lack of family support;
- both lone mothers and one/more of their children had health problems;
- inadequate housing.

ACTIVITY 1.3

You might like to think about the following:

- The efficacy of the focus on paid work as a solution to lone parents' social exclusion and barriers to lone-parent employment other than those highlighted in the extract.
- Are there aspects of these initiatives that you agree with? Perhaps you feel that paid work has advantages for lone parents?
- Jane Ahrend identifies one type of barrier to lone parents' employment. What other barriers can you think of?
- Are there other issues that need to be addressed to ensure the social inclusion of lone parents?

Chapter 2
People with Disabilities

OVERVIEW

- Disability – a socially constructed concept
- Finkelstein's evolutionary model of disability
- The medical model of disability
- The social model of disability
- The negative life experiences of disabled people
- An evaluation of political initiatives aimed at disabled people
- Conclusions
- Suggestions for further study

INTRODUCTION

In this chapter, the term 'disability' will be used in its broadest sense and will refer to physical and mental disabilities. Measuring disability is problematic due to the fact that it is not a static condition, it can be caused by a wide range of impairments and for many there are transitions in and out of disability. The reliability of statistics on disability has also been questioned; this is because they are influenced by factors such as increased public awareness of disability. Nonetheless, it is estimated that 21 per cent of the adult population in the United Kingdom is disabled and that this equates to one in five people of working age (National Statistics, 2002; Disability Rights Commission, 2006).

People with disabilities suffer more inequalities, such as exclusion from employment, poverty and welfare dependency, than many other groups and have frequently been described as the most socially excluded group in society (Howard, 1999; Humphrey, 2000; Hyde, 2000a; Gardiner and Millar, 2006; Gannon and Nolan, 2007). An understanding of their vulnerability requires the exploration of several issues, such as the way disability is constructed in our society, the disadvantages experienced by those who live with a disability and the political initiatives that have focused on disabled people. These will be addressed in this chapter.

THE SOCIAL CONSTRUCTION OF DISABILITY

ACTIVITY 2.1

Below are some examples of approaches to disability. Read through them and think what they tell you about the concept of disability. Further guidance on this is provided at the end of the chapter.

'disabled children have been regarded as changelings and taken as evidence of the mother's involvement in sorcery or witchcraft' (Fawcett, 2000)

disability is ... 'the disadvantage or restriction of activity caused by a contemporary social organisation which takes no or little account of people with physical impairments and thus excludes them from participation in the mainstream of social activities' (Union of Physically Impaired against Segregation, 1976: 4)

disability is ... 'the functional limitation within the individual caused by physical, mental or sensory impairment' (DPI, 1982: 105)

disability is ... 'permanent physical or mental incapacity' (*Pocket Oxford Dictionary*, 1992)

'a person has a disability for the purposes of this Act if he has a physical or mental impairment which has a substantial and long-term adverse effect on his ability to carry out normal day-to-day activities' (Disability Discrimination Act, 1995).

There are different ways of defining disability, with definitions varying according to historical, social and cultural contexts. This indicates that disability is more a question of social definition than a statement of fact or an objective truth. Sociologists, such as Oliver (1990, 1996, 1998), argue that the concept of 'disability' is ***socially constructed***. This refers to the way that aspects of society or behaviour are actively created or 'constructed' in a particular way as a result of social relations and human agency rather than being 'natural' or biological in origin. Social constructions change and will vary from one historical period to another and from one society and culture to another. For instance, homosexuality was constructed as a criminal offence until the 1970s (Hughes, 1998; Fawcett, 2000).

Oliver (1990, 1996, 1998) maintains that disability has been socially constructed through the activities of powerful groups, vested interests, historical and cultural developments and language that is heavily influenced by ideology. As a result, the way disability is constructed has changed over time. The argument that disability is socially constructed is supported by evidence of historical changes in the way that disability has been viewed. Finkelstein (1981) is one of the most well-known writers in this area. Writing in the late 1970s and early 1980s, he developed an evolutionary model of disability that linked changing social constructions of disability with three different phases in history. These are as follows:

Phase 1

In pre-industrial Britain disabled people were not segregated or excluded from the rest of society; the feudal economy was based around cooperative small-scale industry and agriculture in which disabled people were able to participate. Thus they had a role, albeit limited in some cases, in the production process. The nature of the scattered rural communities existing at that time also meant that they were able to be more easily absorbed into the life of communities without special provision. Using the example of those who were visually impaired or blind, the uncongested rural surroundings posed less problems for them than the towns and cities that developed during industrialization.

Phase 2

Changes that occurred during industrialisation and the period after it led to a change in the way that disabled people were socially constructed. This was because during industrialisation there was an increasing requirement for people to work separately from home, and also to adapt and conform to the machinery and imperatives of industrial production. Disabled people obviously found this harder to do and were seen as slower and less productive. This hastened their exclusion from paid labour and 'normal' participation in the community to being considered 'unemployable'. In the eighteenth and nineteenth centuries unemployed people and unemployable disabled people in the cities became a 'problem' for civil authorities. From the early 1800s onwards, they were treated in secure, long-stay institutions, such as special schools, colonies, workhouses and asylums. They had to endure a custodial regime and segregation from the rest of society.

In addition, Finkelstein argues that the rise of **biomedicine** that has dominated our thinking about health and disease for the last 175 years influenced the construction of disabled people in Phase 2. Biomedicine rests on an assumption that all causes of disease – mental disorders as well as physical disease – are understood in biological terms and it views disease and sickness as deviations from normal functioning, which medicine has the power to put right with its scientific knowledge and understanding of the human body. Finkelstein's argument is that the rise of biomedicine meant that since the nineteenth century disability has been medicalised. Disabled people have been viewed as medical problems who need to be 'helped' by the medical profession. They have often been subjected to regimes of moral management, discipline and segregation.

Phase 3

In Phase 3, according to Finkelstein, disabled people will be liberated and included in society once more. This will be because of the reconstruction of disability as a social restriction. The consequences of this, such as the introduction and utilisation of new technologies and collaboration between professional and disabled people, would lead to the end of segregative practices.

ACTIVITY 2.2

The following is an account of institutional life by a child called Mary Baker, who had a dislocated hip and walked with a limp. In 1935 her mother died and her local authority decided that her father could not cope with caring for her and her three brothers. She was sent to Halliwick House for Crippled Girls, a Church of England institution for physically and mentally disabled girls. As you read it, think about which of Finkelstein's three phases it illustrates. See the end of the chapter for the answer and an explanation.

When I arrived at Halliwick the nurse took me into this bathroom and she stripped me off completely. She cut my hair short, right above the ears. And then I was deloused with powder of some description. Then they put me in a bath and scrubbed me down with carbolic soap. ... Then I was dressed in the Halliwick uniform ... and taken up into a Dormitory ... with about ten beds in it. ... I had entered a different life ... the next morning you were given a number and you had to remember it. My number was twenty-nine and when I got up and went to wash, my towel and flannel had my number on them. Twenty-nine was engraved on all my hairbrushes and things ... everything I owned had a marking of twenty-nine on ... our lockers in the playroom had the same number and our clothes were marked with our numbers. ... We were hardly ever called by our first names ... if matron wanted you she called you by twenty-nine or whatever number you had. We never had names, we were just numbers there. It was all very disciplined.

(Adapted from Humphries and Gordon, 1992)

Finkelstein's work has been criticised for being oversimplistic and over-optimistic in that it idealises the 'community' in Phase 1 and implies that attitudes towards, and treatment of, disabled people were somehow positive. The likelihood that the social inclusion of disabled people in Phase 3 is occurring as Finkelstein predicted has also been questioned (Oliver, 1990). Nonetheless, there have been many developments that have influenced the way disabled people are socially constructed that have led to their increased integration into society.

One of these is the growth in the power of the disability movement since the 1960s; in the 1960s and 1970s, there were only organisations *for* disabled people as opposed to organisations *of* disabled people. The former are run by able-bodied people who work in partnership with national and local government agencies. Examples are the Royal National Institute for the Blind (RNIB) and the Royal Association for Disability and Rehabilitation (RADAR). The 1980s saw a change to organisations *of* disabled people; the British Council of Disabled People, which was founded in 1981, specifically stated its support for the development of organisations *of* disabled people. These are run exclusively by disabled people. Furthermore, their number has increased and the disability movement has developed a political agenda that has challenged the dominant discourses about disability, mobilised mass support and taken action that has been of a direct, collective and political nature. They have been and continue to be involved in various successful campaigns for issues to do with health, access, raising awareness and improving benefits; in 1998 disabled activists besieged Downing Street. Paint was thrown, wheelchairs were padlocked to the railings, and some of the activists lay down in the road to protest against proposed changes to benefits (Hughes, 1998; Hyde, 2000a).

Another development is the growth of an increasingly influential body of literature written by activists, such as Oliver, in the disability movement since the early 1990s. There have also been many attempts to counter the dominant cultural imagery of dependence in the arts and media, and challenge the use of negative language in relation to disability (Hughes, 1998). Furthermore, the introduction of community care in the late 1980s heralded the end of long-stay institutions and the start of disabled people being provided with care at home or in 'homely' settings rather than being separated from the rest of the population (Blakemore, 2001).

Such moves towards a more inclusive society in relation to disabled people have also been interpreted as signs of the underlying change from a medical model of disability to the adoption of a social model of disability. It is to these two models that we now turn.

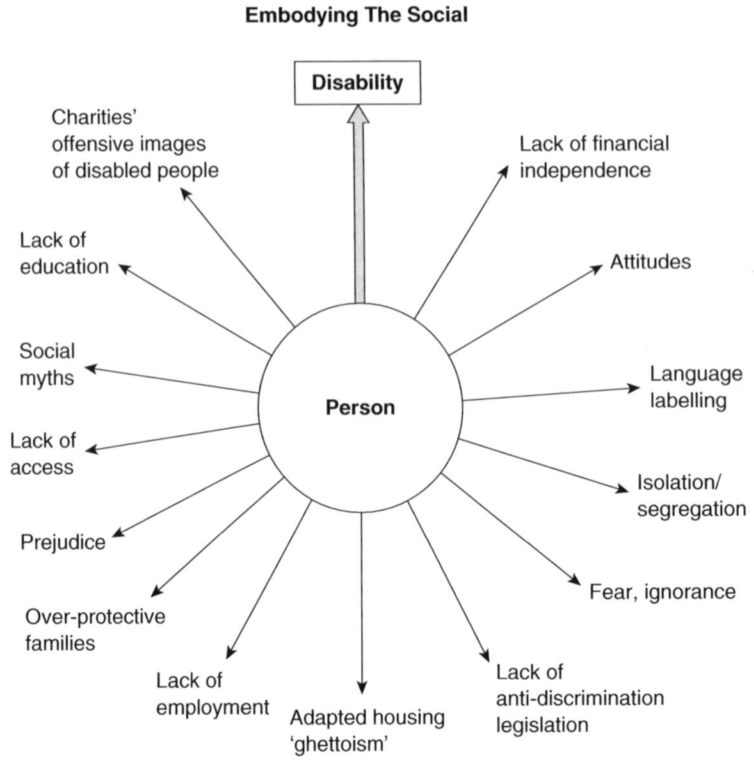

Embodying The Social

Figure 2.1   The medical model of disability
Source: From Hughes (1998)

THE MEDICAL MODEL OF DISABILITY

As discussed above, the rise of biomedicine meant that, since the nineteenth century, disability was medicalised, with disabled people being viewed as medical problems, who if not curable, needed to be 'helped', and were dependent on medical care and the medical profession. This approach to disability is called the 'medical' model of disability and is illustrated in Figure 2.1.

This individualistic model has dominated disability during the last two centuries. It involves medicine colonizing disability and the individualization of disability in terms of individual pathology; impairments are classified and those with disabilities treated as patients. Thus the emphasis is on the impairment rather than the person and it is regarded as their individual problem. Disabled people are also labelled as abnormal. Moreover, the power to decide how the person with the disability is treated resides with the medical and other allied professions. The resultant treatment does not necessarily improve the quality of the 'patient's' life or fit well with the overall economy of their lives. Nor does it involve disabled people in a meaningful way but rather treats them as passive objects of 'intervention, treatment and rehabilitation' (Oliver, 1990: 5).

The medical model has been adopted in legislation about the disabled and disability; policy interventions have been based on medicalised and individualised views of disability. These have focused on individuals' impairments and vulnerabilities rather than the social constraints on social participation for people with disabilities. Many different services have been developed by able-bodied people to address individual need and functional rehabilitation.

Therefore, not only does this model ignore the experiential, social and situational components of disability but it has also had lifelong and oppressive consequences for disabled people (Oliver, 1990, 1996; Hughes, 1998; Hyde, 2000a). Unsurprisingly, the hegemony of the medical model has been challenged and, since the 1990s, a new conceptual framework for understanding disability has emerged – the social model of disability.

THE SOCIAL MODEL OF DISABILITY

This model of disability is illustrated in Figure 2.2 below.

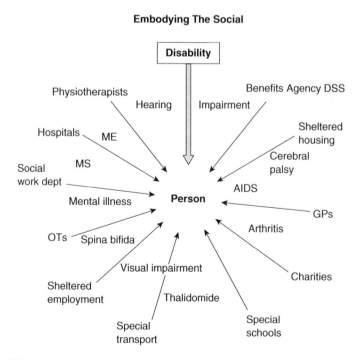

Figure 2.2   The social model of disability

Source: From Hughes (1998)

The social model of disability or, as it is sometimes called, the social barriers model of disability, was campaigned for by disabled activists throughout the 1980s and became embedded in the disability movement. It constructs disability in a radically different way from the medical model; it argues that disability is not the problem of an individual's impairment but rather it is the attitudinal and physical constraints imposed by a society geared towards a norm of able-bodiedness that oppress disabled people and curtail their opportunities and capabilities.

This model concentrates on what society does to construct disability. This involves examining how society needs to change in order to cease disabling people with disabilities and to emancipate them so that they can participate in society and are empowered as citizens with rights. Adoption of the social model has resulted in a distinct set of policies that have aimed to abolish the fixed notion of 'normality' that disabled people have to aspire to and to make the physical, cultural and economic environment accessible and less discriminatory for people with disabilities. Consequently, there have been changes such as ramps and chairlifts, and equal opportunities policies. There have also been policies to alleviate the oppression of disabled people. Examples include the legislation in the 1970s and 1980s to reclassify people once regarded as idiots, mongols, retarded, mentally deficient, mentally handicapped and so forth. There have also been policies to integrate them into ordinary life, to make them more independent and equip them with social and practical skills (Oliver, 1990, 2004; Fawcett, 2000; Hyde, 2000a; O'Grady et al., 2004).

ACTIVITY 2.3

Read through the outlines of both models again. To ensure that you have fully understood them, list their differences.

Some points of comparison to help you with this exercise are set out in the 'Post-activity Comments' section.

Although this change in approach to disability, heralded by the emergence of the social model, has been popular with many, it has been subject to criticisms. Some critics have drawn attention to the way that it prioritises disability as a main form of oppression and excludes other forms of oppression (Oliver, 2004; Matthewman et al., 2007). Others have argued that it does not acknowledge the role of impairment in restricting social participation; in some debilitating cases, whatever the definition of the impairment, the ability to perform social activities is severely limited (Hyde, 2000a; Oliver, 2004). More recent criticisms have focused on the way that the social model does not engage with the personal and experiential aspects of disability, particularly the lived experience of the body for disabled people (Twigg, 2006). The experiential dimension of disability is discussed in the next section.

EXPERIENCING DISABILITY

Although the adoption of the social model over the past two decades has had many positive outcomes for disabled people (Tregakis, 2002), as mentioned at the beginning of the chapter, they still experience many inequalities in their lives that contribute to their continuing exclusion. The exploration of these inequalities that follows in the rest of this section includes the way in which they overlap and interact with each other and with other social divisions.

Employment

Disabled people experience high rates of unemployment; figures show that they are about twice as likely to be unemployed as non-disabled people. They are also more likely to do part-time work, which generally has lower status and pay, less job security and fewer employment rights. Age, gender and ethnicity also interact with disability in this aspect of disabled people's lives; levels of their labour market disadvantage increase from middle age onwards and are greater for disabled women and disabled people from ethnic minority groups. These findings have been partly explained by the fact that many disabled people face a number of potential barriers to employment such as concerns about benefit entitlements, conditions and hours, a lack of relevant experience or skills and discrimination from employers. With reference to the latter, research has shown that employers often misunderstand disability and associate it with 'risk and uncertainty' (Heenan, 2002: 387). Despite legislation to counteract this, there is evidence that such discrimination is still widespread; disabled people are six times more likely to be refused an interview than a non-disabled person with similar skills and qualifications (Heenan, 2002; Bailey, 2004; Sapey, 2004; Bambra et al., 2005).

Prejudice and discrimination

Although blatant forms of prejudice towards disabled people seem to be disappearing, as the discussions above show, **discrimination** continues. It has been argued that among the most notable causes are professionals' disabling attitudes (Morris, 2004; Foster et al., 2006). There is also evidence that more subtle forms of prejudice exist in the mass media. For instance, publicity campaigns by disability charities have presented images of disabled people as helpless and pitiable in order to attract public donations. The absence of images of disabled people taking part in everyday life, such as working and taking an active role in their families, has also led to negative views of the extent of their capabilities (Wates, 2004; Deal, 2007). The inevitable internalisation of such stereotyping can cause much distress for disabled people; Grue and Laerum's (2002) study of physically disabled mothers found that they felt constant pressure to show that they were managing 'normally' and feared that their children would be taken from them if they did not appear to live up to societal expectations of being an 'ordinary' mother.

Health and healthcare

Disabled people experience significant health inequalities compared to non-disabled people (Melville, 2005). The barriers that disabled people face when accessing healthcare have been identified as contributing to this. Studies of healthcare in the United States of America have attributed these barriers to the devaluing of the lives of disabled people and their weak bargaining position as consumers of healthcare (Albrecht, 2001). The role of discriminatory attitudes and a lack of appropriate knowledge and internet access have been identified as causal factors in the British literature (Davis, 2002; Melville, 2005).

Education

Those who are disabled are far more likely to have lower or no academic qualifications than non-disabled people (Smith and Twomey, 2002; O'Grady et al., 2004; Disability Rights Commission, 2006). This is because of the way that they are disadvantaged throughout the education system; in primary and secondary education attendance at a special school leads to the segregation of disabled children and they may also be subject to discrimination. There is evidence that the nature and level of provision are inadequate and that educational attainment levels are lower for those who are integrated into mainstream schools. Tertiary education fails to provide the opportunities that they need to compensate for their lower levels of educational achievement while at school. As a result, their chances of entering higher education are much reduced compared to the non-disabled (Howard, 1999; Hyde, 2000a). Indeed disabled people are still only half as likely as non-disabled people to be qualified to degree level. In addition, despite the significant progress that has been made in the development of provision for disabled students in universities, this pattern of inequality has not changed since 1998; those who do enter higher education can still face disadvantage and further improvements are required to ensure the equalisation of opportunities (Tinklin et al., 2004; Disability Rights Commission, 2006).

Income

Their high unemployment rates, health problems and lack of educational qualifications result in disabled people being the largest group in receipt of benefits. It is also estimated that 45 per cent of disabled adults live in poverty (Hyde, 2000a; O'Grady et al., 2004; Bambra et al., 2005).

Housing

Despite the introduction of community care, many disabled people are still segregated in residential homes and those who are not face considerable disadvantages in relation to housing. Choice is often limited when it comes to meeting their housing needs. They are also more likely to live in public housing and less likely to rent privately or have a mortgage than non-disabled people (O'Grady et al., 2004; Stevens, 2004). A recent study showed how disabled people with mobility problems are often excluded from the owner-occupation market. This is because the design of houses for owner occupation automatically renders them unsuitable for their needs (Thomas, 2004).

Social life

A number of factors have negative impacts on the social lives of disabled people; limited disposable income, lack of own transport, inability to use public transport, inaccessibility of buildings and tourist attractions and inadequate provision of suitable leisure activities restrict their social activities to a greater or lesser extent. With reference to access to buildings, although there are now codes of practice for the design of buildings to cater for disabled people's needs, the extent to which these can effectively meet the access needs of disabled people has been questioned (Israeli, 2002; Aitchison, 2003; O'Grady et al., 2004; Imrie, 2006).

There is also much evidence that those who live in the community do not receive adequate support to enable their participation in mainstream society. This has been attributed to the failure of community services to respond to their needs because of inadequate funding, fragmentation, inflexibility and inequitable distribution (Hyde, 2000a; Kemp, 2002; Gardiner and Millar, 2006).

Personal life

The conditions surrounding permissible sex restrict the sex lives of some groups of disabled people (Spieker and Stetal, 2002). Overall, disabled people are less likely to have children (O'Grady et al., 2004).

These sorts of experiences constitute barriers to social inclusion. It is the combination of the continuation of such experiences and the powerful way in which they interact that has led, as discussed in the introduction to this chapter, to disabled people being described as the most socially excluded group in society (O'Grady et al., 2004). The political focus on the elimination of social exclusion has therefore resulted in many initiatives aimed at disabled people.

POLITICAL INITIATIVES AND DISABILITY

Some of the more recent legislation has already been discussed in relation to the adoption of the social model. An analysis of policies about disability and disabled people introduced over that past two decades shows that cost reductions have been a constant theme. As already mentioned, disabled people are the largest group in receipt of welfare benefits. Indeed, they account for about 25 per cent of benefit expenditure (Bambra et al., 2005). The cost of their welfare dependence rose particularly sharply in the 1980s and 1990s. For instance, the cost of benefits such as Severe Disablement Allowance, Attendance Allowance and Industrial Injuries Disablement Allowance almost doubled from 1988/1989 to 1997/1998. Various moves have been made to impose restrictions on benefit claimants, such as introducing more stringent medical controls and scrutinising claims for benefits more rigorously, to address this issue of rising costs (Deacon, 2002; Heenan, 2002). It can be argued that such measures have been influenced by the political re-emergence of citizenship with its emphasis on individual obligations and conformity to social norms.

Despite these attempts at cost-reduction, the expenditure on state benefits for disabled people remains an ongoing cause of concern (Bambra et al., 2005; Grover and Piggott, 2005). In line with New Labour's welfare-to-work strategies and its focus on social exclusion, there has also been an emphasis on reducing costs by moving disabled people from benefits into work. Welfare-to-work and discrimination have been the other two main themes in recent policy initiatives aimed at disabled people. These and the extent to which they address the social exclusion of disabled people are discussed below.

Welfare-to-work

The growing emphasis on increasing workforce participation among those who are disabled during the past ten years has received mixed reviews. There are five main welfare-to-work strategies aimed at reducing the welfare dependency rates of disabled people by promoting their transition from benefits into paid employment. These are shown in Table 2.1.

Table 2.1   Welfare-to-work strategies

Education, training and work placements	Vocational advice and support services	In-work benefits for employees	Employer incentives	Improving accessibility of work environment
New Deal Innovative Schemes	New Deal Personal Adviser Service	Working Tax Credit Travel to Work	Job Introduction Scheme	Access to Work
Work Preparation		Job finder's Grant	Work Trial	
		Jobmatch		
Residential Training		52-week linking rule		

Source: From Bambra et al. (2005)

The first three focus on individuals with disabilities and the second two concentrate on the work environment. In their evaluation of all of these strategies, Bambra et al. (2005) found that the first two (education, training and work placement, and vocational advice and support services) were felt to be the most useful. Neither of these strategies stood out as being the best way of solving the problems of low employment rates among disabled people and reducing the cost of their benefit payments. Indeed initiatives within both these strategies have been criticised. An example is the 'New Deal for Disabled People' (an outline of the New Deal strategy is on page 4 in the introductory chapter). This voluntary scheme was introduced in 2001 and is designed to enable sick and disabled people to exercise their right to work. The idea behind it is that it addresses social exclusion by removing the obstacles into paid work for disabled people, helps those who obtain jobs and who are already in work to retain their employment and ensures that they are financially better off when in employment.

Research into the New Deal for Disabled People has highlighted some of its positive features; those taking part in this initiative found that the emotional support provided while they were trying to obtain a job and once employment started was invaluable. They also felt that it was a welcome life-changing experience, and that they benefited psychologically from undertaking paid employment in terms of increased self-esteem and social contacts. However there have been criticisms of the way that it fails to take into account the intermittent nature of disability, the way that some groups face more obstacles than others and that not all disabled people can be employed (Heenan, 2002; Wistow and Schneider, 2007).

Critics of the welfare-to-work strategies in general have argued that, although they claim to alleviate the vulnerability of disabled people and reflect the approach within the social model, the recent emphasis on employment for disabled people does not represent an original approach; there have been various political initiatives to increase the workforce participation of disabled people since the early part of the twentieth century. In fact Hyde (2000b) maintains that disabled people were actively encouraged to work in the Second World War in order to replace able-bodied people conscripted into the armed forces. Another criticism is that disabled people cannot be freed from welfare dependency because they tend to be in lower-income jobs and have to be subsidised by tax credits. In addition, despite further development of these strategies to increase disabled people's workforce participation, they have not delivered the expected reduction in unemployment rates for disabled people; there has been an increase of around 8 per cent since 1998, but the employment rate for disabled people is still estimated to be no more than 50 per cent, compared to 87 per cent for the population as a whole (Hyde, 2000b; Grover and Piggott, 2005; Danieli and Wheeler, 2006; Wistow and Schneider, 2007).

Given that there is evidence that disabled people want to work if they can (Heenan, 2002) and that the United Kingdom still does not have an effective strategy to enable them to do so, it has been suggested that there is a need to look at alternative strategies in operation in other countries. For instance, in Sweden policies have focused on preventing disabled individuals from leaving paid employment in the first place, as opposed to helping them back into work once they have left (Bambra et al., 2005). Some of the anti-discriminatory legislation aimed at disabled people in this country has been developed with the intention of enabling them to remain in work by reducing discrimination against them. This is one area that maybe needs further development in order to increase the workforce participation for disabled people. The reduction of discrimination in general is the second main theme in recent initiatives to address the social exclusion of disabled people and it is to this that we now turn.

Discrimination

As discussed earlier in the chapter, discrimination plays a major role in the exclusion of disabled people. There have been attempts at national and European level to achieve equal rights and independence for disabled people, address the pervasive discrimination that they face and ensure their civil rights. The disability movement (see page 33) has played a major role in the struggle for these improvements and in shaping the legislation. It can also be credited for the shift from a medical model of disability to a social model of disability that these developments represent.

One example of these initiatives is the 1986 Disabled Person's Act. Under this Act, local authorities are required to provide disabled people themselves with information relevant to their needs. Another is the Disability Discrimination Act 1995, which was substantially extended by the Disability Discrimination Act 2005. These two Acts addressed such issues as recruitment and employment, management of premises and the provision of facilities, goods and services (for instance, education and transport) to the public. The Disability Discrimination Act 2005 also provided a more comprehensive definition of discrimination and extended the scope of definition of disability to include people with HIV, cancer and multiple sclerosis. Other initiatives are the Disability Rights Commission, which was set up in 2000 under the Disability Rights Commission Act 1999. Among its roles is the investigation and elimination of discrimination against disabled people and the promotion of the equalisation of opportunities for disabled persons. In addition, it has the power to prosecute. The Special Needs and Disability Act 2001 made it unlawful to discriminate against disabled pupils and students seeking access to education in schools and colleges. The White Paper *Valuing people: a new strategy for learning disability for the 21st century* (2001) takes a lifelong approach to disablity and focuses on civil rights, independence, choice and inclusion. Its proposals are intended to result in improvements in education, social services, health, employment, housing and support for people with learning disabilities and their families and carers.

Action that has been taken at European level includes the European Union Disability Strategy 1996, which aims to prohibit discrimination again disabled people, promote the full participation of disabled people and raise awareness of disability among member states; there is now a European Disability Forum, a 'European Day of Disabled People' in December each year, and 2003 was the European Year of Disabled People (European Commission, 2007).

However, not all the anti-discriminatory legislation has been totally successful; the disability movement has been critical of legislation that foregrounds the needs of carers instead of introducing legislation that gives equal opportunities to disabled people themselves. Although the 1986 Disabled Person's Act requires local authorities to provide disabled people with information relevant to their the needs, in reality few do so. Simm et al. (2007) found that, although there have been many positive developments since the introduction of the Disability Discrimination Act 2005, more needs to be done to support smaller organisations in the effective implementation of the Act.

Moreover, the disability movement itself has been accused of not being truly representative of all disabled people and running out of steam (Hyde, 2000a). The former accusation is compounded by the fact that many people do not see themselves as disabled or identify themselves as a disabled person (Watson, 2002). They therefore do not take part in the movement. These criticisms naturally raise questions about its ability to continue to effectively campaign to reduce the discrimination experienced by disabled people.

Hence, while these initiatives have contributed to some reductions in the social exclusion of disabled people, there are limitations to the extent of their success.

CONCLUSION

This chapter has shown that, despite the social, political and cultural changes in approaches towards disabled people, this vulnerable group still has many negative life experiences that result in their social exclusion. Evidence about the persistence of such oppressive experiences has led to claims that disabled people are being denied full citizenship rights (Lister, 1998; Beckett, 2005).

The suggestions in the literature about the ways of working towards the future inclusion of this group and ensuring its members' citizenship are many and varied. At one end of the continuum, there are suggestions that focus on increases in resources. These include the need for a decent disability income (to include, for example, more direct payments) regardless of employment status, and improved service provision. Those at the other end of the continuum argue more for enhancing the role of disabled people in our society. Among these are proposals about the greater inclusion of disabled people in policy forums, more opportunities for disabled people (other than those afforded by paid work) to undertake citizenship duties in their communities, and a move to equal citizenship in society so that everyone is regarded as worthwhile (Fawcett, 2000; Van Hoten and Bellemakers, 2002; Rummery, 2006). While these sorts of suggestions place the responsibility for change on society, there are those who maintain that both individuals with a disability *and* society have a mutual responsibility to work towards greater inclusion (van de Ven et al., 2005). Others focus on the ways in which the social model should be developed; Tregakis (2002: 467) argues that there is a need to concentrate more on non-disabled people in order to address the persistence of disabling attitudes and encourage them to adopt more inclusive practice.

There are also those who point to new forms of exclusion for disabled people that are emerging. These have been linked to the new types of inequalities created by **globalisation**, rapidly changing technology and the move towards a consumer culture (Barton, 2004; Hughes et al., 2005). With reference to the latter, Hughes et al. (2005) argue that at the heart of the move towards a consumer culture are aesthetics such as choice, beauty and youthfulness. These conflict with disability and represent yet another form of exclusion for disabled young people in particular.

Therefore, everyone in society has a responsibility to work towards the goal of social inclusion for disabled people. This also involves the thorough assessment of a range of options in terms of their ability to effectively address both the existing and emerging vulnerabilities of this group.

DISCUSSION POINTS

How tenable is Finkelstein's evolutionary model of disability?

To what extent has the social model led to the social inclusion of disabled people?

What do you think can be done to further reduce the social exclusion of this vulnerable group?

FURTHER STUDY

The emergence of the social model of disability is well documented in Oliver's work (1990, 1996). Different perspectives on the social model can be found in Chapter 4 in Twigg (2006) and the chapters in Parts 1, 2 and 5 in Swain et al. (2004). For recent research on the experiences of those who are disabled, it is worth doing an electronic database search, selecting articles that have appeared during the past five years. Articles in the *Journal of Disability and Society* are particularly useful and informative.

Key readings

Oliver, M. (1998). *Disabled people and social policy: from exclusion to inclusion.* London: Longman

Swain, J., French, S., Barnes, C. and Thomas, C. (eds) (2004). *Disabling barriers, enabling environments.* London: Sage in association with the Open University

Twigg, J. (2006). *The body in health and social care.* Basingstoke: Palgrave Macmillan

POST-ACTIVITY COMMENTS

ACTIVITY 2.1

You will have undoubtedly noticed how much the definitions vary. More specifically, did you see how they varied historically and the types of impairments to which they referred? There were also differences in their views of restrictions of disability, such as whether these are attributed to an individual's impairment or social organization. These sorts of variations have led to the assertion that disability is socially constructed, a view discussed in the first section of the chapter.

ACTIVITY 2.2

The account illustrates a construction of disability that is synonymous with Phase 2 in Finkelstein's model. This is because Mary's disability was medicalised and constructed as a deviation from normal functioning that needs to be treated in a long-stay institution. In this institution Mary was subjected to a regime of moral management, discipline and segregation.

ACTIVITY 2.3

Medical model	Social model
Oppressive	Emancipatory
Disability is caused by a mental/physical impairment and therefore the impairment is the focus of attention.	It is society that causes disabilities. This is because it prevents or excludes people with disabilities from participating in society.
As doctors are trained to cure/alleviate impairments, disability is a medical problem and people with disabilities are patients.	The views of people with disabilities should be listened to and taken into consideration and they should be allowed to manage their own lives.
The emphasis on 'improving' and 'managing' them in order to make them more 'normal' means that their feelings are ignored.	
People with disabilities must adapt to society, rather than society having to adapt to their needs.	It is the collective responsibility of society to alter itself in the areas of, for example, attitudes, transport, architectural barriers, pensions and benefits.

Chapter 3
Older People

OVERVIEW

- Demographic changes and the move to an ageing society
- Disengagement theory
- The social construction of old age
- The experience of being old
- Current policy initiatives
- Conclusions
- Suggestions for further study

INTRODUCTION

Some older people lead independent and active lives, participating in, and contributing to their families, communities and society in numerous ways. However, others are among the most socially excluded and vulnerable in society (Sanatana, 2002; Department for Work and Pensions, 2005a; Shelter, 2007b). Over the past decade older people in general have received much media and political attention; there have been a plethora of policies aimed at older people and various media campaigns to highlight their plight. A pivotal concern is the increasing numbers of older people which have led to frequent references to an 'ageing society'. Consequent concerns are meeting the needs of the vulnerable members of this continually expanding group in society. This chapter will therefore start by exploring the concept of an 'ageing society'. The vulnerabilities of older people will then be considered, followed by an evaluation of political initiatives that have aimed to address these. Recent statistical data will be used to supplement the literature discussed in the chapter.

AN 'AGEING SOCIETY'?

The phrase 'ageing society' is often used but what does this really mean? An explanation requires an examination of relevant demographic data, such as that set out below. Although the social category of 'old age' is extremely broad and many people designated as elderly do not self-identify as old (Degnen, 2007), for statistical and policy purposes, people over 65 are classified as being 'older people'.

ACTIVITY 3.1

Examine Figures 3.1 and 3.2. Which age groups in the United Kingdom are getting smaller and which are expanding? Which age group in the United Kingdom is predicated to expand the most? Now read the text that immediately follows Figures 3.1 and 3.2.

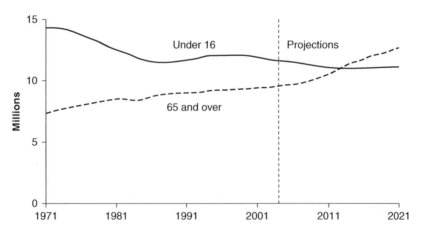

Figure 3.1   People aged under 16 and over 65 in the United Kingdom

Source: Adapted from National Statistics, 2007b

Figure 3.1 shows that since 1971 the numbers of those under 16 have been decreasing while the numbers of those over 65 have increased. Figure 3.2 illustrates these trends in terms of percentages; the percentage of the population over 65 has increased and the percentage of those under 16 has decreased since 1971. Both Figures 3.1 and 3.2 show how these trends are predicted to continue, and the fastest growing age group in the United Kingdom population will remain the over-65s.

There are currently around 11 million people in the United Kingdom over 65 (four million men and seven million women), which is 18 per cent of the

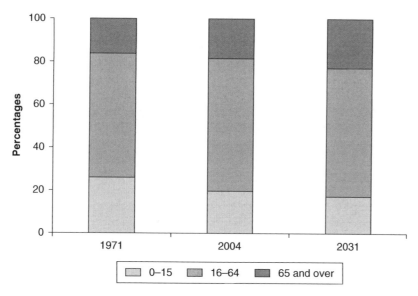

Figure 3.2   Age structure of United Kingdom population
Source: National Statistics, 2007b

population. These figures are double those for 1931 and it is estimated that by 2021, 20 per cent of people (one in five) in the United Kingdom will be over 65. This is mainly due to the decline in fertility and the increase in life expectancy; average family size is now standardising at one or two children. While there are variations in life expectancy between socio-economic groups, with those in the higher groups living longer, average life expectancy has increased dramatically over the past 100 years; in 1901 this was 45 for males and 49 for females. By 2002 it was 76 and 81 for males and females respectively, and, these figures are projected to rise to 79 and 84 respectively by 2020. Within the over-65 age group, the most substantial growth has occurred among those aged 85 and above. The proportion of the United Kingdom population aged 85 or over more than doubled between 1971 and 2004 to reach a record 1.2 million, of which about a third of a million are aged 90 and over. Again this trend is predicted to continue (Stewart and Vaitilingham, 2004; National Statistics, 2006a; Patsios, 2006; Vincent, 2006).

These demographic changes in the United Kingdom over the past 30 years mean that there are now fewer people under 16 than there are over 65; by 2005 the proportion of those aged under 16 had dropped to approximately one in five and the proportion of those aged 65 and over had increased to one in six people. Although Figure 3.2 shows that this decline in the under-16s and increase in those over 65 are likely to continue until 2031, figures released very recently indicate that this inversion in the numbers in these two groups is set to continue until 2050. Thus the United Kingdom's population is ageing and the phrase 'ageing society' is now widely used. These trends are not just confined to the United Kingdom;

ageing populations are an international phenomenon for the same reasons discussed above in relation to the United Kingdom (National Statistics, 2006a; Vincent, 2006).

THEORIES OF AGEING AND OLD AGE

ACTIVITY 3.2

An old lady, Kate, who lived in a residential home for the last few years of her life, wrote the poem below. She was unable to speak, but the nurses noticed that she often scribbled on bits of paper. When she died, they found this in her locker. Read it carefully and note down what she is saying about ageing and old people in our society.

What do you see nurses
What do you see?
Are you thinking
when you are thinking of me
A crabbit old woman
not very wise,
Uncertain of habit
with far away eyes,
Who dribbles her food
and makes no reply
When you say in a loud voice
'I do wish you'd try'
Who seems not to notice
the things that you do,
And forever is losing
a stoeking or a shoe,
Who unresisting or not
lets you do as you will
with bathing and feeding
the long day to fill,
Is that what you're thinking,
Is that what you see?
Then open your eyes nurse,
You're not looking at me.
I'll tell you who I am
as I sit here so still.
As I use at your bidding
as I eat at your will.

A young woman of thirty
My young now grow fast,
Bound to each other
with ties that should last.
At forty my young ones
now grown will soon be gone.
But my man stays beside me
to see I don't mourn.
At fifty once more
Babies play around my knee,
Again we know children
my loved one and me.
Dark days are upon me,
my husband is dead.
I look at the future
I shudder with dread.
For my young are all busy
rearing young of their own.
And I think of the years
and the love I have known
I'm an old woman now
and nature is cruel.
'Tis her jest to make
old age look like a fool.
The body it crumbles
grace and vigour depart.
There is now a stone
where once I had a heart.

I'm a small child of ten
with a father and mother,
Brothers and sisters
Who love one another.
A young girl of sixteen
with wings on her feet.
Dreaming that soon now
a lover she'll meet.
A bride soon at twenty,
my heart gives a leap
Remembering the vows
that I promised to keep.
At twenty-five now
I have young of my own
Who need me to build
a secure happy home.

But inside this old carcase
a young girl still dwells.
And now and again
my battered heart still swells,
I remember the joys.
I remember the pain.
And I'm loving and living
life over again.
I think of the years
all too few – gone too fast,
And crept the stark fact
that nothing can last.
So open your eyes nurses,
Open and see
Not a crabbit old woman
look closer – see ME.

from Carver and Liddiard (1978)

Now compare your notes with the ideas in the discussion of this poem at the end of the chapter.

Different perspectives have attempted to explain why ageing and old age should be experienced in this way. As you read through the following outlines of two of these perspectives, see if you can identify which particular aspects of the experiences of ageing and old age highlighted in the poem are addressed by each one. Some suggestions are made in the 'Post-activity Comments' section.

There are many different theories of ageing and old age. Disengagement theory and those which focus on the way old age is socially constructed have been selected to illustrate the variations in approach that exist.

Disengagement theory

This argues that as people become older they gradually disengage from society in terms of their roles, social contacts and responsibilities. The process of disengagement means that older people retain a much more limited range of activities and circle of friends, which prepares them for the ultimate disengagement in terms of death or incapacity. This is conceptualised as an entirely natural and socially appropriate process. It is based on a functionalist view of society in which people fulfil roles in order for society to run smoothly. By disengaging, such as through retirement and withdrawal from family responsibilities, individuals cease to be essential to the functioning of the social structure and their death does not result in any significant disruption. This process also facilitates the smooth transfer of power from one generation to another (Biggs, 2000; Hockey and James, 2003).

Objections to this functionalist view have focused on the way that old age is portrayed as problematic and the ageing process is seen as leading to individuals' physical and mental deterioration. Other theories have concentrated on the role of social factors in ageing. It is to these that we now turn.

The social construction of old age

There are arguments in the sociological literature that old age is socially constructed in that it is neither natural nor inevitable because functional age is a social condition. Evidence used to support this view includes the way that what is thought to constitute old age varies historically, cross-culturally and within cultures (Hunt, 2005; Vera-Sanso, 2006; Degnen, 2007).

The **life-course perspective** is an example of these arguments that old age is socially constructed. Although there are different strands to this perspective, a predominant theme is that stages in life are not necessarily standardised, chronological, biologically fixed, sequential or gendered but are subject to a variety of social, historical and cultural influences.

One approach within the life-course perspective has focused on the increasing number of, and variation in, life stages that have arisen relatively recently in historical times. These are childhood, adolescence, adulthood, engagement, homeownership, parenthood, grandparenthood and old age. It maintains that these are not just based on biological differentiation but are socially constructed through the cumulative effects of 'socio-economic and cultural changes' (Hareven, 1995: 132). With respect to old age, this approach identifies the sources and nature of these sorts of changes that culminated in the emergence of old age as a life stage. For example, certain social, demographic, cultural and economic changes that occurred as a result of industrialisation changes were highly influential; old age as a life stage did not exist in preindustrial society. As communities were self-sufficient, and older people were still land and property owners, everyone worked for most of their lifetime and there was far less of a distinction between those in their middle years and those in their later years. Families were also large and individual members were closely engaged with each other. Thus older people were afforded considerable economic, social, familial and social power. However, during industrialisation the move from the land to cities for work meant that older people lost the status previously derived from their work, land and property. There was also a reduction in family size and these smaller families were likely to live in the cities. Consequently, older people became socially and economically segregated. This constellation of changes gradually led to their differentiation from other age groups and created a recognised formal phase of life for older people in society that was not solely related to bio-logical ageing (Cohen, 1987; Hareven, 1995; Hockey and James, 2003; Hunt, 2005).

As indicated, these changes also impacted negatively on the lives and experiences of older people. Other social and cultural changes occurred that had further negative implications for this group in society. These included the proliferation of negative stereotypes about older people, the growth in the literature on gerontology, which high-lighted the psychological and social problems of old age, and the estab-lishment of mandatory retirement and its concomitant association with a dependency on social security (Hareven, 1995).

Thus this approach within the life-course perspective argues that not only was the life stage of old age socially constructed but that it was also denigrated and became associated with economic and social dependence, segregation and low status. Although the emphasis is much more on the way capitalism works, similar themes can found in the work of those who have adopted a Marxist approach to the social construction of old age. For instance, Walker (1992) argues that one of the consequences of the constant search for greater profits and the maximisation of profit inherent in capitalism is that the cost and pro-ductivity of workers are closely scrutinised. In the early part of the twentieth century, it became apparent that older workers were more expensive than younger workers and, because of **ageism**, it was also assumed that they were less productive. Thus fixed-age retirement policies (initially at age 60) were introduced to reduce the cost of pay-ing older workers, reconstitute the workforce and optimise its produc-tivity. This reduced the numbers of those over 65 in employment considerably; between 1881 and 1981 the percentage of employed males over 65 in the British population fell from 73 per cent to 11 per cent. Furthermore, there was, on average, a halving of the income of those subjected to these fixed-age retirement policies (Vincent, 2006).

As this twentieth-century phenomenon of age-barrier retirement excluded those over 60 from work and considerably reduced their income, Walker maintains that it institutionalised a generally lower social and economic status for older people. In combination with pen-sions and social services policies, it also legitimated and enforced the dependency of older people on the state and others for support. Walker goes on to argue that increased economic and social dependence con-tributes to physical and mental dependence. Thus he concludes that dependency in older age is neither natural nor an inevitable result of chronological age itself – it has been 'constructed' by capitalist society.

Other approaches within the life-course perspective place more emphasis on the role of the individual, and the interplay between pri-vate lives and public events. An example of this type of approach is the work done by Holstein and Gubrium (2000). Their view is that, within the constraints of social, cultural and historical circumstances, individuals continuously construct their own life course; they argue that we are the 'everyday authors of our own lives' within 'circumstantial constraints' (Holstein and Gubrium, 2000: 182).

Indeed, the concept of an age-determined life course has recently been challenged. With reference to old age in particular, there have been many developments that have led to a dissolution of the life-course patterns associated with this life stage. These include the raising of the retirement age, the increase in workforce participation rates of older people, changing patterns of marriage and cohabitation and the increasing choice of lifestyles available to older people (Hunt, 2005; Vincent, 2006).

The life-course perspective in general has been accused of being 'vague at the theoretical level' (Arber and Ginn, 1995: 28) and not contributing to sociological theory. The justifications put forward were that while material influences on the transitions in social life are highlighted, their sociological significance (such as their relative power) is not addressed. Nonetheless, despite such criticisms, the life-course perspective and the different approaches within it increase our understanding of the social construction of old age.

BEING OLD

Such perspectives afford useful insights into ageing and old age. They also need to be considered in conjunction with detailed evidence about the reality of life for 'older people' in our society and the barriers to their social inclusion that exist. This evidence is considered in the rest of this section. In order to provide a comprehensive and accurate account of 'being old', it is organised into broad headings. These encompass a range of issues relevant to each heading together with their interrelationships. As with the life experiences of other vulnerable groups discussed in this book, the interaction between these and social divisions is also addressed. While this account acknowledges the fact that older people are as heterogeneous as the rest of the population and avoids taking the social division of age as given, it does also attempt to identify similarities in the life experiences of those who are statistically regarded as being 'older people'.

Income

As Figure 3.3 shows, the income of those over 65 rose by 28 per cent in the eight-year period between 1994/1995 and 2003/2004. This has meant there has been a general improvement in their economic position relative to the rest of society. Indeed, between 1996/1997 and 2002/2003, pensioner poverty was reduced in absolute terms by two-thirds, and, due to the introduction of measures such as pension credits and increases in the basic state pension, all pensioners were better off by

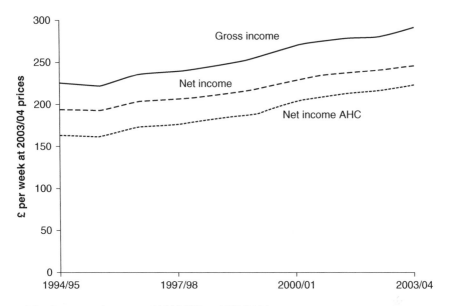

Figure 3.3   Pensioners' incomes 1994/1995 to 2003/2004
Source: National Statistics, 2005

an average of £26 per week (Department for Work and Pensions, 2004; Social Exclusion Unit, 2004a; National Statistics, 2005; Patsios, 2006).

However, 21 per cent of older people are still on low incomes and some groups of pensioners are still much more badly off than others. There is an interaction between age, gender and social class in old-age poverty; the elderly who are most likely to be poor are those who are the older pensioners, women (especially older women) both widowed and single, and those who have been manual workers. In addition, older people on low incomes tend to be concentrated in certain geographical areas, such as the Northeast, Northwest, West Midlands and Greater London. Moreover, despite the fact that the overall proportion of pensioners living in poverty has fallen since 1995/1996, older people, particularly those living alone, represent one of the groups in our society that are likely to live in poverty. Various factors influence statistics about the prevalence of poverty among those over 65, such as the type of measurement used and the fact that, despite drives to improve benefits uptake, there is also a reluctance to claim benefits among this group. The latter has been attributed to the way that older people do not necessarily feel that they are living in poverty. This is because they may compare their own standard of living favourably with a variety of reference groups, such as the older people whom they knew when they were young who lived in much poorer conditions (Evandrou and Falkingham, 2005; National Statistics, 2005; Social Exclusion Unit, 2005; Patsios, 2006; Vincent, 2006; Shelter, 2007b; Zaidi and Gustafsson, 2007).

Health and disability

Although people are living both longer and healthier lives and there have been many initiatives to improve the health and healthcare of older people, age does bring with it a greater incidence of **chronic illness** and disability than that found for other age groups. This is a major contributory factor to their vulnerability. Table 3.1 illustrates the increase in percentages of men and women reporting both physical and mental chronic illness as they age. The significantly higher percentage for women over 65 is due to the fact that women live longer and are therefore more likely to have more years in ill health. With reference to disability, evidence from the Disability Rights Commission (2006) shows how disability rates also increase with age; while 9 per cent of adults aged 16–24 are disabled, this increases to about 44 per cent in the 50 to retirement age category. The sharpest increase in both ill health and disability occurs among those over 80 (National Statistics, 2005; Social Exclusion Unit, 2005; Vincent, 2006; Holmes, 2007).

Figure 3.4   Percentage reporting chronic illness

Age	16–44	45–64	65+
Men	10	24	39
Women	11	25	41

Source: Adapted from General Household Survey, 2003

Increasing years are not the only influence on the ill health and disability rates among those over 65. Another influence that has been identified is low income. For example, the generally lower income of older people referred to above often leads to fuel poverty, which has adverse effects on health; 31,000 older people died of cold-related illnesses between 2001 and 2006 (O'Neill et al., 2006; Riddell, 2007; Shelter, 2007b).

Other findings in the literature on ageing and health confuse the picture about the health of older people. One is the fact that 60 per cent still consider themselves to be in good health, even if they have an illness and/or disability that restricts their daily activities (Social Exclusion Unit, 2005). Indeed, there has been a recent downward trend in those over 70 reporting poor/fair health (1.85 per cent) and disability (1.38 per cent). However, new health problems have emerged with developments in medicine. For instance, the earlier diagnosis and more effective therapies that slow the progression of dementia mean that older people will remain in the early stages of dementia for longer. Although independent living is possible, they do experience considerable emotional turmoil and problems with cognitive loss (Martin et al., 2007; Steeman et al., 2007; Wolf et al., 2007).

Despite such conflicting evidence, it is clear that ill health and disability do increase with age, particularly among those over 80. There is also evidence that this age-related increase in ill health and disability imposes restrictions on the daily activities of both males and females, as illustrated in Figure 3.5.

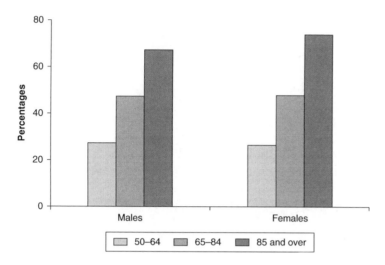

Figure 3.5   Age-standardised rates of long-term illness or disability which restricts daily activities: by gender and age, April 2001

Source: National Statistics, 2005

Daily life

Research on older people shows that there is a general reduction in their activities that tends to lead to an increase in their risk of social isolation. Figure 3.5 clearly illustrates this reduction but, as the discussion below of the data it presents in relation to other findings shows, health is not the only barrier to an active life in older age.

Figure 3.6 provides an overview of the daily lives of older people; it shows how people aged 65 and over in the United Kingdom spend more time than those aged 50 to 64 watching television, reading, listening to the radio or music and resting. They also spend less time socialising and taking part in leisure pursuits; trips out of the house become less frequent and involve less and less distance with advancing years. These trips are also mainly for shopping and other personal business and there is a greater reliance on public transport, in particular local buses. Unsurprisingly, older people also often report difficulties in accessing local amenities such as shops, post offices, banks or hospitals. Compared to non-pensioners, pensioners have lower levels of social contact and poorer social support; they are more likely than any other age group to have infrequent contact with family, friends and neighbours. Some 1 in

5 people over the age of 65 are alone for more than 12 hours a day. Furthermore a quarter of people over 65 do not have a best friend, which is higher than any other age group in the population. Although this is partly because contact with non-family, civic engagement and membership of clubs, groups and organisations tend to decrease with age, whether older people live alone or in a couple is also an important influence, particularly among the very old (National Statistics, 2005; Social Exclusion Unit, 2005; Patsios, 2006; Shelter, 2007b).

In addition to health and mobility problems, the barriers to a more active life that have been identified are poor public transport, a lack of suitable and affordable transport, concerns about personal safety, the fear of crime and a contraction of social networks because of friends and/or relatives dying or moving (Choi and Wodarski, 1996; Burnett, 2002; National Statistics, 2005; Patsios, 2006). However, there is some recent evidence of a reduction in these barriers, such as fear of crime, among older people (Social Exclusion Unit, 2004a).

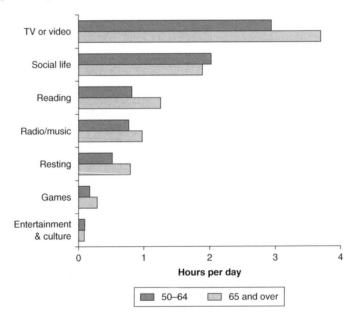

Figure 3.6 Time spent on selected activities: by age, 2000–2001, United Kingdom
Source: National Statistics, 2005

Despite the evidence that there is a contraction in activities undertaken, several studies show that some older people, particularly those under 74, do lead active lives and are involved in their communities; Allender et al. (2006) found that those in the 60–69 age group are more likely to maintain their levels of participation in sport and physical activity than other groups. Volunteering rates for those on the 65–74 age groups are high. More older people are participating in education and learning new skills, including how to use computers and the internet. In

2002, 51 per cent of those aged 60 to 69 in England and Wales engaged in some form of learning as opposed to 47 per cent in 1997 (Home Office, 2003; National Statistics, 2005).

Employment

Labour-market inactivity rates for those over state retirement age are high; 93 per cent of pensioners do not undertake paid work and those that do work tend to be the younger pensioners. Lack of employment among the growing number of older people, who now experience much longer periods of retirement, has been a cause of concern because it can lead to poverty and social exclusion and can increase the costs of funding pensions. As a consequence, there has been considerable political support for extending working lives both in the UK and many other Western countries. A variety of approaches have been used in the United Kingdom. These include raising the state pension age in stages (it will be 68 by 2044) and increasing the participation and retention of older workers in the labour market. One of the key policy initiatives in relation to the latter is the New Deal package called 'New Deal 50 Plus'. This offers opportunities to those over 50 to undertake education and training while on benefits. It also provides subsidies for six months to those employers who recruit people aged 50 plus (Craig, 2004; Mayhew, 2005).

One obvious cause of the low labour-market participation rates of older people is the higher incidence of chronic illness and disability that they experience (as discussed above). Other causes, particularly those affecting younger pensioners, such as ageism, have been addressed through various initiatives and will be discussed in more depth below. Moreover, labour-market non-participation does not automatically mean non-productivity; much unpaid work outside the labour market is undertaken by some older people and this is highly useful to society. Nonetheless, there has been a steady increase in the employment rates for men and women in the 50–64 age range as a result of the political drive to increase labour participation rates for older people (Evandrou and Falkingham, 2005; Social Exclusion Unit, 2005; Patsios, 2006; Vincent, 2006).

Personal relationships

Gott (2005) argues that there are two equally oppressive and inaccurate representations of later-life sexuality; one is 'asexual old age' and the other is the 'sexy oldie'. The first portrays sexuality and ageing as being incompatible and distasteful. It is also exclusionary in that it denies older people the opportunity to be sexual because of the societal intolerance of later-life sexuality that it infers. The second pressurises older people to remain sexual if they wish to remain socially engaged and leaves no room for individual expression and diversity. Both homogenise older people's sexuality.

Indeed, studies focusing on ascertaining older people's attitudes to sexuality support Gott's view that such representations are inaccurate. It has been established that older people see sex as an important component of a close relationship and it is usually ill health, as opposed to age per se, that impacts on the priority that sex has in a relationship. Studies have also highlighted the heterogeneity of the sexuality of older people; as older people's ages can range from 65 to over 90, they will have been subjected to varying social attitudes relating to their particular birth cohort. These can cause significant differences in their attitudes to sexuality. For instance, those who are currently in their 80s are more likely to have seen it as the wife's duty to provide sex for her husband. In contrast, those currently in their 60s were products of the era of the contraceptive pill and the equality of the sexes, which resulted in very different views about sexuality. A further issue relating to the heterogeneity of the sexuality of older people is the recognition that they are not all heterosexual. Despite the fact that 10 per cent of the population is non-heterosexual, those older people who are gay, lesbian or bisexual have been invisible until very recently (Gott and Hinchliff, 2003; Gott, 2005; Williams et al., 2007).

Other research has shown that a new form of personal relationship is developing among elderly people. These types of relationships have been called Living Apart Together (LAT). This arrangement is an increasingly popular alternative to co-residence (with or without marriage) for those who are over 60. It is long-term, combining intimacy with autonomy, and does not involve cohabitation as those involved will maintain their own homes. It has few, if any, of the structural commitments of marriage (such as a common ownership of resources and interwoven kinship networks) and is based on a mutual emotional and moral commitment (Borrell and Ghazanfareeon Karlsson, 2003).

Living arrangements

A further outcome of the decline in health and increase in disability with age means that older people need more help with managing essential aspects of normal daily life. These include climbing the stairs, eating, bathing and taking a shower. Thus the amount of help increases with age and independent living becomes more problematic (Office for National Statistics, 2003; Stewart and Vaitilingham, 2004).

There has been a decline in intergenerational households; only 5 per cent of the over 65s now live with an adult child (McCarthy and Thomas, 2004). Most older people now live either in their own homes or in a residential establishment. If they live in their own homes they are usually owner-occupiers, but some do rent from a local authority, a housing association or privately. Their homes may also be in sheltered and retirement housing complexes where support is provided (National Statistics, 2005; Shelter, 2007a). The move to community care since the 1980s and the more recent increase in intensive home care and community-based services have meant that older people have been able to live in their own homes and there has been a reduction of older people needing to enter residential care (Baggott, 1998; Department for Work and Pensions, 2005a; Social Exclusion Unit, 2005; Patsios, 2006). Although this is viewed as a positive development, it does not necessarily have positive outcomes for all those affected by the changes that have occurred.

With reference to those older people living in their own homes, despite the initiatives to improve the availability and quality of support, many problematic issues can arise for older people and those who care for them. Failures in the delivery of appropriate care and support and the damaging implications that these have for older people are well documented. These failures include the inflexibility and lack of integration of services, poor standards, confusion over the roles of volunteers and professionals, and difficult relationships experienced with some professionals. There have also been concerns about gaps between quality and level of provision and users' needs, and the geographical variations in these gaps. These have increased with recent rationing and changes in the eligibility criteria used by local authorities. Further variations in the services identified have been linked to an older person's race, class and level of education. Indeed, social care arrangements for older people in their own homes compare unfavourably with several other European countries (Chamberlynne and King, 2000; Miller, 2003; Evandrou and Falkingham, 2005; Social Exclusion Unit, 2005; Larsson et al., 2006; Leutz and Capitman, 2007; Revill, 2007; Shelter, 2007b).

Living in your own home when older can also mean living alone; although the proportion of older people in Europe and the United States of America living alone has declined recently in Great Britain, 60 per cent of women over 75 and 29 per cent of men of the same age still live alone (Tomassini et al., 2004). As mentioned above, older people in general experience reduced social contact and social support. However, those living alone spend between 70–90 per cent of their time in their home and are at much greater risk of becoming socially isolated, particularly those in rural areas. It is estimated that one in ten are currently chronically lonely and by 2021 nearly 2.2 million over-65s will be socially isolated (McCarthy and Thomas, 2004; Riddell, 2007). As discussed in Chapter 1, social isolation and a lack of social support can increase susceptability to poorer physical and mental health (Berkman and Syme, 1979; Berkman et al., 2000; Department for Work and Pensions, 2005a).

Moreover, a third of older people live in 'non-decent homes' (as defined by the Decent Homes Standard, 2000). This is a much higher proportion than other groups in the population and means that their houses are more likely to lack central heating, and to have problems such as damp and infestation. Thus when older people live in their own homes, they have a higher-than-average risk of living in poor-quality accommodation. In addition, where older people live in supported accommodation (such as sheltered housing and retirement villages), although it offers many advantages such as the combination of independence and security, it may not meet their needs. This finding has arisen mainly from research into the housing needs of older people; lesbian and gay older people said they would prefer to live in accommodation designed for their needs because they feel that existing accommodation with support is geared to heterosexual older people and is unsuitable and hostile (Johnson et al., 2005; Social Exclusion Unit, 2005; Shelter, 2007b).

Being able to live in his/her own home often depends on an older person having an **unpaid carer**. There are 5.7 million unpaid carers in the United Kingdom, of which half look after someone aged 75 and over (Social Exclusion Unit, 2005). Although carers may choose to care, and there has been a considerable increase in the support for carers over the past two decades, many studies have continued to identify the negative effects of caring on all carers. These include the consequences caring has for their physical and psychological health and social relationships (Lewis and Meredith, 1988; McLaughlin and Ritchie, 1994; Brown and Stetz, 1999; Hirst, 1999; Bond et al., 2003). Studies carried out in several different parts of the world have shown that carers over retirement age are more prone to these and other detrimental effects of caring. For instance, they are more likely to have a pre-existing medical condition that compounds the negative effects of caring on their health (Bandeira et al., 2007; Chun et al., 2007; Hanratty et al., 2007). Indeed retired carers have been referred to as a 'vulnerable group' (Hanratty et al., 2007: 35).

Those who care for older people are usually spouses or adult children. Spousal carers of older people are likely to be retired. Increases in longevity mean that many of those adult children caring for the over-85s are also 65 and over (Social Exclusion Unit, 2005). Therefore the increase in older people living in their own homes can have adverse consequences for those caring for them because of their own advancing years.

Moreover, international trends indicate that in the future, families will be less likely to be able to care for elderly relatives. One of these trends is geographical mobility, both in the search for jobs and as a result of social mobility, which makes it more likely that children will move away from their parents. Others are the reduction in family size and increase in voluntary childlessness; these two trends will mean that the elderly will have fewer or no children to call upon for help than in previous generations. The final trend is the increase in marital breakdown; those parents who are not awarded custody may have weaker links with their children and therefore their risk of being isolated in their old age increases (Phillipson, 1998; Vincent, 2006; Williams et al., 2007).

Even though one of the consequences of the increase in older people living in their own homes has been that there are fewer older people in

residential care, significant numbers of older old people are living in residential establishments. The proportion of older people living in residential care increases with age; in 2001, among those aged 75–84, only
5.2 per cent of women and 3.2 per cent of men were in residential care.
The corresponding figures for those aged 90 and over were 34 per cent
and 20 per cent. Although the higher percentages for women mainly
reflect the difference in life expectancy between males and females, gen-
ders differences in the marital status of older people are also a contributory factor; as a consequence of men's lower life expectancy, among
older people there are more women who are widowed than men. Hence
older women are less likely to have a spouse to take care of them and
more likely to live in a residential establishment.

As with living in their own homes, despite initiatives to ensure quality
of care (such as the Care Standards Act, 2001), living in a residential
establishment can also have negative effects on older people; residential
care is associated with a lack of privacy, a loss of independence, exclusion
from everyday life, high levels of depression, and nearly half of older
people admitted to residential or nursing homes die within 18 months of
admission (Biggs, 2000; Gott, 2005; Social Exclusion Unit, 2005; Davison
et al., 2007). Although standards of care and models of good practice have
been developed, a significant number of residential establishments are
still classified as 'poor'. Thus quality of care in residential establishments
for older people is not necessarily guaranteed (Evandrou and
Falkingham, 2005; Riddell, 2007).

This discussion has shown that older people are at risk of vulnerability whether they live on their own or in a residential establishment.
Nonetheless, when evaluating living arrangements for older people, it
is important not to romanticise the care of the elderly in the past.
These arrangements evolved as a result of different demographic, historical and cultural factors and no ideal system exists as every form of
living arrangement for older people will have its drawbacks.

Abuse of older people

Elder abuse can include physical, psychological, financial or sexual abuse
and neglect. Although accurate statistics are difficult to obtain because elder
abuse is often unreported, it is estimated that 5 per cent of older people suffer psychological abuse and 2 per cent suffer physical abuse. Perpetrators are
commonly partners, family members, neighbours and domiciliary care
workers. Those aged 70 and over (particularly women over 70) are most vulnerable to abuse. A significant number of incidences will take place in their
own homes, with those living on their own being more vulnerable; a recent
analysis of calls made to the Action on Elder Abuse Helpline showed that 64
per cent of cases of abuse had occurred in an individual's own home and 23
per cent had occurred in a residential care home (Action on Elder Abuse,
2004, 2007; Department of Health, 2004a; Pritchard, 2006).

Discrimination

Discrimination has already been referred to in passing during the discussions above about employment and sexuality. A further exploration of the literature on the former shows that there is much evidence of age discrimination; a recent study by the Social Exclusion Unit (2005) found that 1.5 million jobs were vacant on any day and over 1 million people over 50 would like to be working. In addition, 10 per cent of companies do not employ any over-50s, and nine out of ten older people believe that employers discriminate against them. With reference to sexuality, research has shown that gay, lesbian, bisexual and transgender older people experience discrimination from staff and residents in retirement care facilities (Johnson et al., 2005). This is linked to the discrimination that older people experience in health and social care generally; although the Age Limits of Health Care Act, 1999 prohibits the refusal or delay of treatment on the basis of age, there is evidence that age discrimination in healthcare continues. For example, there are restrictions on screening and cardiac care. In social care it has been found that older people, particularly those living in deprived and rural areas, are more likely to receive poorer-quality care than other social care clients (Roberts, 2000; Levenson, 2003; Department for Work and Pensions, 2005a; Social Exclusion Unit, 2005).

Such discrimination has been linked to negative images of old age and the way that old age is culturally devalued. More specifically, the discrimination that older people experience in health and social care has been attributed to the less favourable treatment they receive from professionals working in health and social care (Roberts, 2000; Degnen, 2007). Although discrimination on the grounds of age is not illegal in the same way as sexism or racism, there have been many initiatives aimed at addressing this and improving practice (Evandrou and Falkingham, 2005; Vincent, 2006). There has also been a cultural shift over the past decade in attitudes to the elderly. This has been attributed in part to media attention to age discrimination and changes in advertising representations of older people; there has been a move from negative representations of them as being feeble and senile to more positive ones such as being healthy, fit, active and even sexual (Bytheway, 2003; Williams et al., 2007).

ACTIVITY 3.3

Talk to someone you know who is over 70 and try to establish the extent to which the above experiences feature in their lives. What do you think can be done to improve their situation? Recent initiatives to address the continuing vulnerability and exclusion of older people as well as suggestions for future policy development are discussed below. As you read through them, identify the similarities and differences between your ideas and those presented.

The preceding discussions demonstrate that there have been some recent improvements in the life experiences of older people. These include reductions in poverty, increases in living standards, choice of living arrangements, employment rates and more positive representations of older people. Such progress can in part be attributed to the initiatives that have attempted to weaken the relationship between older people and vulnerability referred to during these discussions. Several of these have formed part of the ongoing political drive to help the most vulnerable. The effectiveness of the approach taken to vulnerable and socially excluded older people has recently been assessed and the future direction of polices required to sustain the progress made to date has been identified (Social Exclusion Unit, 2004a, 2004b, 2005). As mentioned in the introduction to this chapter, there is now a clear commitment to the elderly because of concerns about our ageing society. Indeed, consideration has also been given to the appointment of a Minister for Older People as an indication of the government's commitment to older people's well-being.

However, it is also clear from the above exploration of the experience of ageing and old age that many older people are still socially excluded. The direction of policies that are currently being devised and implemented to address some of the outstanding challenges in the reduction of the social exclusion of older people is discussed in the next section.

CURRENT POLICY INITIATIVES

There have been several recent initiatives that aim to address factors continuing to contributing to the social exclusion of older people. An example is an interim report by the Social Exclusion Unit entitled 'Excluded Older People' (Social Exclusion Unit, 2005). Another is 'Opportunity Age' (Department for Work and Pensions, 2005a), which is the government's first ever strategy to set out its agenda for meeting the challenge of an ageing society. A cross-government SureStart programme for older people was also piloted in 2006 (Social Exclusion Unit, 2006). This is an extension of the SureStart programme for children and families (discussed in Chapter 4). It aims to promote well-being in older age by addressing poor health, poverty and social exclusion with effective joined-up services at key times.

The discussions below outline the sort of policies planned to address specific aspects of the continuing vulnerability and social exclusion of older people. They focus on three main areas and include references to a range of initiatives, including those briefly outlined above.

Income and employment

Although there have been improvements in the income levels of older people in general, low take-up levels of benefits remain the main contributory factor to pensioner poverty, particularly among certain groups (Craig, 2004). There are proposals about ways of maximising take-up by simplifying application processes and providing more localised support (Department for Work and Pensions, 2005).

Criticisms of the political emphasis on paid work as the solution to poverty and social exclusion, and as a means to social citizenship, have been highlighted in relation to the other vulnerable groups discussed in this book. There are several problems with the initiatives that have encouraged older people into paid employment as a means to more active citizenship. One is the way that the concept of citizenship is exclusionary in terms of age (see the Introduction); by seeing paid work as a complete proxy for citizenship, such initiatives actually deny older people this status because they ignore the other activities through which older people achieve citizenship. These include voluntary work and the substantial contribution to caring for others that they make. Furthermore, while it has been shown that these activities do enable more active citizenship, there is a need for the adoption of a broader view of social exclusion and for initiatives to focus much more on participation in mainstream society as a means to combating the social exclusion of older people. It is to the efforts to reduce the social isolation of older people and improve their social participation that we now turn (Craig, 2004; Vincent, 2006).

Social participation

In order to truly unlock the potential of older people to contribute to society, many proposals aim to remove the obstacles that prevent older people from participating more fully in society in general. A fundamental barrier is discrimination; steps are being taken to address the root causes of persistent age discrimination both in and beyond employment, and to simplify current discrimination legislation (Department for Work and Pensions, 2005a). As mentioned in the discussions on the experiences of being old, age-related ill health and disability can restrict older people's opportunities to play a full and active role in society. There is a two-pronged attack on ill health among older people; one is the drive to promote healthy living at all ages, which should lay the foundations for better health in old age. The other is through the promotion of mental and physical activity, healthy diet and smoking cessation among older people. Other barriers that have been identified are fear of crime as well as security at home and on the streets; anticrime initiatives will be continued and older people will be involved in the design of local policies and strategies to help address their concerns. With respect to overcoming the problems that older people have with getting out and about, local authorities are being encouraged to provide more accessible transport and concessionary fare schemes (Department of Health, 2004b, 2004c; Department for Work and Pensions, 2005a).

It is anticipated that the removal of these barriers will increase older people's independence and enable them to take full advantage of the schemes being introduced to involve them more in mainstream society. Examples are the availability of more opportunities to be active citizens by being involved in decision-making and voluntary work in their communities. In addition, more learning and training opportunities will arise from the proposed removal of the upper age limits for higher education fees. The accessibility of leisure facilities is being extended too, for instance, libraries are developing further support for older people who are struggling with disabilities (Department for Work and Pensions, 2005a; Social Exclusion Unit, 2005).

Services for older people

The emphasis on older people living more independent lives also features in planned service developments. As mentioned in previous discussions, many older people are living in their own homes with the support of community-based services. There is a commitment to raising awareness and improving the delivery of these services, and providing more choice and opportunities for user involvement. With reference to health services, these include strengthening such services for old-age conditions, increasing their flexibility, making them more person-centred and providing better management for complex and longstanding conditions. Additional support is to be made available for those who care for older people in their own homes; steps are being taken to further protect carers' income and to encourage wider neighbourhood support for them by promoting more active citizenship within communities. Moves are also being made to tackle inappropriate housing, increase levels of housing-related services (such as good neighbour and handymen services) and provide more home adaptations to enable older people to stay in their own homes (Department for Work and Pensions, 2005a; Social Exclusion Unit, 2005).

It has been argued that this political concern about the social exclusion for older people has been driven by alarms about the costs of supporting them and meeting these costs when relatively fewer people in society will be of working age; at worst, social care costs could double within 25 years and by 2050 expenditure on long-term care could be four times as much as it is currently (Social Exclusion Unit, 2005; Vincent, 2006; Wanless, 2006). There is clear evidence that costs are reduced by the type of interventions already introduced and those planned. For instance, adaptations to older people's houses in order to help them live in their own homes work out at around £4.74 per week. This compares very favourably to the £338 that is the average cost of keeping an older person in residential care (Heywood, 2001). The development of health services so that more older people can receive healthcare in own homes has reduced the length of costly hospital stays and number of admissions to long-term care (Social Exclusion Unit, 2005; Holmes, 2007).

This evidence is presented not to deny the benefits to older people that such developments bring. Indeed some of these developments have reduced mortality among the elderly (Social Exclusion Unit, 2005). However, it has to be asked how effective the focus on social exclusion with respect to older people can be because of the complexity of the exclusionary processes involved (Bowes, 2006). One reason for this complexity is that some of the processes are very hard to control. For instance, the way that exclusionary factors due to the disadvantages associated with low income, poor health and educational status persist and accumulate throughout the life course (Taylor-Gooby, 2005; Patsios, 2006; Price, 2006). Others argue that a major influence on the social exclusion of older people is their own construction of themselves as being 'past it'. Hence addressing their social exclusion also entails addressing the self-perceptions of older people (Degnen, 2007; Hutton, 2007).

CONCLUSIONS

The exploration of the life experiences of older people in this chapter has highlighted the extent to which these continue to contribute to the social exclusion of significant proportions of this group in society. The evaluation of the recent and planned policies highlighted some of the problems inherent in addressing the vulnerability of older people. The details that have been given about the demographic structure of society show that the challenge of ensuring the inclusion of older people is not going to lessen. While policy-makers have clearly attempted to be creative in their approach, several conclusions about what could be usefully focused on in future initiatives aimed at reducing older people's social exclusion can be drawn from the discussions.

The variation between different groups of older people has been demonstrated throughout the chapter. More specifically, some groups are far more likely to be vulnerable than others. For instance, those who still experience poverty, those over 85 and those who live alone. The increased vulnerability of these groups of older people means that overcoming their social exclusion involves tackling specific and often more complex barriers than those found within some other groups of older people. In order to work towards the social inclusion of all older people, the particular needs of the most vulnerable older people should be carefully researched and targeted through policies.

As mentioned in the section on the theories of ageing, the life course is not always closely related to biological ageing; both individual and social processes are influential. Therefore it is also important that policies are sensitive to an individual's own construction of their old age and to changes in the life-course patterns associated with the later years. Moreover, the concept of citizenship for older people requires revisiting to fully and publicly acknowledge their citizenship in relation to their unpaid and voluntary contributions to society. An examination of the welfare systems in other European countries, such as Sweden, can provide further ideas about extending the citizenship of older people in the UK.

Finally, as discussed above, exclusionary factors accumulate over the life course and adversely affect old age. Thus, there is a need to continue finding effective ways of breaking the cycle of disadvantage to address social exclusion in people's lives. In order to achieve the objective of breaking this cycle, another vulnerable group has been subject to much political scrutiny and activity. This is children – the subject of the next chapter.

DISCUSSION POINTS

To what extent is the social exclusion of older people in the United Kingdom socially constructed?

Do you think the relationship between older people and vulnerability has weakened over the past decade?

Is social inclusion a realistic goal in relation to this vulnerable group?

What further steps need to be taken to reduce the exclusionary factors that accumulate over the life course and adversely affect old age?

FURTHER STUDY

Chapter 1 in Hunt (2005) provides a useful account of the development of the life-course perspective and gives details of recent changes within this perspective. For a highly readable account of the social construction of old age read Hareven (1995). Although this is written from an American perspective, it explains the process and factors involved in the creation of this life stage very well. Up-to-date statistics on older people can be found in the Focus On series produced by the Office for National Statistics. If you want to explore the relationship between gender and ageing in more depth, both Arber and Ginn (1995) and Arber et al. (2003)

(Continued)

cover a wide range of issues about this relationship. A visit to the Social Exclusion Taskforce website will provide information about recent initiatives to address the social exclusion of this vulnerable group.

Key readings

Hareven, T.K. (1995). 'Changing images of aging and the social construction of the life course' in Featherstone, M. and Wernick, A. (eds) *Images of aging: cultural representations of later life*. London: Routledge

Patsios, D. (2006). 'Pensioners, poverty and social exclusion' in Pantazis, C., Gordon, D. and Levitas, R. (eds) *Poverty and social exclusion in Britain: the millennium survey*. Bristol: Policy Press

Phillipson, C. (1998). *Reconstructing old age: new agendas in social theory and practice*. London: Sage

Social Exclusion Unit (2005). *Excluded older people: Social Exclusion Unit interim report*. London: Office of the Deputy Prime Minister

Vincent, J.A (2006). 'Age and old age' in Payne, G. (ed.) *Social divisions*. Basingstoke: Macmillan

POST-ACTIVITY COMMENTS

ACTIVITY 3.2

Did you notice that Kate talks about how she used to fulfil many roles that involved status and responsibilities to others, especially her family? In contrast, in her old age she interacts with a very limited number of people, seems to be isolated from her family and no one is dependent on her. She talks about how the physical effects of ageing influence her and her dependency on those who are caring for her. With reference to the latter, she clearly feels that the nurses in her residential home perceive her negatively and do not treat her as an individual.

Disengagement theory would focus on the gradual withdrawal from social roles and responsibilities that occurs as people enter their later years that is highlighted in Kate's poem. Her death does not seem to cause any social discontinuity. This would be interpreted by disengagement theorists as being the result of the withdrawal process.

Kate's experiences of lack of status, isolation from mainstream society and her family, unwelcome dependency and negative attitudes can be explained by the theories that argue old age is socially constructed. In addition, the fact that she is in a residential home is the outcome of contemporary policies about care of the elderly and therefore reflects the way that dependency is socially constructed through social policies.

Chapter 4

Children

OVERVIEW

- The social construction of childhood
- Factors that contribute to the vulnerability of children
- Policy initiatives that address children's vulnerability
- Conclusions
- Suggestions for further study

INTRODUCTION

Unlike older people in our society, the number of children has been declining since 1971; they represent just under 20 per cent of the population at the moment and the decline in their numbers is expected to continue (see Figures 3.1 and 3.2 in Chapter 3). While meeting the needs of an *expanding* group in society is therefore obviously not an issue with this vulnerable group, there is a cross-national political concern with the well-being of children because of their acknowledged importance to the future of a society. More specifically, the past five years have seen an emphasis on the social inclusion of children in international comparisons. Such research has highlighted many of the ways in which childhood in the United Kingdom compares unfavourably with other industrialised countries (Bradshaw et al., 2006). Consequently, there have been many initiatives in the United Kingdom to reduce children's levels of vulnerability and address factors which could contribute to their social exclusion in adulthood.

The concept of childhood will be explored at the beginning of this chapter. This will be followed by discussions of several key vulnerability factors in children's lives and some of the policies in the United Kingdom introduced to prevent their social exclusion in the longer term.

WHAT IS CHILDHOOD?

ACTIVITY 4.1

Briefly describe what you think a fairly typical 1950s' 10-year-old child would have been like, for example, their clothes, their leisure activities, their schooling and their family life. Now do the same for a 10-year-old child today. List the differences between the two descriptions. What does this tell you about the nature of childhood? (See the 'Post-activity Comments' at the end of the chapter.)

The arguments in the sociological literature that stages in life are socially constructed were introduced in Chapter 3 in relation to old age. The life-course perspective was given as one example of these arguments. The way that this approach focuses on how stages in life are not necessarily biologically determined but rather the result of the cumulative effects of social, cultural and historical influences was explained (Hareven, 1995; Hunt, 2005).

Similar arguments have been put forward in relation to childhood; a major proponent of the view that childhood is socially constructed is Aries (1965). He used historical material to argue that in pre-industrial societies, childhood was not a distinct stage of life in most cultures in that children were not regarded as significantly different from adults. For instance, they were integrated into adult working and social life, treated and dressed as miniature adults who gradually assumed adult roles and slowly matured into adulthood. Those in the lower classes worked at a very early age and for long hours.

Several social and economic developments changed this; as life became more complex, there was an increasing emphasis on the importance of education and the acquisition of skills, which led to the beginning of a period in which children were educated and prepared for the adult world. Industrialisation separated the world of work and home. This had two implications: one was a greater emphasis on the sentimental relations of family life as opposed to their previous, more instrumental basis, leading to a new child-centredness. Another was that working children became more visible and offensive to the middle-class philanthropists. The legislation that ensued throughout the nineteenth century meant that children's paid work was gradually limited; compulsory schooling was introduced; and many laws were passed to protect children's welfare. Hence childhood began to be defined as a separate life stage and the continuation of these developments contributed to the consolidation of the demarcation between childhood and adulthood that had previously not existed (Aries, 1965; Hareven, 1995).

Aries' views have been challenged; there is evidence that the integration of children into the adult world was not as complete as he suggested and that they were still viewed as being subordinate within the patriarchal and feudal social order of pre-industrial societies. Furthermore, his construction of childhood is not universal as in many third world countries young children still work, often in demanding circumstances. In addition, the fact that children are not passive actors and construct their own everyday reality should not be ignored. Nonetheless, by the mid-twentieth century the first twelve years of life had become a clear and distinct stage of life recognised as childhood. It tended to be romanticised as a time of freedom, of play rather than work and protection from the 'real' world without responsibilities. A plethora of literature on child-rearing and family life emerged (Hunt, 2005; Jackson and Scott, 2006).

More recently, however, there have been concerns that childhood in the West is being eroded and that childhood is in 'crisis'; technological and social developments such as the ease with which children now have access to adult information and adult lives, mass conspicuous consumption and precocious sexuality have led to a blurring of the boundaries between adulthood and childhood. Thus, new notions of childhood in the West are emerging. Globalisation has also meant that these are being imposed on those cultures that still have more benign conceptions of childhood. Alongside such changes in the construction of childhood there have been growing national and international concerns about children's vulnerability, and an awareness that their lives and experience can be adversely affected by many factors (Postman, 1983; Garbarino et al., 1992; Hareven, 1995; Stephens, 1995; Jackson and Scott, 2006). It is to the realities of children's lives today that we now turn.

CHILDREN'S VULNERABILITY

As mentioned in the introduction to this chapter, children and young people's vulnerability and/or 'well-being' has been high on the political agenda. However, there is no agreement on indicators of both vulnerability and well-being and a comprehensive analysis of either of these concepts in relation to children and young people (Bradshaw and Mayhew, 2005; Bradshaw et al., 2006; Buchanen, 2007). Thus, not only is there an absence of a general consensus about what constitutes 'childhood' but also as to what are the factors that contribute to children's vulnerability. A review of the relevant literature and policy documents established that the most accurate and comprehensive explanation of why today's children are vulnerable would be to define 'children' as those under 16 years of age and focus on several key factors that were identified. These factors together with the interactions between them and other social divisions are discussed below.

Poverty

The measurement of poverty in childhood is notoriously controversial and is further complicated by the fact that definitions of poverty vary; a distinction is often made between **relative** and **absolute poverty**. The former refers to the lack of basic resources to sustain a physically healthy existence. Absolute poverty refers to poverty relative to standards in a particular society and reflects differences in living standards between societies and across time within the same society. Many different indicators of poverty are also used in studies into childhood poverty. Nonetheless, there is clear evidence that around a fifth of children in the United Kingdom are living in poverty. Studies have also shown that childhood poverty tends to lead to adult poverty and its persistence across generations is of particular concern in relation to the intergenerational nature of social exclusion (Social Exclusion Unit, 2004a; Mogadi and Middleton, 2005; Blanden and Gibbons, 2006; Buchanen, 2007).

Parents will often try to protect their children from poverty and will go without necessities themselves. Indeed, spending on children in poor families is proportionally higher than it is in richer families. Nonetheless, studies show that children in poorer families are more vulnerable than those in better-off families. For instance, they have higher malnutrition, acute and chronic illness rates, experience more injuries, are less likely to take part in school, hobbies and leisure activities, and to have holidays. Childhood poverty also has negative effects on cognitive and social development. Although some of the impacts of childhood poverty are mediated by factors like the quality of family relations, their adverse impacts increase with age. This is reflected in, for example, low educational performance, and in higher adulthood rates of ill health, offending, drug and alcohol abuse, and reduced employment and earnings prospects (Bradshaw et al., 2006).

Some groups of children are far more vulnerable to severe and persistent poverty than others. These include homeless children, some ethnic minority groups and those in particular types of families such as asylum seeker and lone-parent families, large families and families in which people have a disability. In addition to the above negative experiences, such children are more likely to experience problems at school (including higher school truancy and expulsion rates) and with housing conditions, and to feel lonely and unhappy. It is therefore these groups of children in the severest form of poverty that are the most vulnerable to social exclusion (Bradshaw, 2002; Mogadi and Middleton, 2005; Brewer et al., 2006).

Diet and obesity

The diets of children in the United Kingdom, particularly those in poorer households, have been found to be nutritionally inadequate in that they generally contain an excess of fat and sugar and not enough fruit, vegetables and high-fibre products. Indeed, the quality and variety of their diets are among the worst in industrialised nations (Finch and Searle, 2005). Poor nutrition can result in many physical and mental health problems, such as high cholesterol, cardiovascular diseases, diabetes, high blood pressure, and impaired muscular and neurological growth and development (Desai, 2000).

While government interventions have focused on the quality of children's diets and the risks to their health, it is the steady increase in childhood obesity rates that has had a particularly high political profile; in 1995, fewer than 10 per cent of primary schoolchildren were classified as obese. In 2007, obesity rates had jumped to 16.9 per cent of boys and 16.8 per cent of girls aged between 2 and 10, with a third of all children leaving primary school overweight. It is now estimated that 24 per cent of boys and 32 per cent of girls will be overweight by 2025. Apart from the fact that obesity is a disease in its own right, as children who are overweight tend to carry obesity into later life, it can also cause many chronic diseases into adulthood. For instance, heart disease, cancer, diabetes, stroke, high blood pressure, high cholesterol levels and mental illness (Finch and Searle, 2005; Foresight, 2007).

These alarming increases have been attributed to a variety of factors, including the fact that children in the United Kingdom tend to consume more energy-dense foods compared to children in other countries. In addition, they lead far less active lives; less than one-third of school-children participate in regular physical activity at school; parents are reluctant to let children play outdoors or walk/cycle to school; and there is a greater use of TV and computers by children in general. Negative correlations between obesity and both education and future socio-conomic status have also been identified, which further increase the risks of vulnerability in adulthood (Finch and Searle, 2005; Foresight, 2007).

Risk-taking behaviour

The ways in which alcohol consumption, smoking and illicit drug use increase vulnerability to health and other problems are well established. Therefore, these lifestyle factors have been selected to illustrate risk-taking behaviours in children.

The number of children drinking alcohol increases with their age. On average, a third of children in the United Kingdom are reported to drink at least once a week, with drinking more prevalent among boys than girls. Alcohol consumption among children in the United Kingdom is higher than in other countries (Finch and Searle, 2005). What is also of concern is the amount of alcohol consumed in one session. Public attention has turned to 'binge-drinking' and this has certainly increased for older children over the past decade. Such drinking patterns make children in the United Kingdom more vulnerable to unsafe sexual behaviour, violence, accidents, permanent disabilities and death (World Health Organization, 2001).

As with alcohol consumption, children are more likely to smoke as they get older. Smoking rates are also higher for boys than for girls. Statistics show that smoking rates for both boys and girls aged 11 to 14 in this country are on average higher than other countries. By the age of 15, boys' smoking rates drop to below average but rates are still higher than average for girls (Finch and Searle, 2005). Daily smoking in children and young people has been associated with psychological problems and smoking-related illnesses in later life (Bradshaw et al., 2006).

With reference to illicit substance abuse, although usage does increase between 11 and 16, it is relatively uncommon among children up to 16 years old compared to 18–25 year olds. There has also been little change in illegal substance misuse in recent years. While use of drugs cuts across the social spectrum, the more problematic use, which is likely to lead to serious and/or persistent offending, is concentrated among the poorest in society. In addition, certain groups are more vulnerable to such problematic use. These include children in care, those who truant or are excluded from school, those who are mentally ill and those involved in prostitution (Neale, 2005; Bradshaw et al., 2006).

Interestingly, any changes in risk-taking behaviour are not reflected in youth offending. As the age of criminal responsibility is 10, relevant statistics are only available for children between 10 and 17, and there has been little change in crime rates for this group in recent years (Neale, 2005; Bradshaw et al., 2006).

Many factors influence vulnerability to smoking, drug and alcohol abuse among young people. These include personality, personal situation, behaviour of parents and peers, living in a deprived area, low income and the experience of stress that they cannot manage with positive coping strategies. Nonetheless, there is evidence that their vulnerability to these risk-taking behaviours does not persist into adulthood. For instance, many young people do overcome their youth drug abuse experience in adulthood (Stewart and Vaitilingham, 2004; Finch and Searle, 2005; Neale, 2005; Bradshaw et al., 2006).

Child maltreatment

This term is used to encompass various forms of physical and emotional abuse, both of which are contested concepts in themselves. While there is a dearth of information that allows for the identification of trends over time, there is evidence that such abuse does affect a substantial minority of children. For instance, in a survey carried out by the National Society for the Prevention of Cruelty to Children 21 per cent of children had been physically abused, 16 per cent had experienced sexual abuse and 6 per cent had been emotionally abused (Cawson et al., 2000).

Bullying by peers is often classified as a form of child abuse; the aforementioned survey found that 43 per cent reported bullying. This can lead to self-harm, social anxiety, depression and can have a negative impact on educational attainment. Bullied children are also at risk of being victimised in later life. Those who are bullies in childhood are more likely to exhibit antisocial behaviour in adulthood and have problems maintaining stable relationships and long-term employment (Hooper, 2005; Bradshaw et al., 2006). However, there are those who argue that the level of bullying is exaggerated and that learning to cope with a certain amount of unpleasant behaviour from other children helps develop resilience and skills for adult life (Gill, 2007).

Although child abuse often occurs in families across generations, some children are at a greater risk of abuse than others. For instance, if they are female, live in poverty, have a disability, and/or belong to a lone-parent or stepfamily. Any form of child abuse significantly increases children's vulnerability to drug abuse, mental health problems and offending and antisocial behaviour (Hooper, 2002, 2005; Jackson and Scott, 2006).

Health

The discussions of each of the vulnerability factors addressed so far have shown the varying degrees to which they all impact on children's health. It is therefore appropriate at this point to explore health in childhood and its association with other aspects of vulnerability in more depth.

Despite the fact that the comprehensiveness and the validity of the data on child physical and mental health have been criticised, some clear trends have emerged (Beresford, 2002; Timimi, 2004). While children living in poverty still suffer from more health problems, the health of children in general in the United Kingdom has dramatically improved over the last century. This has been attributed to the eradication of contagious diseases, such as measles, diptheria, polio and tuberculosis and the continuing development of successful treatments for previously fatal diseases. Nonethleless, as indicated above, new childhood health issues have emerged, such as poor nutrition and obesity. Other new issues in childhood health include increases in particular illnesses; when comparing age groups in the population, the greatest relative rise in the prevalence of chronic illnesses has been among children. Examples of such chronic illnesses are Type 1 (or insulin-dependent) diabetes and asthma; Britain has one of the highest prevalence rates for asthma in the world and it has been statistically associated with deprivation. The increases have been highest in those in the lower socio-economic groups and those of Asian origin.

Survivors of childhood chronic illnesses more likely to be disadvantaged in terms of educational opportunities and employment than those who had not experienced such illnesses (Beresford, 2002; Blanden and Gibbons, 2006; Bradshaw et al., 2006).

There has also been a growth in the number of sexually transmitted infections in the under-16s. While the incidence of childhood cancers has increased, there have been improvements in five-year survival rates. Levels of mental health problems among children, particularly among boys, have been rising since the Second World War. This has been attributed to factors such as the growing exam culture and leads to decreased employment opportunities and increased probability of criminal activity in adulthood (Beresford, 2002; Bradshaw et al., 2006; Lloyd, 2006; Pilgrim, 2007).

With reference to infant and childhood mortality rates (including accidental deaths), these have decreased substantially over the past two decades but there are broad-based variations; child mortality rates are higher in lower socio-economic groups, in economically depressed areas and among children born to mothers from the new Commonwealth. Furthermore, the United Kingdom does not compare favourably with other European Union countries (Sloper and Quilgars, 2002; Bradshaw et al., 2006).

The above shows that poverty itself is not only a key vulnerability factor, but that it is also an underlying theme in the other factors identified that contribute to children's vulnerability. In addition, the discussions highlight how a wide range of influences, including social divisions, interact in complicated ways and both contribute to children's vulnerability as well as impact on their adult lives. Moreover, the intergenerational dimension to many of these factors is evident. Although there have been some recent improvements in children's lives, these aspects of their vulnerability clearly determine the extent to which social exclusion can be a lifetime experience. The explorations of each of the vulnerability factors also demonstrate that children are not socially homogeneous. Indeed, recent research has highlighted those children who are particularly vulnerable, such as young carers and asylum seekers' children; being a young carer has been found to adversely affect educational performance, school attendance, emotional and physical health and transitions into adulthood. However, there are some positive outcomes, such as close parent–child relationships (Aldridge and Becker, 1999, 2003; Becker, 2000). The vulnerability of children of asylum seekers will be addressed in detail in Chapter 8.

ADDRESSING CHILDREN'S VULNERABILITY

ACTIVITY 4.2

The introduction to this book included an outline of 'inclusive politics'. This explained how it aims to:

- prevent the exclusion of vulnerable groups from full participation in society;
- make sure that mainstream services are delivered for everyone;
- reintegrate people who have fallen through the net;
- address both the structural causes and individual causes of social exclusion.

Find examples of policy initiatives discussed below which achieve these aims. Some suggestions are set out at the end of the chapter.

Children's vulnerability has been a major political concern in the United Kingdom over the last decade; initiatives from 1997 have emphasised that the state has a legitimate interest in ensuring the next generation has the best start in life and has worked to develop its strategy to tackle children's social exclusion. There has been a raft of policy measures such as cash/tax benefits and increased expenditure in many areas, for example, education, health and childcare.

The political prominence of children and children's issues is probably best signified by the establishment of the Department for Children, Schools and Families, the appointments of a Minister for Children and a Children's Commissioner. Since 2000, the focus on the most vulnerable children has increased and overall spending has become more pro-vulnerable children (Department of Health, 2001; Bradshaw and Mayhew, 2005). There have also been recent attempts to address the unfavourable comparisons that have been made between childhood in Britain and in other industrialised countries (Department for Children, Schools and Families, 2007a).

Many current initiatives have emanated from the Green Paper *Every Child Matters* (2003). This recommended a closer alignment between social services and education. It advocated a drive to interdisciplinary practice in order to break down professional barriers and to ensure that professionals such as health workers, social care and education workers cooperate to ensure that children's needs are met effectively. Preventative services, sustained support, protection and quality services for children and families were key areas of concern. The emphasis was on concentrating on outcomes that children and young people themselves have said are important, rather than prescribing organisational change. The Children Act 2004 was produced in light of the consultation on the Green Paper and gave effect to legislative proposals that created clear accountability for all children's services and more targeted services for those with additional needs (such as looked-after children), enabled better joint working and secured a better focus on safeguarding children. Alongside this Act, the government also published *Every Child Matters: Next Steps*, that provided details of the changes to be made to promote the well-being of all children.

The discussion of initiatives is divided into three groups: the first focuses on initiatives that have addressed some of the key vulnerability factors identified in the previous section. The second group contains examples of the initiatives aimed at causal factors and the third focuses on the most vulnerable children who may require reintegration to prevent their long-term social exclusion. Further relevant policy documents will be referred to as appropriate.

Initiatives aimed at key vulnerability factors

As demonstrated above, childhood poverty is a key vulnerability; it damages the lives of those who suffer from it, and persists into adulthood and across generations. More generally, it also damages society in terms of its costs, for example, remedial services, conduct disorders, crime, ill health and low employment. Indeed it has been recently estimated that child poverty costs British taxpayers more than £40 billion per year (Blanden and Gibbons, 2006; Buchanen, 2007).

There were alarming increases in child poverty in the 1980s and 1990s. Given the political focus on the elimination of social exclusion, and the wider costs of childhood poverty, New Labour aimed to halve child poverty by 2010 and eradicate it by 2020. A series of initiatives has been introduced; examples of policies to date are out-of-work benefits, improving parental employment, in-work benefits and tax credits. Public spending per child increased in real terms between 1996–7 and 2001–2 by almost 20 per cent and there have been some positive developments such as the improvement in housing conditions (Department for Work and Pensions, 1999; Social Exclusion Unit, 2004a). Nonetheless, there has only been a slight reduction in child poverty; as already mentioned, a fifth of children in the United Kingdom are still living in poverty and Britain's child poverty rates continue to be among the worst in the European Union. Furthermore, a recent analysis of the major policy areas aimed at eradicating childhood poverty by 2020 concluded that this target will not be achieved unless progress is made in reducing the poverty levels of those children who are vulnerable to persistent poverty (Bradshaw, 2002; Mogadi and Middleton, 2005; Bradshaw et al., 2006; Brewer et al., 2006; Evans and Scarborough, 2006; Buchanen, 2007).

Other key vulnerability factors currently being addressed are children's diets and childhood obesity. The government has set targets to improve children's diets and to reverse the rising tide of childhood obesity by 2010. Many initiatives have been introduced to achieve these targets, such as banning the sale of chocolate bars, sweets and crisps in schools, limiting the number of fast-food outlets near parks and schools, curbing the advertising of junk food and encouraging parents to support anti-obesity measures (Asthana and McNeil, 2007). However, critics point to the evidence of the inexorable increase in childhood obesity and argue that this target will have to be pushed back to 2015 or even 2020. In addition, international studies show that the efficacy of some of these measures, such as bans on food marketing to children, is still unproven (Foresight, 2007).

Initiatives aimed at causal factors

The examples of initiatives aimed at the underlying causes of children's vulnerability illustrate the focus on interdisciplinary practice in many recent policies.

1 **Parenting:** Supporting parents in improving their children's lives has featured in several initiatives; a Parenting Fund of £25 million was created from 2003–6. The *Respect Drive*, a cross-government strategy that aims to tackle bad behaviour and nurture good behaviour among children and young people includes a parenting programme. This is designed to meet the individual needs of parents so as to help them address their child's misbehaviour (Home Office, 2003, 2006a, 2007). The National Academy for Parenting Practitioners was set up in the autumn of 2007. It is provided by a consortium consisting of the Family and Parenting Institute, Parenting UK and King's College London. The academy acts as a national centre and source of advice on high-quality academic research evidence on parenting and parenting support, combined with practical knowledge of what works and has worked in different situations and with different client groups. It also has a strong training role. For instance, it supports the training of a range of professionals, such as social workers, clinical psychologists, community safety officers and youth justice workers liaising with parents (Department for Education and Skills, 2003).

   Such initiatives have been criticised because they ignore certain important influences on parenting. These include the social context in which parenting occurs, which can make it easier or more difficult, and the quality of parent-child relationships (Bradshaw et al., 2006; Buchanen, 2007; Sutton et al., 2007).

2   **Early Years services:** The recognition that good-quality care, education and play for all children in their early years are pivotal in raising educational standards and enhancing children's social development has led to the drive to expand and improve early education and childcare services. For instance, since April 2004 all 3- and 4-year-olds have been entitled to a free, part-time early education place (12½ hours per week) in the maintained, private, voluntary and independent sectors. Initiatives such as the *National Childcare Strategy* and *Children's Workforce Strategy* have meant that the stock of good-quality, affordable childcare for children aged 0 to 14 in every neighbourhood doubled between 1997 and 2007.

   SureStart aims to bring together early education, childcare, health and family support in order to deliver the best start in life for every child from birth. Its programmes have included SureStart Local Programmes, Neighbourhood Nurseries and Early Excellence Centres. This initiative is constantly being enhanced; a recent development is the introduction of 3,500 SureStart Children's Centres, which will build on existing successful initiatives and provide high-quality integrated services. The intention is for there to be one for every community by 2010, so that every family has easy access to their services and the benefits of SureStart can be felt nationwide (Department for Children, Schools and Families, 2007b; Department for Work and Pensions, 2007).

3   **Extended schools:** Under this initiative, schools will offer access to a range of services for children, young people, their families and communities often beyond the school day. These services will reflect community demand and will include childcare from 8 am–6 pm, which offers a varied menu of activities all year round, parenting programmes, family learning sessions, access to a wide range of specialist support services, ICT, sports, arts and educational facilities. Where they are co-located, some of these schools will offer joint services with Children's Centres (Department for Children, Schools and Families, 2007c).

   Although this policy initiative has been well received, it has been argued that it may be of limited benefit to more disadvantaged children because they are more likely to see school as boring. Therefore they will be unwilling to participate in school-based activities outside of the normal school day (Sutton et al., 2007).

Initiatives aimed at the most vulnerable children

Other new policies being developed reflect the government's concerns about the most vulnerable children in that they focus on monitoring children to ensure that they do not fall between agencies. They include single information systems that can be accessed by all agencies, which can also tag the records of children deemed to be at risk. Policies specifically aimed at these children include:

1 **Parenting orders:** Where it is deemed that parental involvement would help prevent a child who has been involved in, for example, truancy, criminal activity and antisocial behaviour, from re-engaging in such activities, a parenting order can be issued. Youth Offending Teams work with the parents of young offenders who receive parenting orders.

2 **Vulnerable children's grant:** Between 2003–6, a grant of £252 million was made available to provide additional support for children most in need, including children in care. An extra £113 million was also made available to improve care placements and stability (Buchanen, 2007).

Some of the criticisms of the above policies have already been mentioned. Evaluation studies of the sort of initiatives described can be hindered by changes in levels of vulnerability and social exclusion that occur following policy implementation, which may be influenced by a range of other factors unrelated to the policies being reviewed. Those studies which have been undertaken put forward different views about the effectiveness of the political drive to reduce children's vulnerability. There are those who argue that, although there have been some improvements, the United Kingdom's performance is disappointing given all the government's efforts and that there is a need to consider new approaches such as developing children's competences, resources, skills and ability to take control of their lives. Some have shown how initiatives vary in success and highlight the problems of engaging certain groups of children, such as those from black and ethnic minority communities. Others highlight problematic issues in relation to specific aspects of the policies. For instance, the *Every Child Matters* initiatives emphasise the importance of listening to children but studies have shown that children may not want to talk, and that responses vary between groups; older and higher-achieving groups furnished elaborate answers whereas younger and lower-achieving groups did not answer all the questions, gave shorter answers and lost concentration and interest more easily (Bradshaw and Mayhew, 2005; Aubrey and Dahl, 2006; Bradshaw et al., 2006; Buchanen, 2007).

As discussed, the processes involved in the social exclusion of children are complex and addressing them represents a huge commitment for policy-makers. The whole issue is also shrouded by a variety of controversies. These include the extent to which state intervention undermines the rights of both children and parents; the need to protect children from risk without overprotecting them; the way that the very nature of childhood inevitably entails dependence and vulnerability; and the interpretation of citizenship in relation to children. With reference to the latter, there have been disagreements about the relationship between children and citizenship. There are those who argue that some aspects of citizenship are more compatible with childhood than others. For instance, the emphasis on active participation in community life is problematic because of the inevitable limits to children's capacity to be participatory citizens. In the last decade new discourses on children's citizenship have emerged; the notion of the 'citizen child' has gained increasing popularity and within this the child is seen as a rights holder and a subject who should be afforded opportunities to become a full and active member of his/her community. This is often referred to as 'citizen now' as opposed to 'citizen becoming' and the adoption of this discourse is reflected in the increased investment in children. Nonetheless, the concept of the 'citizen child' has been debated as it is argued that it overemphasises children's rights and requires a clearer articulation of the responsibilities and obligations of children. Hence the introduction of citizenship education into primary and secondary schools in 2000 and 2002, which focuses on both the rights and obligations of young people in relation to citizenship (Fortin, 2008; Lister, 2008; Morrow, 2008).

Furthermore, there are those who maintain that the increased investment in children is not so genuinely child-focused as it appears; Lister (2003) argues that the new investment in children is less concerned with improving their citizenship status during their childhood and more about ensuring that they are appropriately equipped for their future role as waged contributors to society, or, more specifically 'citizen workers'. She therefore concludes that it is the child as the 'citizen worker' of the future rather than the 'citizen child' of the present who is really at the heart of recent initiatives.

CONCLUSIONS

This chapter has shown that concerns about children's levels of vulnerability in the United Kingdom are justified. The efforts that have been made to improve their lives have also been discussed at length. These have adopted many different strategies at a range of levels and have involved considerable political and social investment to effectively address the myriad of interacting factors that contribute to this highly complicated social problem.

As demonstrated, the success of some of these initiatives has been questioned. However, in view of the strong intergenerational element in children's vulnerability, if the persistence of social exclusion into the next generation is to be halted, it is essential to monitor and evaluate polices that are introduced and use the information generated to inform new policies. Furthermore, there is a need to continue to focus on the most vulnerable groups of children. Most importantly, positive outcomes will not be achieved if policies are introduced for rapid political return. Therefore, an unhurried and persistent political approach is required in order to achieve a reduction in children's levels of vulnerability and their more certain social inclusion as adults.

DISCUSSION POINTS

Why are some children in the United Kingdom more vulnerable than others?

Why do you think that childhood in the United Kingdom compares unfavourably with childhoods in other industrialised countries?

How useful is the concept of 'citizen child' in relation to children's vulnerability?

FURTHER STUDY

Chapters 3 and 4 in Hunt (2005) provide useful overviews of the main approaches to the social construction of childhood. Jonathan Bradshaw has carried out extensive research into the lives of children in the United Kingdom and in other countries. Thus, further details about different aspects of their vulnerability can be found in his work. Valuable sources of information about recent research are the Social Policy Research Unit (University of York), the Centre for Research in Social Policy (Loughborough University) and the Centre for Child and Family Research (Loughborough University). The Home Office, the Department for Children, Schools and Families and SureStart websites can help with up-to-date information on recent policies aimed at children. If you are particularly interested in citizenship in relation to children, Invernizzi and Williams's (2008) book contains an excellent collection of reflections on complementary and contrasting perspectives on children's citizenship.

Key readings

Bradshaw, J. and Mayhew, E. (eds) (2005). *The well-being of children in the UK*, 2nd edn. London: Save the Children Fund

Hunt, S. (2005). *The life course: a sociological introduction*. Basingstoke: Palgrave Macmillian

Invernizzi, A. and Williams, J. (eds) (2008). *Children and citizenship*. London: Sage

POST-ACTIVITY COMMENTS

ACTIVITY 4.1

Your list of differences should show how the nature of childhood changes over time. It should therefore also demonstrate how the observation and evidence of such changes led to the development of the idea that childhood is socially constructed. This is discussed in detail in the first section of the chapter.

ACTIVITY 4.2

What examples did you find? Some suggestions are:

- preventing the exclusion of vulnerable groups from full participation in society: *increases in levels of out-of-work and in-work benefits, and the improvements made to tax credits and parental employment rates*

- making sure mainstream services are delivered for everyone: *the continued enhancement of Early Years services*

- reintegrating people who have fallen through the net: *the efforts to ensure that children do not get overlooked because they fall between agencies and those initiatives aimed at the most vulnerable children, such as parenting orders and the vulnerable children's grant*

- *addressing both the structural causes and individual causes of social exclusion: many of the initiatives that support parents and reduce poverty operate at both a structural and individual level in that they address the underlying causes of children's vulnerability as well as meeting individual needs.*

Chapter 5
Ethnic Minority Groups

OVERVIEW

- Definitions of race, ethnicity and ethnic minority groups
- Inequalities experienced by those in ethnic minority groups
- Racial divisions
- Marxist explanations of racial divisions
- Postmodernist explanations of racial divisions
- Current and future policies
- Conclusions
- Suggestions for further study

INTRODUCTION

After the Second World War a significant number of people emigrated from Britain's old colonies to settle in Britain. Many were responding to the demand for labour in various sectors of the British economy as opportunities were often more limited in their countries of origin. There had been waves of immigration before in Britain. For instance in the nineteenth century, rising populations and bad harvests led to a mass influx of Irish people. At the turn of the twentieth century, virulent anti-Semitism prompted the movement of Jews from Eastern Europe. However, immigration from the New Commonwealth and Pakistan since the Second World War has brought a significant increase in the proportion of people of colour in Britain and they now make up just under 8 per cent of the population. This has made Britain a more ethnically diverse society and increased the visibility of ethnic minority groups (Mason, 2006).

Definitions of ethnic minority groups vary widely. In addition, the concepts of **race** and **ethnicity** are often confused and used interchangeably in relation to these minority groups. Both of these concepts have also been understood in a variety of different ways since the end of the eighteenth century. Systems of classification are also continually being contested and revised. In order to unfathom these complexities, for the purposes of this chapter, ethnic minority groups are defined as those non-white groups who are from or descended from the populations of the countries of the New Commonwealth as classified by the methods adopted in the United Kingdom census. Race will be used to refer to physical differences between people whereas ethnicity will refer to cultural differences such as language, religion, dress, eating habits, literature, history and shared learned customs. Notions of shared experiences, similarities and connections are therefore integral to ethnicity. This means that there is generally a strong sense of identity among such groups irrespective of any blood relationships that exist. They are also often characterised by extensive and supportive social and kinship networks. Nonetheless, there is an inherent fluidity in the concept of ethnicity in that it varies across situations and generations, and with time (Bond, 2006; Mason, 2006; Platt, 2007a).

Research over the past 25 years has highlighted the **social inequalities** experienced by many of those who belong to ethnic minority groups in British society. Concerted efforts have been made at local and national level to address these inequalities and their causes. Indeed, the multiple disadvantages faced by some people from ethnic minority groups have been prioritised within the social exclusion agenda (Social Exclusion Unit, 2004a; Bhopal, 2007; Platt, 2007a). This chapter will start by giving an overview of the inequalities still experienced by those in this vulnerable group in our society. The relationship between these vulnerabilities and racial divisions will be explored before assessing the implications of this relationship for the success of existing policies and the direction of future policy initiatives. While the dynamism of the concept of ethnicity is acknowledged in the discussions, fixed categories for ethnic minority groups are employed. Where this occurs, these will reflect those used in the literature under discussion, and when comparisons are made between studies, every effort will be made to ensure that the categories in question share the same characteristics.

ETHNIC INEQUALITIES

ACTIVITY 5.1

The following is an extract from an article written after the allegations about racism in *Big Brother* when housemates attempted to think up words that began with "Paki". Read through it and then think about the questions set below.

> Discrimination is not cooked up in the *Big Brother* kitchen. It seeps down from the top, not in rivers of blood but in such meandering streams of cause and effect that people barely notice how shamingly endemic it has become. A quarter of white children live in poverty, compared to 74 per cent of Bangladeshis, 60 per cent of Pakistanis and 56 per cent of black Africans. Stephen Byers, a former cabinet minister, tells our political editor today, that in part of the country, we are 'sleep-walking towards the segregation of schools on racial grounds'.
>
> This shadowy apartheid means that a child's future is dictated by race, not by ability. Employers overlook or underpay non-whites, and black people are five times as likely as white ones to be stopped and searched. On Prison Reform Trust figures for 2002, more African Caribbean entrants went to jail (11,500) than to university. Far from highlighting these imbalances, the *Big Brother* row has diverted attention from real scandals.
> (*The Observer*, 21 January 2007)

- What sort of inequalities between ethnic minority groups and white people are highlighted in this extract?
- According to the author, what is to blame for such inequalities?

As you read through the next section, see if there are any similarities between these inequalities and those discussed in the next section. Further guidance on this can be found at the end of the chapter.

Although there have been significant reductions in some inequalities, there is still much evidence that testifies to the continued vulnerability of many who belong to a minority ethnic group. Generalising can be problematic because of revisions in official measurement and categorisation methods. However, examples of these inequalities, together with the variation between and within ethnic minority groups, are discussed below.

Employment

In employment, an area of central importance to life chances, ethnic minority groups are disadvantaged relative to white people. Overall, although unemployment rates for ethnic minority groups have decreased, they are twice those for the total working age population. These rates also compare unfavourably with other countries; while the employment rate in Great

Britain is the highest of all the G8 countries at 75 per cent, ethnic minority employment is 15 per cent lower.

There are considerable variations between groups and between males and females in certain groups. Figure 5.1 illustrates some of these: Indian men have a similar level of unemployment to white men (7 per cent and 6 per cent respectively). In contrast, the unemployment rates for black Caribbean, black African, Bangladeshi and mixed race men are around three times the rates for white British and white Irish men (between 13 per cent and 14 per cent). Pakistani women have the lowest employment rates whereas the unemployment rate for Pakistani men is just over the average (National Statistics, 2004; Clark and Drinkwater, 2007).

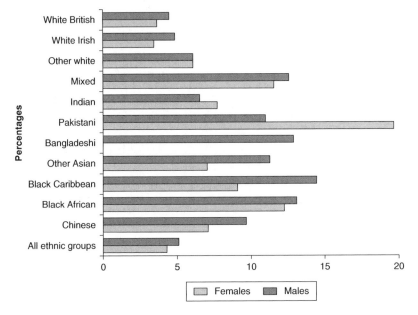

Figure 5.1   Unemployment, by ethnic group and sex, 2004, Great Britain

Source: National Statistics, 2006c

When in employment, research from the 1960s to 1980s showed consistent patterning in ethnic minority groups' employment, namely, that they were concentrated in particular industries and occupations and more likely to be in less skilled jobs than other groups in the population. Although there have been improvements for most ethnic minority groups in educational attainment, which have contributed to intergenerational mobility and positive changes in this patterning, there are still some continuities. Differences between and within ethnic minority groups are emerging too; while the proportion of those from all ethnic groups with managerial jobs has increased, the biggest increases are for black Caribbean, black African and Indian men as well as Indian women. In contrast, Bangladeshi men remain concentrated in the lower-skilled jobs (Social Exclusion Unit, 2004a; Department for Work and Pensions, 2006; Mason, 2006).

Improvements in occupational attainment have been most marked for those who have obtained higher qualifications. Nonetheless, there is statistical evidence that graduates from ethnic minority groups, particularly women, are less likely to be employed than white graduates and are increasingly experiencing more problems obtaining high-status jobs. Such inequalities also have longer-term implications for retirement planning and pension entitlement (Clark and Drinkwater, 2007; Platt, 2007a).

Income

The differences in occupational attainment just described are reflected in the way that the incomes of those in ethnic minority groups are generally lower than those of white people. Those who are most vulnerable to such income differentials are Bangladeshi men, who on average earn 27 per cent less than white men. There are also substantial earnings gaps within occupations. For example, black Africans and Bangladeshis in professional and managerial occupations earn up to 25 per cent less than white men in similar positions. These pervasive earnings disadvantages in the British labour market, in combination with their higher unemployment levels and low uptake of some benefits, means that income poverty rates among ethnic minority groups are, on average, twice as high as for white British people. Moreover, this is despite a national reduction in income poverty over the last decade in this country. Some groups are particularly vulnerable; as Figure 5.2 shows, income poverty rates are highest for Bangladeshis and Pakistanis (Clark and Drinkwater, 2007; Palmer and Kenway, 2007; Platt, 2007a).

Housing

Although both urban and rural areas are increasingly ethnically diverse, those in ethnic minority groups tend to be concentrated in certain parts of the most densely populated urban areas, such as London and the West Midlands. There are many reasons for this, for instance, the location of particular industries. Some studies have also shown that a residential concentration of ethnic groups is driven by a preference for co-ethnic neighbours due to fear of discrimination and hostility (Clark and Drinkwater, 2007). Whatever the reasons, the outcome is that these groups live in some of the most deprived areas and experience the many disadvantages inevitably associated with living in such areas, such as poorer employment prospects and higher crime rates. They are also less likely to be homeowners and to be living in social housing (Mason, 2006; Platt, 2007a; Shelter, 2007b).

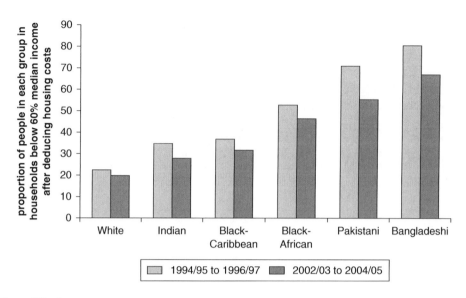

Figure 5.2   Income poverty rates

Source: National Statistics, 2006c

Crime

As Figure 5.3 shows, those from a mixed race or Asian background are more likely than those from other ethnic groups to be victims of crime in England and Wales. When overall crime rates are analysed in terms of personal crime (common assault, robbery, theft from the person and other personal theft) and household crime (which includes vehicle

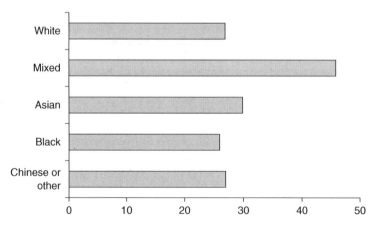

Figure 5.3   Proportion of adults who have experienced a crime in the last 12 months: by ethnic group, 2002/03, England & Wales

Source: National Statistics, 2006c

theft, vandalism and burglary), those with mixed race backgrounds are at a higher risk of experiencing both types of crime. People from mixed race backgrounds are also at greater risk than other ethnic groups of experiencing violence and being the victim of a racially motivated incident.

People from ethnic minority groups, particularly Asian people, are much more likely than white people to report that they are 'very worried' about crime. For instance, 43 per cent of Asian people are very worried about violent crime compared with 19 per cent of white people.

Health

The way official statistics were compiled meant that the links between race, ethnicity and health were not established until the 1980s. Since then there has been much research into the health status of ethnic minority groups in the United Kingdom. This consistently shows that minority ethnic groups are more vulnerable to physical and mental ill health than the white British group.

However, as demonstrated in the discussions of the other inequalities above, there is considerable variation between and within groups. For example, Pakistani, Bangladeshi and black Caribbean people report the worst health. In contrast, black African, Indian, and East African Asian groups report the same health as white British. Chinese people tend to report the best health of all white and non-white groups. Some groups are more prone to particular illnesses; Bangladeshi, Pakistani and Indian men are 50 per cent more likely to have ischaemic heart disease (heart attack or angina) than other men in the population. Although Caribbean men are less likely to die from coronary heart disease, they are 50 per cent more likely to die of a stroke than the general population. Variations in long-term illness between ethnic minority groups are shown in Figure 5.4 (Department of Health, 2000; Bradshaw, 2002; Parliamentary Office of Science and Technology, 2007).

The research about the incidence of mental health among ethnic minority groups is more controversial. Surveys based on treatment rates show that they are more likely to be diagnosed as having a mental illness than white British. Once again, there are significant variations: the diagnosis of psychosis is seven times higher for black Caribbean people than white British, and the Chinese have considerably lower rates of mental illness diagnoses. There are also variations between in-patient and community-based treatment rates; one in five mental health in-patients come from an ethnic minority background, compared to about one in ten of the population as a whole. However, surveys that have looked at the prevalence of mental illness in the community show smaller ethnic differences. The reasons put forward for these discrepancies include discrimination in mental health services and a lack of cultural sensitivity (Department of Health, 2000; Social Exclusion Unit, 2004c; Parliamentary Office of Science and

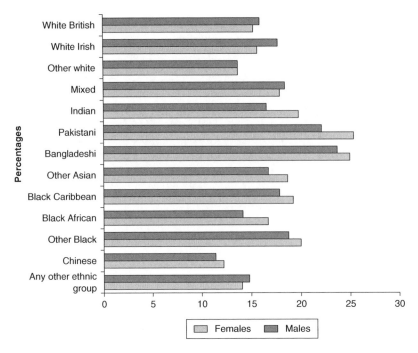

Figure 5.4   Age-standardised limiting long-term illness, by ethnic group, England and Wales, for persons aged 16–74

Source: National Statistics, 2006c

Technology, 2007). These points about mental health services link with ethnic minority groups' reported negative experiences of health and social care generally (Lester and Glasby, 2006).

While the above have been presented as discrete inequalities, interactions clearly occur between them. For instance, level of income also affects sources of inequalities for ethnic minority groups, such as health and housing. There is also evidence of the influence of gender in several of these, such as employment and income. Despite the sorts of heterogeneities highlighted, such inequalities, through their various relationships to each other and social factors, have led to the development of racial divisions now regarded, along with class and gender, as one of the major social divisions in society (Payne, 2006; Ahmad and Bradby, 2008). There is much evidence that the continued existence of this social division means that many members of ethnic minority groups will remain vulnerable to exclusion from full participation in mainstream society (Department for Work and Pensions, 2004; Social Exclusion Unit, 2004a, 2006; Buchanen, 2007).

In order to assess the policy implications of improving the social inclusion of this vulnerable group, it is necessary to explore the explanations that have been put forward as to why racial divisions exist.

EXPLANATIONS OF RACIAL DIVISIONS

The role of discrimination in the creation of some aspects of the inequalities and exclusion discussed above has been highlighted. Discrimination is a dimension of **racism** and some explanations of racial divisions have focused on the relationship between racism and racial divisions. Before outlining these, it is necessary to explore the concept of racism further.

Racism manifests itself when those groups who believe themselves to be inherently 'superior' discriminate against those who belong to ethnic groups because they deem them to be 'inferior'. Such judgments are bound up with the idea that certain biological and racial characteristics make people different and less acceptable in terms of their social activities and abilities. There are different types of racism: **institutional racism** has received the most attention in recent years, particularly in relation to policing and healthcare. Racism can also be **direct** and **indirect**. The former can take the form of physical and/or verbal abuse whereas indirect racism is the fear of direct racism and the stress that this inevitably causes (Mason, 2006; Barry and Yuill, 2008).

Despite initiatives to address racism, it still exists in many areas of life. These include the paid labour market, education and housing. Recent research has also highlighted that racism is not only common in the urban conurbations where many ethnic groups are concentrated but, as rural communities gradually become more ethnically diverse, is also a cause of exclusion from mainstream community activities in rural locations (Tikly et al., 2005; Neal and Agyeman, 2006; Clark and Drinkwater, 2007; Garland and Chakraborti, 2007; Lewis and Gunn, 2007; van der Laan Boumadoff, 2007).

Both the Marxist and **Weberian perspectives** have put forward explanations of racial divisions which link them with racism: Marxist explanations argue that racial divisions developed in the context of the development of international capitalism. In the search for profit, capitalist countries such as the United Kingdom exploited the colonies and, during colonialism, assumptions about the inherent inferiority of the people inhabiting the colonies and negative attitudes towards them were reinforced to justify further colonialism. Such views became commonplace throughout Britain and were sustained when migrants from the then ex-colonies responded to the demand for labour in Britain after the Second World War. Such workers were mainly recruited into the lower-paid jobs and were highly vulnerable to irregular employment as the demand for labour in such jobs fluctuates considerably. Divisions have occurred because of the way that these sorts of jobs affect life chances and because these workers were not viewed as part of the class system but as a subordinate fraction of the working class, referred to as the '**reserve army of labour**'.

Weberian explanations go back to colonialism too and also argue that the belief in the superiority of white people developed under colonialism. They have different views from Marxist perspectives about what happened when migrants from the then ex-colonies responded to the demand for labour in Britain after the Second World War. Weberian explanations focus on the way that these migrants not only faced the status division between 'black' and 'white', with its concomitant belief in the superiority of being white but also had to compete with the rest of the predominantly white British population for the resources necessary to make a life over here, such as jobs, houses and so forth. They refer to this as '**competition for scarce resources**'.

A key concept in Weber's theory of class is **social closure**. This is engaged to describe how groups try to preserve their prestige by restricting entry into their ranks, for example, through education, networks, setting various conditions for entry such as certain qualifications and payments. These are within reach of most members of society. Weberians argue that the predominantly white population operated social closure, with race functioning as an attribute for the exclusion of people from ethnic minority groups. Hence those from ethnic minority groups were excluded because of their racial background and racial divisions developed (White, 2002).

In contrast to the images presented in the Marxist and Weberian perspectives of people from ethnic minority groups as passive victims of the processes described, recent work within the social sciences has focused on the fluid and provisional nature of ethnic identities and experiences, mentioned in the introduction to this chapter. An example of this work is found in **postmodernist** writing. This rejects the views that the social world can be conceptualised in terms of stable social categories. It argues that identity is multifaceted and that all individuals in the postmodern world have multiple identity choices that are situational. Hence ethnic identity is dynamic and a question of individuals' responses to the identity options available to them in the particular situations in which they find themselves.

ACTIVITY 5.2

Read through the list of ethnic inequalities in the first section. To what extent do you think people from ethnic minority groups do have the sort of postmodernist choices described above over their life experiences? See 'Post-activity Comments' for a discussion of this question.

ADDRESSING THE SOCIAL EXCLUSION OF ETHNIC MINORITY GROUPS

As demonstrated in this chapter, while there have been improvements for some groups, despite the initiatives to date, many people from ethnic minority groups are still highly vulnerable to social exclusion. This has been attributed to a variety of factors. Inevitably the variation between and within ethnic groups means that there are ethnic variations in the effects of policies. Some have pointed to the fact that, despite the high-level commitment to social inclusion, any services developed have been underfunded and lack integration. Furthermore, racial equality monitoring and mainstreaming has been patchy. Studies have also shown that there are problems with engaging families in initiatives to reduce social exclusion from ethnic minority communities. For instance, language, gender and age can be barriers to accessing services and information about them (Social Exclusion Unit, 2005; Aspinall and Mitton, 2007; Buchanen, 2007; Platt, 2007b). The rest of this section will reflect on policy developments in the sort of areas addressed in the first section and highlight possible ways forward identified by recent research.

Employment

Employment policies for the past few years have focused on encouraging ethnic minority groups into paid work in order to reduce their unemployment through the use of innovative employment packages, incentives to work and changes in the delivery of support in finding employment. The aim now is to raise employment rates to 80 per cent and target those who have the very lowest employment rates, such as Pakistani and Bangladeshi women. This is being done by building on existing programmes, and tailoring programmes to the localities in which people live. An example of a programme in operation is the City Strategy, which gives local representatives of disadvantaged communities greater flexibility over funding designed to address worklessness and poverty. In addition, as part of the government's welfare reform agenda to boost employment opportunities for ethnic minorities, the Ethnic Minority Advisory Group (EMAG) was set up in 2006. This is taking forward the work of the Ethnic Minority Employment Task Force Stakeholder Group and the National Employment Panel's Minority Ethnic Group. It comprises 22 representatives from across ethnic communities working in partnership with local communites and aims to help get more people closer to the workplace by targeting both public- and private-sector employment practices to increase ethnic minority representation (Department for Work and Pensions, 2004, 2007).

There are initiatives that promote equality within the workplace itself by tackling discrimination at work, and supporting the retention, management and progression of staff from ethnic minority groups. Monitoring of workforce data on selection, access to training, career progression, grievances and disciplinaries in relation to ethnicity is also taking place (Race Relations (Amendment) Act, 2000; Race for Health, 2007).

Recommendations have been made about ways of increasing and improving the effectiveness of such interventions; it has been argued that targeted policies, such as the City Strategy and the Ethnic Minority Advisory Group, need to focus specifically on areas with high concentrations of ethnic minority people in order to be effective in improving employment for these groups in particular. A further means by which people from ethnic minority groups can improve their employability and employment prospects emphasised recently is by obtaining higher qualifications. As mentioned earlier, these improve job prospects for both men and women in ethnic minorities. Moreover, those with the lowest employment rates have recently been identified as experiencing some of the biggest improvements in their employability. These findings indicate that even greater encouragement to invest in such qualifications is one way to improve employment prospects for these groups. Another suggestion is that the full diversity and dynamics of ethnic minority labour-market activity need to be understood in order to formulate appropriate policies. This could include wider acknowledgment of the need to accommodate religious practices within employment policy initiatives (Clark and Drinkwater, 2007; Platt, 2007b).

Poverty

As we have seen, social exclusion is multi-dimensional. Thus initiatives, such as those just described, which focus solely on employment and employment-related issues cannot effectively address the high poverty rates among ethnic minority groups without the adoption of other measures. It is also important that income maintenance policies prioritise the take-up of benefits among those eligible in these groups, and give consideration to the ways in which the contributory system can disadvantage some groups. In addition, analysis and monitoring of the different and complex routes into poverty for different ethnic groups could usefully inform policy-making about ways of meeting the needs of different groups. Policies also need to be sensitive to cultural influences, such as the emphasis on caring responsibilities in some cultures (Platt, 2007a, 2007b).

Health inequalities between ethnic groups

A major source of inequality discussed in the first section was health. New Labour has been very concerned about health inequalities between ethnic groups and there have been attempts to specifically consider the needs of ethnic minority groups in the development and implementation of policies aimed at reducing inequalities. The emphasis has been on addressing the root causes, such as poverty and social exclusion, of health inequalities. As a result, cross-departmental initiatives, such as Tackling Health Inequalities: A Programme for Action (2003) have been set up to address the wide range of interconnecting contributory factors (Parliamentary Office of Science and Technology, 2007).

An example of a recent initiative is Delivering Race Equality in Mental Health Care (2005). This is a five-year action plan for eliminating discrimination and achieving equality in mental health care for all people of ethnic minority status. It aims to help mental health services provide care that fully meets the needs of ethnic minority patients and to build stronger links with diverse communities. However, this action plan has not been without its critics; there are those who argue that it has been implemented patchily and that it does not acknowledge the underlying differences in prevalence of mental illness among ethnic minority groups (Parliamentary Office of Science and Technology, 2007).

New approaches have been adopted too; for instance, the South Asian Community Health Education (SACHE) campaign was launched at the end of 2007. This campaign means that healthcare professionals from within local communities go into temples, mosques, gurudwaras and community centres to deliver health education to combat health inequalities. Thus, health education about issues that directly affect those in the South Asian community (such as heart disease and strokes) is delivered directly to communities, usually in their first language, by health professionals from those communities.

Suggestions about future directions for policies that aim to address health equalities between ethnic groups include increased consultation with user groups in health and social care, in order to understand traditional values and to help the development of ethnic-sensitive practices (Bowes, 2006).

Discrimination and racism

A theme running through the discussions about the above initiatives has been tackling the underlying cause of inequalities – discrimination and racism. Some initiatives have explictly addressed these issues. For example, the Race Relations (Amendment) Act, 2000, outlawed both direct and indirect discrimination in all public authority functions. Much of the research into racial divisions highlights the need for more intervention to combat discrimination in many different areas such as the labour market (Clark and Drinkwater, 2007), schools (Dass-Braillsford, 2007) and policing (Delsol and Shiner, 2006). Some also see focusing more on the varying demographic structures, situations and circumstances of each group to ensure that ethnic minority groups do not miss out on opportunities as essential in the drive to eliminate discrimination (Dale et al., 2006).

ACTIVITY 5.3

Choose one of the recent policies mentioned above. Find out more about it by looking it up on the relevant websites. Assess its potential to reduce the vulnerability of those in ethnic minority groups. Questions you could bear in mind as you do this are:

- Does it address the root causes of inequalities?
- Is the multidimensional nature of social exclusion addressed?
- To what extent has it been implemented effectively?
- How adequate are the funding arrangements?
- Can you identify any barriers to accessing the services provided?
- How realistic do you think the targets set are?
- Does it recognise differences between ethnic minority groups?
- Is it sensitive to cultural practices?
- How could it be improved and why?

Apart from the fact that there are still unresolved issues, there are changes that need to be acknowledged in any further policies. One of these is the fact that the United Kingdom will continue to become more ethnically diverse. The composition of our ethnic minority groups will alter; for instance, the nature of the population growth in these groups means that they will account for half the growth in the working population between 1999 and 2009. In addition, it is estimated that the number of older people within ethnic minority groups will double between 2004 and 2026 (Social Exclusion Unit, 2004a; Parliamentary Office of Science and Technology, 2007; Shelter, 2007b). The globalisation of language is predicted to be yet another new source of segregation for those from ethnic minorities (Watson, 2007). Other global changes, such as the exclusionary effects of reactions to global terrorism, are less predictable (Abbas, 2007).

These examples show how it will also be necessary for policy-makers to address evolving needs that arise among these vulnerable people in our society. There are fundamental concerns too. These include the extent to which people from ethnic minority groups are denied full citizenship because of the exclusionary processes discussed and because many feel a sense of exclusion from the 'British' identity. As mentioned in the Introduction, one of the criticisms levelled at the concept of citizenship is that it is exclusionary in relation to ethnicity. One of the main reasons for this is that its universal nature assumes cultural assimilation and affective connections with others in society. This leads to the exclusion and questions the equal status of people from ethnic minority groups. Possible ways forward suggested are to work towards multicultural citizenship whereby negative views of difference are replaced by positive ones. Within multicultural citizenship, Britishness is seen as being a more plural concept and difference is not seen as problematic. Everyone as a citizen has common rights and responsibilities, including the right to be supported in relation to their specific cultural situations. However, the dynamism of ethnicity may hinder the successful adoption of multicultural citizenship (Lister, 1997; Modood, 1997).

More recent work has focused on the role of **social capital** in relation to addressing the vulnerabilities of ethnic minority groups. This concept is generally used to describe those features inherent in the interconnections that take place in community social life that become resources for individuals when they actively participate in their communities. Examples of these resources are networks, norms, reciprocity and a sense of trust, solidarity and belonging. Being able to use them brings many benefits and advantages. These include access to information and empowerment, which in turn enable community members to act more effectively in pursuing shared objectives and improving their economic prosperity and life chances. Thus social capital can make individuals 'healthy, wealthy and wise' (Putman, 2000: 288).

It has been argued that the strong social ties and networks that exist within ethnic minority communities should be mobilised and used with the aim of transforming them into social capital. The empowering nature of social capital would help those within these communities overcome the inequalities that they face and pursue improved life chances, social advantage and upward mobility. There are a variety of suggestions about how the use of social capital in this way can be supported. One is to conduct further empirical research into the nature of the networks across and within ethnic groups to gain a better understanding of how their productivity can be increased. Another is to ensure that ethnic ties are socially valued within ethnic categories and by society as a whole. Criticisms of this approach include the way that concentrating on social capital ignores the underlying structural causes of inequalities in society (Putman, 2000; Anthias, 2007; Platt, 2007a). Furthermore, the concept of social capital itself has been accused of being 'elusive' and 'nebulous' (Morrow, 2008).

CONCLUSIONS

This chapter has demonstrated the extent of the existing inequalities faced by members of ethnic minority groups and how addressing their social exclusion is highly complex. It has also drawn attention to the need for future policy initiatives to be targeted and creative in their approaches to meeting the needs of such a diverse group in society.

One of the most important points to emerge from the evidence presented is the dynamic, heterogeneous, multilayered and entrenched nature of the vulnerability of this group. Moreover, reducing its social exclusion involves addressing a major social division. Hence breaking the 'cycle of disadvantage' (Social Exclusion Unit, 2004a: 4) still faced by so many in ethnic minority groups must remain a social and political priority if we are to achieve an inclusive society.

DISCUSSION POINTS

Compare the findings presented about the social exclusion of ethnic minority groups with the experiences of those of you in your class/seminar group who are from an ethnic minority background.

To what extent do you think racism contributes to the continuing social exclusion of many members of ethnic minority groups from full participation in mainstream society?

Explore the concept of social capital further. How effective do you think it can be when used in relation to addressing the vulnerabilities of ethnic minority groups?

FURTHER STUDY

Up-to-date statistics on ethnic minority groups can be found in the Focus On Series produced by the Office for National Statistics. A visit to the Joseph Rowntree Foundation website will provide some interesting insights into current research projects focusing on the social exclusion of ethnic minority groups. Recent publications by Lucinda Platt on poverty and ethnicity are very helpful for a more detailed analysis and under-standing of ethnic differences in poverty rates. The Department of Health website is essential for further exploration of the relationship between ethnicity and health and details of current policies.

Putman and Halpern's work is well worth looking at if you are interested in the concept of social capital. If you are particularly interested in social capital and health, you could look at the following Health Development Agency publications: Morgan, A. and Swann, C. (2004). *Social capital and health.* London: HAD; and Cropper, S. (2002). *What contribution might ideas of social capital make to policy implementations for reducing health inequalities?* London: HAD.

Key readings

Bhopal, R.S. (2007) *Ethnicity, race and health in multicultural societies.* Oxford: Oxford University Press
Mason, D. (2006). 'Ethnicity' in Payne, G. (ed.) *Social divisions.* Basingstoke: Macmillan
Platt, L. (2007a). *Poverty and ethnicity in the UK.* Abingdon: Policy Press

POST-ACTIVITY COMMENTS

ACTIVITY 5.1

There were many similarities in the inequalities identified in the *Observer* article and those described in the first section, for instance, the way that the education and employment prospects for ethnic minority groups compare unfavourably with white people, their higher poverty rates and increased chances of being involved with the police. The disparities between different ethnic groups were also highlighted. The first section provides evidence of additional inequalities, such as poorer health.

The author of the article blames discrimination that she says is 'endemic'. The second section explores the explanations for these inequalities, and discrimination is addressed in detail.

ACTIVITY 5.2

The evidence presented in the first section shows that many of their life experiences are constrained by social processes. Examples are:

- Some minority groups, such as Pakistani women, are consistently more likely to be unemployed than others. Cultural constraints such as traditional or religious attitudes have been identified as having a significant role in these differences in employment rates (Dale et al., 2006; Clark and Drinkwater, 2007).

- Despite choosing to obtain a degree, graduates from ethnic minorities, particularly women, are disadvantaged in terms of their career progressions when compared to white graduates. This points to factors, such as a lack of equal opportunities and the role of gender in society, over which individuals themselves have little control.

- While there is some evidence that people from ethnic minorities may choose to live in more deprived areas so that they can have co-ethnic neighbours, this 'choice' may be dictated by their fear of discrimination and hostility from others in society.

There are many examples of Britain's minority citizens challenging the constraints on their life chances, such as self-help groups, community support groups and even political action (Mason, 2006). Nonetheless, it would seem that the sort of relationship between choice and constraint central to postmodernist thinking needs to be approached with some sceptism when applied to racial divisions.

Chapter 6
The Mentally Ill

OVERVIEW

- The contested nature of mental illness
- Social constructionist perspectives on mental illness
- Social causation perspectives on mental illness
- The vulnerabilities of those living with mental ill health
- The social inclusion of the mentally ill
- Conclusions
- Suggestions for further study

INTRODUCTION

Mental illness is notoriously difficult to define; the nature of mental illness itself is contested and both its meaning and measurement changes over time, across cultures, and between disciplines. In addition, there are often no clear-cut objective signs that someone is suffering from a mental illness. Indeed many people have real psychiatric problems but never receive any help. However, statistics relating to those suffering from mental ill health are regularly produced and these indicate that its incidence is both high and increasing. For instance, it has been estimated that around one in six people has significant mental distress at any one time, one in seven have considered suicide at some point in their lives and 1 in 200 have a psychotic disorder such as psychosis or schizophrenia. There is also evidence that there is a global growth in the number of people suffering from a mental illness.

The treatment of mental illness costs £100 billion per year and it is now the most expensive health problem of all. Furthermore, the annual cost to the economy in terms of welfare benefits and reduced productivity from those who work and have a mental illness is £10 billion.

While the numbers and costs are matters of political concern, mental illness also raises important social issues. The move from segregation and institutional care to community-based care that began in the 1980s for those with mental health illnesses is well documented. This, combined with the more recent switch in emphasis from hospital to community care, has meant that by the end of the twentieth century, most people with a mental illness, including those with serious mental illnesses, were cared for in the community. There are many positive aspects to these developments, but they have inevitably led to the emergence of a new set of problems. One of these has been the extent to which the increasing number of vulnerable people with a mental illness now living in our communities are excluded from many aspects of life, such as employment and civic involvement, that others take for granted. This has been acknowledged for some time and mental health has become one of the key priorities within the social exclusion agenda. Nonetheless, there is still plenty of evidence about the vulnerabilities of people with mental health problems and the extent to which they are socially excluded (Social Exclusion Unit, 2004a; Lester and Glasby, 2006; National Statistics, 2006b; Hill, 2007; Pilgrim, 2007; Merritt, 2008).

This chapter begins with an exploration of the debates about mental illness. The experiences of living with a mental illness and how these lead to vulnerability are then discussed. The chapter ends with a critical evaluation of the initiatives that have been introduced to reduce the vulnerability of this group.

THE DEBATES ABOUT MENTAL ILLNESS

Given the above definitional problems, not unsurprisingly, there are many different explanations of mental illness. These fall into two broad camps – biological and social explanations.

Mental health professionals tend to opt for biological or medical explanations. These argue that mental illness is a physical disease like polio or cancer. The emphasis in such explanations is on the recurring behaviour, or 'pathological symptoms' of a disease as well as 'diagnosis' and 'treatment with drugs' as in physical medicine. For example, low serotonin levels are associated with depression and hence this has been treated with pharmaceutical interventions such as SSRIs (selective serotonin reuptake inhibitors).

There are two types of social explanations; one argues that mental illness is socially constructed, in that is an artefact created by social processes. The other maintains that social forces (such as the inequalities in society like disparities in status, wealth and power) cause mental illness. These are usually referred to as the social constructionist and **social causation** perspectives respectively.

ACTIVITY 6.1

What does the following account tell you about the diagnosis of mental disorders? See the 'Post-activity Comments' section if you need some suggestions.

The Diagnostic and Statistical Manual of Mental Disorders (DSM) is widely used by mental health professionals as a diagnosis guide and an evidence-based reference point to classify mental disorders. Classification is carried out on the basis of manifest symptoms, which are organised into subtypes of psychiatric disorders. The original version, DSM-I, was produced in 1952 and it has been subsequently revised many times; DSM-II was produced in 1968, DSM-III in 1980, DSM-IV in 1994 and it is anticipated that the next version, DSM-V, will be published in 2011. In order to reflect research and changes in knowledge, it is not uncommon for interim revised versions to be produced, for instance, there was a DSM-III-R, and DSM-IV-TR was published in May 2000.

The impact of these changes in the diagnostic system on diagnoses of mental disorders have been studied. For example, the change from DSM-II to DSM-III meant that:

- Some diagnoses were placed in different categories under the DSM-III system, for example, schizophrenia latent type in DSM-II would be categorised under non-organic psychosis in DSM-III.
- A previous history of treatment was related more significantly to a diagnosis of schizophrenia under DSM-III.
- Under DSM-II homosexuality was eliminated as a mental disorder.
- The proportion being diagnosed as having a personality disorder was lower under DSM-III than under DSM-II.
- Autism was included in DSM-III for the first time in 1980 in a new class of conditions called Pervasive Developmental Disorders.

(Shulman and Hammer, 1988; American Psychiatric Association, 2004)

The view that mental illness is socially constructed has been influenced by the work of Foucault (1961), who argues that there is no single incontestable truth as both individuals and powerful groups construct society through their ideas and conceptualisations. Central to his argument is the notion of **discourse,** which he uses to describe the accepted conceptualisations about mental illness that are constructed by powerful groups, such as psychiatrists. As with other such discourses, these can remain dominant in society over a period of time.

Those who adopt a social constructionist approach to mental illness point to the historical and cultural variations in the way that mental disorder is defined. With reference to historical variations, in the Middle Ages mental illness was constructed as being caused by demonic forces at work in the brain. Mentally ill people were often killed or tortured. During the eighteenth century, people thought to be mad were regarded as deviant and incarcerated with other 'deviants' such as criminals and paupers. Treatment was punitive. Even now, when there is a more humanitarian social construction, the assessment of mental illness lacks objectivity and still varies over time; changing classification systems and the role of values in the diagnosis of mental illness have been found to lead to disagreement among psychiatrists in around 54 per cent of cases. Indeed, the **anti-psychiatry movement** in the 1960s and 1970s focused on the way that psychiatry is a fraudulent medical speciality as it only uses symptoms (that is, what people say and do) rather than clinical evidence as in other areas of medicine (Manning, 2000; Rogers and Pilgrim, 2005).

Szasz (1961) went as far as accusing psychiatry of manufacturing the criteria on which behaviour is evaluated and coined the term 'the myth of mental illness'. He and others within the anti-psychiatry movement also argued that mental disorder involves **labelling**. Using Szasz's work again to illustrate this, he maintained that there are no brain changes in madness and that mental illness is the result of the unfortunate experiences of socially powerless individuals who commit deviant acts, much like those committed by everyone at one time or another during a lifetime (for example, losing your temper really badly or getting very drunk). However, such individuals are caught by socially powerful others and given the label of mentally ill. The type of behaviour acted out by those who have been so labelled is viewed as mentally aberrant, and it is given the status of mental illness. In other words, the fact of the illness is inferred from the behaviour so that the behaviour itself constitutes the illness. Thus, individuals who are labelled as mentally ill may only have failed to manage their lives within the demands of the social environment, but their behaviour, which may represent nothing more than 'problems in living', violates prescribed behaviour.

In contrast, the social causation model of mental health points to the remarkably consistent social patterning in mental illness as evidence that mental illness is produced by social forces. For statistical purposes, neurotic disorders are normally used as indicators of mental illness. These include depression, anxiety, obsessive-compulsive disorder, panic disorder and phobias. Some examples of this social patterning are as set out below:

Class

As Table 6.1 shows, mental illness is generally greatest among the lower classes. However, there are exceptions; some diagnoses are more likely to occur in higher social class groups, such as eating and obsessive-compulsive personality disorders (National Statistics, 2006b; Pilgrim, 2007).

Table 6.1   Prevalence of neurotic disorders, by social class

SOCIAL CLASS	I	II	III Non-manual	III Manual	IV	V
PERCENTAGE	7	15	17	15	17	19.5

Source: Adapted from National Statistics, 2006b

Gender

There are variations in the types of mental illnesses that men and women suffer from: Figure 6.1 shows that, while neurotic disorders are more common in women than men, panic disorders are equally common in both sexes. Other studies have identified that men are more likely to have antisocial personality disorders and are three times more likely to commit suicide than women (Pilgrim, 2007; Merritt, 2008).

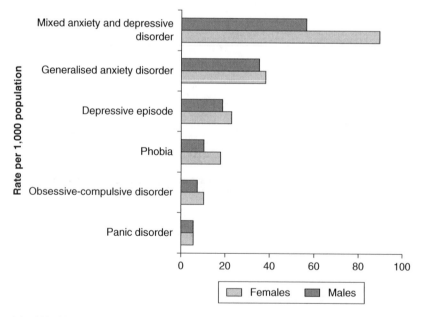

Figure 6.1   Weekly prevalence of neurotic disorders, by sex, 2000, Great Britain

Source: National Statistics, 2006b

As discussed in Chapter 5, ethnicity has also been found to lead to higher rates of mental illness. Those that argue that mental illness is caused by such social factors have developed many explanations about the nature of the processes involved. One of the best-known studies of the relationship between social class and depression is that carried out by Brown and Harris (1978). When they compared working-class and middle-class women with children living in London, about a quarter of the working-class women suffered from depression whereas the middle-class women suffered depression at only a quarter of the working-class rate. They put forward a model about the factors that are in some way involved in bringing about depression.

The term *provoking agents* was adopted to denote those life events, such as severe and life-threatening difficulties, which provoke depression. However, these provoking agents do not necessarily cause depression unless two other sets of factors are present. These are *vulnerability factors* and *symptom formation factors*. The former included the absence of an intimate relationship with a husband or boyfriend, having three or more children under the age of 15 at home, unemployment and the loss of a mother before the age of 11. The presence of these factors greatly increased the chances of a breakdown in the presence of provoking agents. Symptom formation factors included other past losses of close relatives in childhood and adolescence and these may influence the type and severity of depression. For example, loss by death is strongly associated with psychotic-like depressive symptoms, whereas loss by other means (such as parents separating) leads to neurotic-like symptoms. This is represented diagrammatically in Figure 6.2.

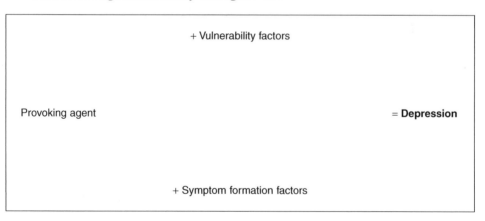

Figure 6.2   Brown and Harris's model

Brown and Harris claimed that, because of their social class, working-class women experience more untoward life events and difficulties (provoking agents) and have an excess of vulnerability factors, which explains their higher rates of depression. However, this model has been criticised for not including a broader analysis of the structure of society. Indeed, feminists have argued that the higher rates of mental illness among women are the product of the inequalities and exploitation that exist in contemporary society, and point to the social oppression of women in our society in particular. The terms 'victims of our social order' and 'patriarchal power' feature in feminist arguments. They say that mental illness is caused by features of society that control, coerce and constrain women, such as the burden of childcare, the low status of their domestic work and the 'double burden' that they carry if they are employed outside the home as well (Doyal, 1995).

These different views of mental illness are not totally incompatible; for example, both social constructionist and social causation models can involve power. Nonetheless, it is clear that no one approach is sufficient to address the complexity of mental illness. This complexity is further illustrated in the exploration of the experiences of those who suffer from mental illness in the next section of this chapter.

LIVING WITH A MENTAL ILLNESS

The experiences of this vulnerable group discussed below have been selected for several reasons. One is to give as comprehensive a picture as possible of what it is to live with a mental illness. Another is to highlight the differences in the vulnerabilities between members of this group in society. The third reason behind their selection is to demonstrate the complicated relationships between the various factors, and the implications that these have for conclusions about the social exclusion of those with mental health problems.

Discrimination

Although attitudes to mental illness have become more positive in the past couple of decades, the **stigma** attached to mental illness remains (Social Exclusion Unit, 2004c; Corrigan, 2007). Goffman (1963) produced seminal work about stigma; he maintained that stigmatisation involves the association of socially constructed negative characteristics with members of a particular social group. This stereotyping produces negative emotional reactions in others, which include contempt, disgust and fear. Such reactions make those who are stigmatised feel disempowered, rejected and depersonalised. This leads to self-doubt and a crumbling of self-image, which can ultimately 'spoil' the self-identity of those experiencing the stigma.

Those who argue that the media are culpable for the aforementioned ongoing stigmatisation point to discriminatory reporting that reinforces and maintains public hostility towards people with mental health problems. For instance, despite recent efforts to adopt a more considered approach to mental health matters, two-thirds of all British press coverage of mental health has been found to include a link with violence, 40 per cent of daily tabloids and nearly half of the Sunday tabloids contained derogatory headlines such as 'schizophrenic kills' and references to 'nutters' and 'loonies'. Media stereotypes have been further fuelled by high-profile and brutal murders such as those of Jonathan Zito, Lin and Megan Russell and John Curran. However, there is much evidence that these negative stereotypes are unfounded; although the rates of violence and arrest among the mentally ill may be higher when compared to the general population, statistics since 1957 show that very few people with mental illnesses commit homicides and there is little fluctuation in the numbers. The discharge from long-stay institutions means that this also represents a fall of 3 per cent in the overall homicide rate for people with mental illnesses. Indeed people with mental illnesses are more likely to be the victims of crime (Social Exclusion Unit, 2004c; Lester and Glasby, 2006; Markowitz, 2006; Pilgrim, 2007).

Whatever the cause(s) of this stigma, it manifests itself in the continued discrimination against those who have a mental illness. For instance, people with mental health problems are attributed with qualities such as violence and unintelligibility, fewer than four in ten employers said that they would consider hiring someone with mental health problems and they are systematically excluded from full participation in civic, social and political life. The loss of confidence, impaired social relations and well-being that the experience, fear and/or perception of such a stigma produce in a mentally ill person can lead to the development of a 'spoiled identity' (Rogers and Pilgrim, 2003; Social Exclusion Unit, 2004c; Kelly, 2006).

Poverty

Mental illness is also associated with living in poverty (S. Payne, 2006). While there is evidence that 90 per cent of users of mental health services want to work, those with a mental illness have the lowest employment rate of any of the main groups of disabled people. Even when they have a job their chance of losing their job is twice that of others and on average they only earn two-thirds of the national hourly rate. Benefit dependency is high; recent statistics show that 34 per cent of incapacity benefit claimants have a mental health problem. Studies have shown that they are also three times as likely to be in debt (Meltzer et al., 2002; Kelly, 2006).

Housing

One of the consequences of living in poverty is that those with poor mental health, particularly those with more severe mental illnesses, tend to live in poor-quality accommodation that is inadequate, noisy, crowded and located in undesirable neighbourhoods characterised by high deprivation and unemployment rates (Payne, 2006; Kyle and Dunn, 2008).

Social isolation

People with mental illnesses have fewer social and family networks than average; many of their contacts are related to health services rather than to employment, family, friends, leisure, social and community activities. In addition, they experience considerable difficulties in establishing and maintaining long-term intimate partner relationships. The relationships of those with serious mental illnesses in particular tend to be characterised by a lack of intimacy and commitment. One of the consequences of these problems is that those with a mental illness are three times as likely to be divorced (Perry and Wright, 2006; Wright et al., 2007). The social isolation that results from this lack of social networks and personal relationships can also contribute to a deterioration in mental health (Meltzer et al., 2002; Huxley and Thornicroft, 2003).

Increased morbidity

Mental ill health often goes hand in hand with poorer physical health. For example, links have been established between the chronic stress experienced as a result of some mental illnesses and cardiovascular disease, as well as between serious mental illness and an increased risk of cancer. The relationship between social isolation and a relative lack of personal and social support to poorer physical and mental health has been addressed in other chapters in this book. Given the findings reported above, it not surprising that one of the reasons put forward for the decrease in sufferers' physical health is the concomitant isolation that mental ill health often entails. Other explanations have focused on the enmeshment of physical and mental health among the mentally ill; some physical illnesses or acquired disabilities, such as a cancer diagnosis or amputation, can lead to severe emotional distress and personality changes. Some drugs used to treat a physical illness can also cause temporary psychological disturbances (Office for National Statistics, 2004; Pandiani et al., 2006; Pilgrim, 2007).

Increased mortality

Those with a mental illness have higher rates of mortality than those who are not mentally ill. Mortality rates do vary with the nature of the illness, for example, people suffering from schizophrenia or an eating disorder are more at risk than those with depression. However, much of this mortality profile can be attributed to the generally raised suicides rates among those with mental ill health (Office for National Statistics, 2004; McCusker et al., 2006).

Quality of care

There has been much criticism of the care provided for people with mental illnesses. Indeed, the mental health system has been accused of being discriminatory and 'at breaking point' (Hill, 2007). These criticisms have been directed at both hospital and community-based care. Reports focus on overflowing hospital wards that represent dangerous environments, how the staff working in them are exhausted and over-worked, and the ways that long waiting lists and the pressures on beds mean that many patients do not receive the appropriate levels of care. In the community, piecemeal development, a lack of funds and the failures of partnership working have contributed to individual neglect, oversights and allegations that patients 'fall through the net'. Early intervention work, such as helping people to stay in work and maintain their social contacts, often does not take place, leading to an escalation of less serious mental health problems (Lester and Glasby, 2006).

Persistence across generations

The children of those with a mental illness may also experience mental ill health. This is because untreated mental illness in a parent can affect their children's social and mental development, which in turn leads to emotional problems and educational failure. The consequent increase in their chance of unemployment reduces their social contact and networks. These factors increase their own risks of mental illness in their later lives (Social Exclusion Unit, 2004c; Payne, 2006).

The above discussions of the experiences of those living with a mental illness show that multiple interlocking and reinforcing processes can contribute to their social exclusion. For instance, in addition to money, employment provides social contact and support. Hence the increased chances of unemployment faced by those with a mental illness to reduces their social contact and networks. Without the income from a job, they are also more likely to live in poverty, which negatively affects social relations and community participation. The resultant paucity of social contact adversely affects the self-esteem of an already vulnerable individual and engenders feelings of powerlessness. Consequently, further mental health problems may be induced. Moreover, poverty means fewer stress-reduction activities, such as leisure activities and holidays. Stress levels are therefore not lowered and existing mental health problems may increase (S. Payne, 2006; Pilgrim, 2007).

This example also illustrates the complicated relationship between mental ill health and social exclusion – mental illness can cause social exclusion but socially excluding forces can also contribute to and exacerbate mental illness. Thus, addressing social exclusion within the context of mental illness is highly problematic.

However, the overall conclusion drawn from the existing evidence is that many people who are mentally ill suffer from social exclusion to a greater or lesser extent. Furthermore, those with more serious mental illnesses are among the most excluded in British society and are being denied access to levels of citizenship (Social Exclusion Unit, 2004c; Pilgrim, 2007). The approaches adopted to address the social exclusion of this vulnerable group are critically analysed in the next section.

WORKING TOWARDS THE SOCIAL INCLUSION OF THE MENTALLY ILL

Mental illness is part of the wider social inclusion agenda. A key document was the Social Exclusion Unit's *Mental health and social exclusion* (2004d). This set out a 27-point action plan to ensure that government departments and other organisations worked together to 'challenge attitudes, enable people to fulfil their aspirations and significantly improve opportunities and outcomes for this excluded group' (Social Exclusion Unit, 2004c: 6). Parallel publications included *Action on mental health* (Social Exclusion Unit, 2004d), which provided practical guidance for action by frontline staff and service providers, people affected by mental health problems, local agencies and employers about ways to promote social inclusion. In the same year, the National Social Inclusion Programme (NSIP) was created to coordinate the implementation of the 27 action points. It produces annual updates on progress made and information about planned developments.

Within this agenda, the main focus of concern has been the persistence of mental ill health across generations. As a result, many mental health initiatives not only promote the social inclusion of those with a mental illness but also aim to reduce social exclusion across the life course. The emphasis in these is on the integration of policy areas, such as housing and employment, and close collaboration across government departments and with the private and voluntary sectors. Some of the main issues addressed and key policy documents are as follows.

Reduction of stigma and discrimination

An example of an initiative that involves a partnership between a range of government departments and other organisations in challenging attitudes and ensuring that those with a mental illness have the same rights and opportunities as others in society is *Action on stigma* (Department of Health, 2004d). This is a five-year plan (2004–09) designed to tackle stigma and discrimination around mental health issues. It works in areas where people say that they have experienced discrimination most, paying particular attention to issues of multiple discrimination, including discrimination on grounds of race and gender. The emphasis is on drawing on relevant expertise (such as in public health and mental health promotion, communications, disability rights, service redesign, research); explaining the ways in which people with mental health problems make a positive contribution to society; and monitoring and evaluating the work undertaken.

Employment

As part of New Labour's welfare-to-work strategy, initiatives have been introduced to support people with mental health problems in finding and retaining work. For instance, the Pathways to Work initiative promotes employment for people receiving incapacity benefit. Comprehensive packages of support in the transition back into employment are also available. These include re-vocational training to help prepare individuals for paid work and supported employment (that is, on-the-job support). There has been a recent drive to accelerate and supplement such measures for those suffering from more severe mental health problems. Additional approaches currently include individual placement and support, anti-stigma employer-based campaigns and a training pack aimed at job-broking advisors to help them be more confident when working with people with mental health problems and employers (Department for Work and Pensions, 2007; National Social Inclusion Programme, 2007).

Housing

Several initiatives aim to ensure that adults with mental health problems have a stable home. One is Public Service Agreement 16 (2007), which sets out a strategy to help them access and maintain **settled accommodation** in both the social and private sectors. The National Social Inclusion Programme is working closely with the Cabinet Office and regional stakeholders to ensure that this is effectively implemented at a local level (National Social Inclusion Programme, 2007).

Service delivery

As part of New Labour's **modernisation agenda** for mental health, the National Service Framework for Mental Health set out national standards for mental health that are closely monitored throughout the country. The National Institute for Mental Health in England (launched in 2002) is responsible for supporting the implementation of positive change in mental health services. Measures have also been introduced to address inequalities in access to healthcare, including the provision for training health and social care professionals on improving social inclusion. Government departments are actively trying to work together and with the voluntary sector to deliver services more effectively in the setting where people live their lives. Finally, as this book goes to press, a major review of the future funding of mental health services is being carried out in partnership with researchers from the Institute of Psychiatry at King's College London and the Personal Social Services Research Unit at the London School of Economics. The aim of this review is to ensure high-quality, cost-effective mental health care.

Community involvement

Positive practice in community participation includes the improved avail-ability of and access to education, the arts, sports and leisure activities, as well as the provision of more training opportunities. Plans are in place to remove some of the barriers to community participation that have to date restricted the activities of those with a mental illness, such as preventing then from being school governors or undertaking jury service.

Empowerment of mental health service users

There has been a recent emphasis on strengthening the rights of those with mental illness. Examples include the growth of user involvement and engagement; those who use the services have a say in their individual care plans and how services are organised and planned. There is now a Patient and Public Involvement Resource Centre to support the delivery of patient and public involvement in health services. Nonetheless, there are those who argue that the unequal distribution of **power** between users and professionals limits the extent to which users' contributions can serve to address the social exclusion of those who are mentally ill (Rogers and Pilgrim, 2003).

Another example is the introduction of further measures to empower and protect mentally ill people who are not able to make their own decisions: the Mental Capacity Act, 2005 and Mental Health Act, 2007 provide statutory frameworks to this effect.

These efforts, together with the way that important drivers against social exclusion are being addressed at national level, should go some way to facilitating the participation of the mentally ill in society. However, as indicated above, there are inherent problems associated with successfully addressing social exclusion within the context of mental illness. Unsurprisingly these sorts of changes have therefore had a mixed reception.

ACTIVITY 6.2

What criticism can you make of the type of initiatives discussed above? You might like to think in terms of two main concepts in this book – communitarianism and citizenship.

Some criticisms have been made of specific aspects of the above, such as the emphasis on paid work for people with mental health problems. While employment has been found to be of value, there are several reasons why it may not be a simple protection against poor mental health and social exclusion. One reason is that it has variable effects on mental health, for example, mental health is affected by the level and status of the paid employment. Another is that, if it involves antisocial hours, it restricts social activities outside of work and thus increases, as opposed to reduces, social isolation that can harm mental health (Marmot et al., 2001, Goodwin and Kennedy, 2005). Employment also improves men's mental health more than women's (Nozal et al., 2004). Therefore, for employment to be effective in improving mental health, it needs to meet certain criteria such as improving status and reducing isolation.

Other criticisms have been made at a more conceptual level. Many issues closely allied to mental illness mean that there is a tension between mental ill health and full citizenship; addressing mental health involves complex and controversial processes such as compulsory detention and the administration of medical treatments without consent. Whatever the rights or wrongs of these, they erode the citizenship rights of those who are subjected to them.

New Labour's incorporation of communitarianism has been criticised as being a further source of exclusion for people with mental health problems. As explained in Chapter 1, within this ideology, communities are seen as a means for ensuring social cohesion. As we have seen, even though many more people with mental illness now live in the community, they are not necessarily accepted by the community at large nor can they participate in their communities. Thus the extent to which communities can be a vehicle for social inclusion is limited and will remain so until people with mental illnesses are included within society as part of a community of interest.

CONCLUSIONS

The varying theoretical perspectives and the interlocking web of factors that shape the reality of living with mental ill health discussed in this chapter have clearly demonstrated the reasons why reducing the social exclusion of those who suffer from mental illness is such a challenge to policy-makers.

Nonetheless, the increase in numbers of those experiencing mental ill health and both the quantifiable and unquantifiable costs to society identified mean that this social problem will retain political prominence. More importantly, unless solutions are found, the mentally ill will not enjoy their right to full participation and inclusion in society and the associated status of citizenship. Various suggestions have been made about future ways forward: more rights-based approaches (Kelly, 2006) and focusing on helping members of this group in society to gain a sense of control over their lives (S. Payne, 2006). These are certainly valid but what this chapter has shown is the deep-rooted negative attitudes within society about those with mental health problems and the way that these can present more barriers to their social inclusion than is the case with other vulnerable groups. Therefore in addition to and alongside any policy initiatives, individuals and the wider society need to work towards a culture of inclusion in order to effectively address the needs of this vulnerable group.

DISCUSSION POINTS

Why are some groups more vulnerable to mental illness than others?

Which factors are most influential in the social exclusion of those with a mental illness?

What do you think needs to be done to reduce the social exclusion of mentally ill people?

FURTHER STUDY

Publications by Pilgrim and/or Rogers offer an excellent, in-depth understanding of mental illness, its causes and the experiences of those afflicted. For a further exploration of the anti-psychiatry movement, see work by Scheff, Szasz and Laing. Lester and Glasby (2006) provides a readable and useful overview of *mental health services* and both past and current policy developments. A visit to the Department of Health website is recommended for the most up-to-date policy information. Details about the work being undertaken in relation to mental health and social exclusion specifically can be found on the National Social Inclusion Programme (NSIP) website (www.socialinclusion.org.uk).

Key readings

Social Exclusion Unit (2004c). – *full reference as in bibliography*

Lester, H. and Gladsby, J. (2006). *Mental health policy and practice.* Basingstoke: Palgrave Macmillan

National Statistics (2006b). *Focus on health,* National Statistics website: www.statistics.gov.uk

Pilgrim, D. (2007). *Key concepts in mental health.* London: Sage

Rogers, A. and Pilgrim, D. (2005). *A sociology of mental health and illness,* 3rd edn. Maidenhead: Open University Press

Social Exclusion Unit (2004c). *Mental health and social exclusion.* London: Office of the Deputy Prime Minister

POST-ACTIVITY COMMENTS

ACTIVITY 6.1

Some suggestions about what the account says about the diagnosis of mental disorders are:

- ideas about mental disorders change over time;
- diagnoses are not incontestable;
- diagnoses lack objectivity possibly because they are based on symptoms as opposed to clinical evidence;
- category changes reflect attitudinal change, such as attitudes aboout sexuality.

See how these sorts of points feature in the discussion of the arguments about the social construction of mental illness that follows this activity.

Chapter 7
The
Homeless

OVERVIEW

- Defining homelessness
- The 'statutory homeless' and the 'hidden homeless'
- Rough sleepers and street homelessness
- Individualist and structuralist explanations of homelessness
- Living without a home
- Charities and voluntary organisations for the homeless
- Developments in statutory provision for the homeless
- Ways of ensuring that policies are effective
- Conclusions
- Suggestions for further study

INTRODUCTION

Historical records dating back to the seventh century show that homelessness has been a social problem for centuries. Treatment of the homeless has improved; up to the sixteenth century it was punitive. After this time, there were attempts to house the homeless. This was initially in workhouses and, although these were an improvement on the previous provision, they still retained a punitive element and could be spartan, unsanitary and uncaring places. Workhouses were succeeded by spikes, which provided very basic dormitory housing without the punitive aspects of the workhouses (Firth, 2007b).

Public concern about homelessness grew from the 1960s as the numbers of homeless, especially those who were living in temporary accommodation and/or sleeping rough, increased steadily into the 1990s. There have been several initiatives by both the previous Conservative governments and New Labour but, despite such efforts, Britain still has one of the highest rates of homelessness in Europe with four people in every 1,000 without a roof over their head. Furthermore, it is predicted that the current housing situation will increase these numbers. Homeless people are also still among the most vulnerable in society. Indeed homelessness has been described as 'one of the most acute forms of social exclusion' (Shelter, 2007b: 8). In addition to concerns about their numbers and their vulnerability, powerful images in the media of people begging on the streets and sleeping rough have fuelled political debates about the homeless. An indication of the priority given to homelessness by the current government was the creation of the Department for Communities and Local Government (DCLG) on 5 May 2006. This has housing and homelessness as one of its main responsibilities (Social Exclusion Unit, 2004a; Roche, 2004; Cadwalladr, 2007).

As a result, the homeless have emerged as a prime focus of social policy. In order to contextualise and critically reflect on policy developments with regards to this vulnerable group, this chapter will begin with an exploration of the meaning of homelessness. This will involve discussions about who the homeless are, the causes of their homelessness and the extent of their vulnerability. The nature of voluntary and statutory support and services for the homeless will then be described and evaluated, particularly with reference to recent initiatives to alleviate the problem. The chapter will conclude with a reflection on issues that need to be addressed if policies aimed at reducing homelessness are to be effective.

HOMELESSNESS

ACTIVITY 7.1

There is much debate over what homelessness is. Which of the following situations do you think means that someone is homeless?

- temporarily staying with friends or family;
- staying in a hostel or bed and breakfast;

(Continued)

- living in very overcrowded conditions;
- at risk of violence or abuse in their home;
- living in poor conditions that affect their health;
- living somewhere that they have no legal right to stay in (for example, a squat);
- living somewhere that they cannot afford to pay for without depriving themselves of basic essentials;
- forced to live apart from their family, or someone who they would normally live with, because their accommodation is not suitable?

Now see how your answers concur with the definitions of homelessness discussed below.

Many people assume that homelessness means sleeping on the streets. Although there is no generally accepted definition of homelessness, it is not just about having a roof over your head. It is a far broader concept in that a person or a family can be homeless for a variety of different reasons. These include the fact that they do not feel emotionally secure and safe in their home, they do not have any rights to stay there and if their accommodation is substandard and adversely affects their health. Thus, homelessness can arise in any of the circumstances listed in Activity 7.1. These also demonstrate that homelessness can affect a wide variety of both single people and families. Some groups are more vulnerable than others; examples of those who have a greater vulnerability to homelessness include those who are experiencing a relationship breakdown (with parents, a partner or friends), older people (over 50), people with children, people with physical or mental health problems, people with drink- and drug-related health problems, people on benefits or low incomes, young people leaving care, ex-prisoners, ex-service personnel and asylum seekers and refugees. Homelessness is also high among ethnic minority groups. In addition, there are regional variations in the numbers of homeless; they are highest in London and the West Midlands and lowest in the Southeast. Although homelessness is mainly urban-centred, recent research has started to uncover the extent of rural homelessness (Cloke et al., 2007; Department of Communities and Local Government, 2007a; Shelter, 2007b).

Defining homelessness is further complicated by the fact that it is also dependent on the relationship between being homeless and being provided with accommodation; under the Housing Act, 1996, local authorities must consider all applications from people seeking accommodation or assistance in obtaining accommodation. Where they are satisfied that the applicant is eligible for assistance, unintentionally homeless and falls within a priority-need group, they have a statutory duty to provide suitable accommodation for the applicant and his or her household until a settled home becomes available for them. Since the introduction of the Homelessness Act, 2002, priority-need groups have been extended; they originally included households with dependent children or a pregnant woman and people who are vulnerable in some way (e.g. because of mental illness or physical disability). They now also include applicants aged 16 or 17, applicants aged 18 to 20 who were previously in care, applicants vulnerable as a result of time spent in care, in custody, or in HM Forces, and applicants vulnerable as a result of having to flee their home because of violence or the threat of violence. There is provision for those who are intentionally homeless; where households are found to be intentionally homeless or not in priority need, the authority must make an assessment of their housing needs and give advice and assistance to help them find accommodation for themselves. Where applicants are found to be intentionally homeless but fall in to a priority-need category, the authority must ensure that accommodation is available for long enough to give the applicant a reasonable opportunity to find a home (Department of Communities and Local Government, 2007a).

While these categories indicate that official definitions of homelessness are broad, in reality, those accepted as homeless by local authorities only represent a small percentage of all those who are homeless. This is because some are refused help, others are unaware of their entitlements and some are too vulnerable to seek help. The terms **statutory homeless** and **hidden homeless** are therefore used to reflect the distinction between the two types of homeless people. The latter are usually single people and couples without children who live in temporary accommodation, such as **hostels**, squats, **bed and breakfasts**, or with family and friends. They do not feature in government homeless statistics but their numbers can be over twice those who are the statutory homeless. Indeed, it is estimated that there are around 400,000 'hidden homeless' adults at any point in time (Riddell, 2006; Firth, 2007b; New Policy Institute, 2007).

Those people sleeping on the streets are yet another subgroup of homeless people. Although these constitute only a very small proportion of all those who are homeless, they tend to attract the most attention because of their visibility. They are predominantly (90 per cent) men and are between the ages of 26 and 49. Two terms are used in connection with this most visible and extreme form of homelessness; those who are deemed to be **rough sleepers** are defined as 'people sleeping, or bedded down, in the open air, such as on the streets, or in doorways, parks or bus shelters; people in buildings or other places not designed for habitation (such as barns, sheds, car parks, derelict boats, stations, or "bashes"[1])' (Shelter, 2006: 1). **Street homelessness** is a wider term and encompasses the street lives of those who may not necessarily sleep rough. Those who are the street homeless live on the streets in the day and have nowhere to sleep at night. Some end up sleeping in the sorts of places identified in

---

1. A bash is a makeshift shelter usually made with cardboard boxes.

the definition of rough sleeping, while others sleep at friends' houses for short periods of time, in a squat, hostel, prison or hospital. Street lifestyles can involve drinking very heavily in public, begging and sex work. The boundary between rough sleeping and street homelessness is often fluid. It usually takes four weeks to become acclimatised to life on the streets and, after this point, it becomes much harder to move back into mainstream society (Shelter, 2006).

Thus defining homelessness is problematic mainly because of the different types of circumstances that can lead to either a person or a family being homeless, the ways in which policies construct homelessness and the sheer diversity of those who are homeless and the different categories used to describe them. This diversity has also been attributed to the wide range of factors that cause homelessness.

THE CAUSES OF HOMELESSNESS

People become homeless for a variety of reasons; some are precipitated by personal factors, for instance, being evicted by a landlord, becoming unemployed, health, alcohol, drug abuse and relationship problems. Others are outside an individual's control. These include natural disasters (such as fire or flooding) and macro-level economic and social factors. An example of a macro-level economic factor is a downturn in the economy that results in job losses or rises in interest rates which in turn lead to financial problems and an inability to pay rents or a mortgage. An example of a social factor is housing policy that makes homes in the private rented and owner-occupied sectors unaffordable and leads to long waiting lists for social housing.

In reality, the factors that lie within an individual's control and those that do not are often intertwined; an inability to meet mortgage repayments due to an increase in interest rates could be interpreted as poor management of personal finances. Therefore, the ensuing homelessness could be construed as being due to personal influences as well as broader structural factors. Differences in emphasis on the two sets of factors are part of the wider debate about individual culpability with respect to homelessness, and relate to individualist and **structuralist explanations**. These operate at different levels: individualist explanations see social problems, such as homelessness, as being the outcome of actions taken by individuals themselves. In contrast, structuralist explanations operate at a social level and argue that political, economic and social factors are the causes and conditions of problems. The way in which individual and social factors are reflected in policy responses is discussed later in the chapter (Roche, 2004; Phelan and Norris, 2008).

ACTIVITY 7.2

Using the grid below, read through the chapter so far and write against each level of explanation which factors each one would focus on when explaining homelessness. There is a completed grid at the end of the chapter to give you some ideas about factors that you could have identified. Try not to look at the completed grid until you have done the exercise and then compare it with your own grid.

| Individual factors: |
| Structural factors: |

The discussions in this chapter so far have highlighted the fact that there are many different types of homeless people who have followed many different routes into homelessness. This would indicate that commonalities between people who are in this vulnerable group in society are limited. However, research has drawn attention to some of the experiences that they share and these are outlined in the next section. Experiences that relate to specific groups of homeless people are also included.

LIFE WITHOUT A HOME

ACTIVITY 7.3

Visit the websites, such as those for Shelter and Crisis, in the 'Further study' section at the end of the chapter. As you look through them, list the sorts of experiences that the homeless seem to have before reading the rest of this activity.

You probably found that there is a strong focus on those who are single rough sleepers and the extreme nature of their needs and experiences. However, many of these are shared, albeit to a lesser extent, by other groups of homeless people. These are illustrated in the discussions below about the findings from studies into homelessness.

Unemployment

Unemployment is much more common among the homeless than the rest of the population. This has been attributed in part to their lack of basic skills and qualifications; higher rates of learning difficulties have been identified among the homeless and 40 per cent of homeless adults have no qualifications, compared to 10 per cent of the general population. Lack of a permanent address inevitably makes holding down a job extremely difficult and is therefore another cause of high unemployment among the homeless (Doward, 2006; Firth, 2007b).

Low income/poverty

Homelessness is an outcome of extreme poverty, Thus, without stating the obvious, homeless people are inevitably poor and experience a high frequency of insufficient and/or inconsistent income. Their situation is not alleviated by welfare benefits because they often have problems accessing these (Rogers and Pilgrim, 2003; Donnellan, 2004).

Health problems

Homeless people are more likely to have physical and mental health problems than most other members of the population. There are several reasons for this; as explained above, homelessness is often *caused* by health problems, such as mental illness and drink- and drug-related health problems (Firth, 2007b). There is also evidence that homelessness causes a deterioration in health. For example, studies have shown that living in poor accommodation causes poorer health in general, and badly designed housing or dangerous household fittings can lead to injuries. The negative attitudes that are prevalent among the homeless (especially males) towards medical services and the problems that they experience accessing them also contribute to their higher incidence of health problems (Donnellan, 2004; Ensign and Bell, 2004; Riddell, 2006).

The **social drift hypothesis** has been used to explain how homelessness is caused by health problems. This is based on Darwinist theories of natural selection and hypothesises that those who are physically and mentally ill move down the social system and accumulate at the bottom. However, the use of the word 'drift' has been challenged by those who argue that health is determined by a multitude of risk factors that accumulate throughout a lifetime. Despite individuals' efforts to cope, these will repeatedly and systematically destroy their health. Hence the word 'drowning' as opposed to 'drifting' is deemed to be more appropriate (White, 2002).

Those who sleep rough are far more prone to ill health than other homeless groups; it is estimated that around 70 per cent have mental health problems (which can include severe psychiatric problems), 50 per cent are heavy drinkers and one in seven has a drug problem. Their rate of physical health problems is between two and three times higher than the rest of the population. Health problems include chronic chest, respiratory, digestive, musculo-skeletal, wound and skin problems. Tuberculosis rates among rough sleepers are also 200 times that of the rest of the population. The effects of sleeping rough on physical and mental health can also accelerate the ageing process; rough sleepers in their forties and-fifties may have the health problems normally associated with older people (Donnellan, 2004; Firth, 2007b).

Mortality rates

Once again, these are particularly high for rough sleepers; their average age of death is between 42 and 53. They are also four times more likely to die from unnatural causes (such as accidents, assaults and drug or alcohol poisoning) and 35 times more likely to commit suicide than the rest of the population (National Statistics, 2004).

Victims of abuse

Those who are homeless are more likely than members of the domiciled population to have been in a violent or abusive relationship, for instance, with a parent or a partner. Indeed domestic violence accounts for on average 16 per cent of the households accepted as homeless each year (Rogers and Pilgrim, 2003; Hill, 2006).

Isolation and loneliness

Homeless people lack the regular forms of social support to which other social groups have access. A major consequence of this is that loneliness is pervasive among the homeless. This is emotionally painful and has detrimental consequences for physical and mental well-being. Studies have shown that both the causes and the experience of loneliness during homelessness are different from those of the general population. With reference to the causes of loneliness, these encompass personal adequacy, developmental deficits, unfulfilling personal relationships, relocation/significant separations and social marginality, which are significantly different from the causes identified in housed people. In her study of the experience of loneliness, Rokach (2004) found it to be composed of five factors. These are emotional distress, social inadequacy and alienation, interpersonal isolation, growth and discovery and self-alienation. When the loneliness experience of the homeless was compared to that of the rest of the population, the homeless (both male and female) scored higher on each factor except growth and discovery (Rogers and Pilgrim, 2003; Rokach, 2004, 2005).

Stigma and discrimination

Despite efforts to reduce the societal stigma of the homeless, they are still subjected to aggression and victimisation. The media has played a central role in creating less negative images of the homeless in recent years and placed a greater emphasis on gaining an understanding of the homeless. Nonetheless, studies have shown that there is still a tendency in the media to foreground their differences from housed people and overlook aspects of their lives that invoke their 'normality'. There is also a reluctance to engage the homeless in discussions about their needs as part of the solution to homelessness, which can reinforce their exclusion (Hodgetts et al., 2005, 2006; Rokach, 2005; Leipersberger, 2007).

Involvement with crime

Homeless people in general are both more likely to have a criminal history than the rest of the population and to experience high levels of criminal victimisation. Once more, it is rough sleepers who have the worst record, with approximately half of them either having been in prison or a remand centre at some point in their lives. Studies illustrate the complex relationship between crime and homelessness and the impossibility of establishing causality. For instance, around a third of those entering prison had not been living in permanent accommodation prior to their imprisonment. However, imprisonment can often lead to housing problems; it has been estimated that around a third of people lose their homes while in prison. This is due to several reasons, one being the fact that housing benefit is terminated if a sentence is longer than 13 weeks. Thus many prisoners leave prison with no permanent accommodation. This situation is reflected starkly in the statistic that one in ten repeat prisoners ends up sleeping rough (Rogers and Pilgrim, 2003; Doward; 2006; Stevens et al., 2007). Hence the evidence is not clear-cut as it simultaneously shows that homelessness leads to crime and imprisonment leads to homelessness and further criminal activity.

Children in homeless families

These children have been found to suffer from developmental delays, psychological stress, behavioural problems, disturbed sleep, bedwetting, soiling, aggression and hyperactivity. They also miss, on average, a quarter of the school year. This has been attributed to the frequent changes of schools that inevitably occur when a homeless family has to live in temporary accommodation. Such a lack of regular attendance at school for children in homeless families leads to educational disadvantage and poorer educational performance. Nor are the overcrowded facilities in temporary accommodation conducive to the completion of homework and, more specifically, the coursework required for formal qualifications such as GCSEs. Furthermore, this type of accommodation means that they are at greater risk of accidents and their diet is poorer because of inadequate cooking facilities (Keogh et al., 2006; Firth, 2007b).

Such experiences often occur in combination and when they do, this can lead to further deterioration in a homeless person's situation and/or condition. For instance, the development of drink- and drug-related problems while homeless can lead to behavioural problems, an increased chance of entering the criminal justice system and further homelessness. The experiences of children in homeless families have a major impact on their future employment prospects and can lead to poverty in adulthood (Donnellan, 2004; Firth, 2007b).

The nature of these experiences and their interconnections also means that members of this vulnerable group in society are socially excluded and there have been considerable efforts to address their social exclusion. Furthermore, as one of those vulnerable groups identified as requiring additional targeting to ensure their social inclusion, there has also been an emphasis on adopting a lifetime approach in order to break the 'cycle of disadvantage' that they seem to be caught up in (Social Exclusion Unit, 2004a; Cabinet Office, 2006). The factors that drive the social exclusion of homeless people are addressed by several different organisations and have also been the focus of political initiatives. The role of these organisations and examples of the initiatives introduced are the subjects of the next section.

ADDRESSING AND REDUCING HOMELESSNESS

The voluntary sector has traditionally played a central role, directly and indirectly, in the provision of support and services for the homeless. One of the best-known national charities for the homeless is Crisis. This helps vulnerable and marginalised *single* homeless people. It develops innovative services to enable them to progress through education, fulfil their potential and transform their lives, regularly publishes and commissions research, organises events to raise awareness about the causes and nature of homelessness and campaigns for a more inclusive society (Crisis, 2008). Another national voluntary organisation is Shelter. This provides expert information, advice and advocacy for people with housing problems, helps people keep their homes and prevents them from becoming homeless in the future. Their advisors also help clients negotiate with councils and landlords. Specialist Shelter projects have been developed all over the United Kingdom to support those who sleep rough and help them find homes that are decent, affordable, secure and suitable for their needs. These include **day shelters**, **outreach teams**, hostels, **night shelters** and **resettlement teams**. This organisation also has a campaigning role and carries out extensive research. It regularly promotes good practice at a local level, lobbies government and local authorities to implement laws and policies that will improve the lot of people with a housing need, briefs ministers about current housing issues and tables amendments to draft housing bills (Roche, 2004; Shelter, 2008).

Despite the invaluable contribution that the voluntary sector makes to addressing the needs of the homeless, there have been concerns about aspects of the services provided by some voluntary organisations, such as the quality of accommodation and care for single homeless people. As mentioned in the introduction to this chapter the political profile of homelessness has been raised and it has become very much part of the social exclusion agenda. The new policies that have emerged reflect the emphasis on reducing the social exclusion of the homeless and a move away from the previous dependence on the voluntary sector. They have also focused on the role of **statutory services** and homelessness-related targets and are discussed below.

Statutory services

Statutory services have recently been required to develop strategic approaches to address both the causes and the symptoms of homelessness. An example is the Homelessness Act, 2002, which signalled that homelessness had moved from a subsidiary to a core political issue. As a result of this legislation, local authorities are obliged to be more proactive in tackling homelessness and to devise homelessness prevention strategies for which £360 million in grant funding has been made available. The importance of prevention is also emphasised in the strategy document *Sustainable communities: settled homes; changing lives* (2005). This stated that homelessness can be prevented by

> *providing people with the ways and the means to address their housing and other needs in order to avoid homelessness. Prevention activities include those which enable a household to remain in their current home, where appropriate, or to enable a planned and timely move and help sustain independent living. (Office of the Deputy Prime Minister, 2005: 14)*

Such activities include mediation services to prevent relationship breakdown and rent deposit schemes (Roche, 2004; May et al., 2006; Department of Communities and Local Government, 2007b).

Overall, the use of prevention activities has been deemed successful because it has resulted in a decrease in the number of households accepted as homeless by local authorities; as Figure 7.1 shows, the number of households that became homeless (that is accepted by local authorities as statutorily homeless) in England has declined steadily since 2003. For instance, between July 2007 and September 2007 the number was 15 per cent lower than for the same period in 2006 (Department of Communities and Local Government, 2007a).

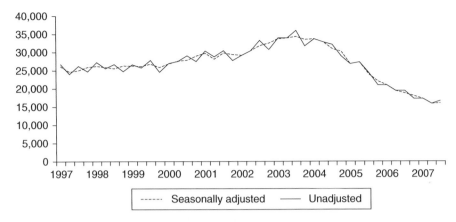

Figure 7.1   Households accepted by local authorities as owed the main homelessness duty, each quarter, England

Source: Department of Communities and Local Government, 2007a

Homelessness-related targets

The political focus on the exclusion of the homeless has also meant that several specific homelessness-related targets have been set for this decade. Past and current examples are:

- eliminating the long-term use of bed and breakfast accommodation for households with/or expecting children by March 2004;
- ending, by 2010, the use of bed and breakfast accommodation by local housing authorities for 16- and 17-year-olds;
- halving the numbers of households housed in insecure temporary accommodation by 2010;
- reducing the number of homeless households with children in temporary accommodation by over 30,000 between 2008 and 2016;
- reducing the number of rough sleepers by at least two-thirds from its 1998 level of 1,850 by 2002;
- increasing the number of social rented homes from 16,000 in 2004 to 28,000 in 2008.

With reference to specific targets, there have been some positive developments: between March 2002 and March 2004 there was a 99.3 per cent decline in the use of bed and breakfast accommodation for housing homeless families with children (Social Exclusion Unit, 2004a). Progress with this target has been further sustained by the Homelessness (Suitability of Accommodation) (England) Order 2003; under this, local authorities can no longer discharge their duty to families with children accepted as homeless by placing them in bed and breakfasts for longer than six weeks (Department of Communities and Local Government, 2007a).

In addition, as Figure 7.2 shows, there has been a downward trend in the number of households in temporary accommodation since the fourth quarter of 2005, which follows a period when numbers had been static at around 101,000. The number of households in temporary housing on 30 September 2007 had fallen by 11 per cent since 30 September 2006. This is 18 per cent lower than the peak in temporary accommodation use during 2004 (Department of Communities and Local Government, 2007a).

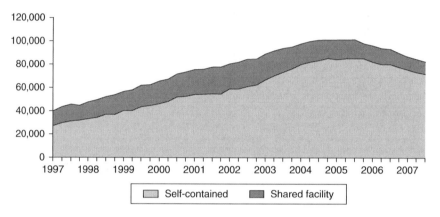

Figure 7.2   Households in temporary accommodation at the end of each quarter, by type, England

Source: Department of Communities and Local Government, 2007a

As a result of reduced recourse to bed and breakfasts and a rise in the provision of self-contained accommodation, when temporary accommodation is enlisted, there is now less chance of a homeless household having to share facilities. The use of housing with shared facilities has been declining in recent years: in 2007 it was only 14 per cent, and 86 per cent of homeless households were in self-contained accommodation. However, although the percentage of households who spend two or more years in temporary homes or are recorded as homeless at home was stable during 2007, it had been increasing until the end of 2006. In addition, with respect to households that include dependent children and/or a pregnant woman, although 92 per cent of them were in self-contained accommodation, for 76 per cent this housing was still temporary (Department of Communities and Local Government, 2007a).

More services have been developed to address youth homelessness; there is now improved access to homelessness mediation across the country, including family mediation for young people, and a new national supported lodgings development scheme has been launched. This provides accommodation, advice and mediation services for young people who can no longer stay in the family home (Department of Communities and Local Government, 2007a, 2007b).

The penultimate target was met ahead of time in 2001 and to date this progress is being sustained; in June 2007 there were just under 500 sleeping rough in England on any single night. Such single-night counts may not reflect the full extent of rough sleeping because, for example, they will not include those who hide themselves in disused buildings or avoid being counted. Nor will they capture the number of people who may have had experience of sleeping rough over the course of a year. However, they enable progress to be measured over time and across regions. This latest figure represents a 73 per cent reduction in rough sleeping since 1998. The government is now committed to reducing rough sleeping to as near to zero as possible. There are outreach teams to help those on the streets, hostels to provide the first step off the streets, day centres and other agencies to offer social and cultural activities, and training and support to help increase employment opportunities. As explained above, The Homeless Act, 2002, extended the categorisation of those considered to be in priority need for housing so that more groups of the street homeless (such as care leavers aged 18 to 20) are entitled to housing. Investment programmes, such as the £90m Hostels Capital Improvement Programme, should help to achieve further reductions in rough sleeping over the next few years (Department of Communities and Local Government, 2007b).

Such targets are monitored and evaluated by the Department of Communities and Local Government. Good practice principles are identified in relation to issues such as using services effectively, homelessness-prevention approaches, service procurement and assessing value for money (Office of the Deputy Prime Minister, 2005; Shelter, 2006; Department of Communities and Local Government, 2007a, 2007b).

ACTIVITY 7.4

Mike's story

This is a case study of a homeless person called Mike. It illustrates some of the benefits of homelessness-prevention strategies implemented through a day shelter. Make a note of the strategies mentioned and the sort of benefits that Mike derived from them as you read it. Some ideas to get you thinking can be found in the 'Post-activity Comments' section.

Over several years, Mike had held various bar management jobs which came with rented accommodation, but each one had ended with his dismissal because of the inappropriate behaviour that inevitably followed his bouts of binge-drinking. The years of financial insecurity and his problematic relationship with alcohol took their toll on his

(Continued)

marriage and when his wife finally asked him to leave, he went to live with his elderly mother. However, his drinking habits led to violent rows and she eventually told him to go. He then went to live with his sister for a short while but the same behaviour patterns led her to tell him that he could no longer stay in her home. He became homeless and lived on the streets for two years.

Other people living on the streets told him about a day shelter where he could get food and advice. During the past six months, he has been attending this day shelter on a regular basis. Here he has attended workshops on how to communicate better with people and prepare for working again. In addition, he has been able to pursue his long-term interest in painting and has also received tuition in how to design websites. As a result of this support, he has set up his own website on which he is now selling his paintings. Staff at the day shelter have also arranged for him to receive medical attention and counselling for his drink problem.

Mike says that selling his paintings has made him feel proud of himself for the first time in many years. He also finds painting therapeutic and motivating. The routine of daily attendance at the day shelter has helped to give a structure to his life that it lacked over the past few years. He enjoys interacting with staff at the centre and is now talking to a resettlement worker about finding accommodation. As a result of the medical treatment he is now receiving, he is beginning to feel physically better than he did before. The counselling is also helping him to start to address his drinking habits.

However, despite all the resources put into addressing homelessness and some successful outcomes, there is still evidence that many of the homeless do not receive the help they need when they need it. Emergency accommodation is unevenly distributed, 25 per cent have been homeless for more than five years and repeat homelessness remains high; two out of every three homeless people have been homeless more than once and one in ten have been homeless more than ten times. Furthermore 95,000 households are still homeless, including more than 130,000 children. There are also concerns that the essential preventative services, which could enable lasting solutions to homelessness, are not being delivered because of the way that funding is allocated. Examples are the Supporting People and Homeless Prevention Grant programmes. Although these have been invested in upgrading hostels into places of change for homeless people, with the intention of providing support services and learning opportunities, funding for the latter has not been available. These are all central to the prevention of homelessness as they give people the skills that they need to tackle their deprivation and increase their chances of employability and social inclusion. An example of such skills are those which enable them to leave past negative behaviours behind in order to interact successfully in work and non-work situations and to access and use services which will ensure that their wider needs are met (see 'Mike's story' above). Although the majority of homeless people recognise the benefits of, and want to utilise, such services and participate in learning and skills development, only a fifth are currently engaging in such opportunities. In addition, there is evidence that those who have been homeless the longest are much less likely to take advantage of services for learning opportunities and skills development. Thus, there are groups that require particular targeting and encouragement if the social exclusion of the homeless is to be effectively addressed (Doward, 2006; May et al., 2006; Riddell, 2006; Firth, 2007b).

FUTURE DIRECTIONS FOR POLICIES

In addtion to identifying the strengths and weaknesses, evaluation studies of these recent polices have also suggested ways forward. Some of these suggestions are as follows:

'Joined-up' working between different services

As explained above, the voluntary sector makes a very significant contribution to meeting the needs of the homeless and over the past decade there has been an expansion of statutory services. Homelessness is multifaceted and, for policies to be effective, there must be more integration of both voluntary and statutory services so that people do not 'fall through the net' and there is a move way from the 'revolving door' culture. Some of the recommendations that have been made have concentrated on the differences in working practices and organisational cultures between the voluntary and statutory sectors and the need to develop relationships between the two, perhaps through service level agreements between agencies. Increased integration of different services can also help to create service provision that is more transparent and less of a deterrent to service users (Roche, 2004; Cabinet Office, 2006).

Adoption of a more holistic approach

Policies have been criticised for being reactive and holding homeless individuals culpable for their predicament. This concentration on the individual causes of homelessness has also meant that more 'challenging' service users are excluded from services. Critics have called for a more holistic approach that incorporates the wider causes of homelessness. These include the underlying socio-economic causes, and the impact of other social policies, such those that have implications for house building and community care (Riddell, 2006; Phelan and Norris, 2008). For instance, one of the outcomes of the house-building programmes during the last three decades of the last century was a mismatch between the number of homes available and the number of households. This was because the number of households rose by 30 per cent but housebuilding fell by a half. Since the closure of mental institutions in the 1980s and 1990s and the introduction of community care, the number of homeless people with mental health problems has almost doubled. In support of their argument, those advocating a more holistic approach point to the growing body of evidence that social policies in other countries that focus on the structural causes of homelessness have lowered their numbers of homeless people and reduced their exclusion (Cohen, 2006; Shinn, 2007).

Targeting 'hard-to-reach' groups of the homeless

Some homeless groups are less responsive to the expansion of service provision that has taken place and therefore remain more vulnerable to homelessness. One of these groups is older people; because of mental health problems, alienation or apathy they are less likely to ask for help from mainstream advice services or helplines. This means that they are often still neglected. Therefore both statutory and voluntary services need to be more proactive in identifying them and 'seeking' them out through home visits and/or visits to lunch clubs or day centres. Services that are specifically tailored to their needs should be developed. Preventative services suggested in the literature include improving mainstream housing for older people on low incomes and the provision of a wider range of housing with care options in later life. Tenancy support is advocated for older people who have experienced long-term street homelessness as this increases the likelihood of them keeping their new home. Such support includes helping older people to become established within their new community and to ease their transition between hostel or institutional living and independent living (Crane and Warnes, 2005; Means, 2007; Shelter, 2007b).

Reducing stigma

The reduction of stigma has been shown to lead to a greater **social integration** of vulnerable groups. This facilitates their participation in mainstream activities in society, such as employment, voluntary work, and social and community life. Social integration is also beneficial in itself as it provides moral support and enables individuals to deal with life's stresses and crises (Durkheim, 1968). Furthermore, it is now recognised that social integration has positive effects on physical and mental health (Berkman, 1995; Berkman et al., 2000; Freund and McGuire, 1995).

Increased social integration would therefore be invaluable in supporting people who have been homeless with their transition from homelessness and could help to prevent repeat homelessness. Consequently, in addition to the arguments for reducing stigma associated with homelessness from a **social justice** point of view, further efforts could be made to reduce this stigma in order to ensure the social integration of the homeless. Recent American studies have produced some useful ideas about both reducing societal stigma and the self-stigma experienced by the homeless themselves; some found that greater exposure to and contact with the homeless can influence public attitudes favourably (Wong et al., 2006). Others found that programmes to reduce the self-stigma of mentally ill homeless people facilitated their social integration. Such findings could be developed in the drive to support and socially include members of this vulnerable group (Lee et al., 2004).

There are also broader issues that need to be considered in ensuring the social inclusion of homeless people. One is the need for adequate government funding; it is estimated that 20,000 more social rented homes are required by 2011 in order to halt the housing crisis. This is 60,000 more over and above current government plans and will cost £1.25 billion. Thus government funding commitments will need revisiting if this crisis is to be averted (Riddell, 2006).

Moreover, there are questions around the citizenship of homeless people. Citizenship requires fulfilling social obligations such as being a community member, helping fellow citizens and ensuring social order and cohesion. The very nature of homelessness and the fact that homeless people do not have permanent accommodation mean that meeting such criteria is unrealistic. It is therefore more appropriate to talk about citizenship in relation to the homeless once they have achieved a non-homeless state and can participate more in mainstream society. Even then, factors such as the stigma of homelessness and the length of time that people have been homeless mean that they may only have marginal connections with mainstream society. Thus there are obstacles to their inclusion and the associated status of citizenship. Rowe et al. (2001) argue that there are more obstacles for some homeless people than others, for instance, those who are mentally ill; this group bears the stigma of both homelessness and mental illness and, whatever the level of funding and service provision, they can rarely overcome their marginalisation and ensure their social inclusion. As a result, they are highly likely to be denied full citizenship.

CONCLUSIONS

It is clear from the discussions in this chapter that the longstanding social problem of homelessness is both multidimensional and dynamic. Moreover, it poses new and unique challenges to the social exclusion agenda for several reasons. These are the complexity of its characteristics and the issues that define it, public attitudes towards homelessness, and the range of organisations and services that work with the homeless.

One of the key points to emerge is that different groups of the homeless, such as homeless families and the hidden homeless, have very different needs, which can also include those of children caught up in a 'cycle of disadvantage'. While progress has been made, there is much more to be done to socially include all members of this vulnerable group and overcome the obstacles to their enjoyment of full citizenship. The evidence presented shows that this requires more coordination between the various sectors and more members of society to fulfil *their* social obligations as citizens towards the homeless. This was summed up in the words of a recent Cabinet document, which stated that 'social exclusion cannot be addressed by government alone. Individuals and the wider community, in addition to the private and third sectors, all have a role to play' (Cabinet Office, 2006: 12).

DISCUSSION POINTS

To what extent is 'homelessness' socially constructed?

Why are 'the homeless' socially excluded?

What are the arguments for extending the role of statutory services in addressing the social exclusion of the homeless?

What directions do you think future policies aimed at addressing the social exclusion of the homeless should take?

FURTHER STUDY

Much information can be gleaned from the websites of the national charities for homeless people, such as Shelter, Crisis and Centrepoint. For up-to-date statistics and information about recent initiatives, visit the Department of

Communities and Local Government website. The series 'Issues' (published by Independence Educational publishers) also includes current information about homelessness and related issues. Buying a copy of the *The Big Issue* both helps the homeless and affords real insights into the realities of homelessness. *Social Work* and *Community Work* journals often have articles about the homeless and strategies for addressing homelessness. If you are interested in the concept of social integration, it is worth looking at the original work on it by Durkheim (1968). Examples of the ways in which this concept has been applied to the study of health can be found in the following articles: Berkman and Syme (1979); Berkman (1995); Berkman et al. (2000).

Key readings

Donnellan, C. (ed.) (2004). *Dealing with homelessness*. Cambridge: Independence

Firth, L. (ed.) (2007b). *Homelessness*. Cambridge: Independence

Roche, M. (2004). 'Complicated problems, complicated solutions? Homelessness and joined-up policy responses.' *Social Policy and Administration*, **38** (7) 758–74

Rowe, M., Kloos, B., Chinman, M., Davidson, L. and Boyle Cross, A. (2001). 'Homelessness, mental illness and citizenship.' *Social Policy and Administration*, 35 **(10)** 14–31

POST-ACTIVITY COMMENTS

ACTIVITY 7.2

Individual factors

- physical or mental health problems;
- drink-and drug-related problems;
- relationship breakdowns.

Structural factors:

- political instability: *as experienced by asylum seekers and refugees*
- ethnic minority group status: *homelessness is high among these groups*
- housing policy: *changes in official definitions of homelessness determine who is accepted as homeless by local authorities and who, consequently, receives help*
- regional economic performance: *can lead to variations in homelessness rates*
- gender: *men are more likely to be sleeping rough than women*
- benefit system: *people on benefits have a greater vulnerability to homelessness*

ACTIVITY 7.4

Some ideas to help you with this activity are:

- the opportunity to attend the day shelter on a regular basis gave Mike's life some structure;

- contact with staff at the day shelter widened his social network;

- the facilities available at the day shelter enabled him to pursue a long-term interest that he found therapeutic;

- the learning and skills development opportunities provided enabled him to undertake productive activities, increasing his confidence, self-esteem and employability skills;

- the services which could be accessed through the day shelter helped Mike to address his health and drinking problems and negative past behaviour.

Chapter 8

Asylum Seekers and Refugees

OVERVIEW

- Definitions
- Reasons for seeking asylum in the United Kingdom
- Vulnerabilities upon arrival
- Life in the United Kingdom for asylum seekers and refugees
- Existing policies and initiatives that address the social exclusion of asylum seekers and refugees
- Directions for future policies
- Conclusions
- Suggestions for further study

INTRODUCTION

Wars, conflicts, human rights abuses and environmental disasters in different parts of the world result in the enforced migration of civilians to other countries. Although their numbers fluctuate, there are around 21 million **asylum seekers** and **refugees** worldwide who have fled their homes in the world's trouble spots. Their plight is a cause for global concern and action at an international level to ensure their protection and to resolve problems is coordinated by the United Nations High Commissioner for Refugees (UNHCR).

Therefore global events and processes influence the ways in which the United Kingdom is affected by asylum and refugee issues; for instance in the 1970s there were asylum seekers from Chile, and then from Vietnam in the early 1980s. The numbers of those coming to the United Kingdom to seek asylum increased in the 1980s and 1990s because of the situations in countries such as Kurdistan, the former Republic of Yugoslavia, Somalia and Uganda. These increases, together with concerns about costly delays in processing their applications and abuse of the asylum system, considerably raised their political profile in the 1990s. Research into the lives of asylum seekers in this country highlighted their marginalisation from mainstream society. The media also played a significant role in increasing their visibility and raising public awareness with images of asylum seekers in holding centres and living in areas of severe deprivation. They have been prioritised within the social exclusion agenda and the Social Exclusion Unit identified them as being amongst the 'hardest to help' (Social Exclusion Unit, 2004a: 5) groups in society. Other sources have described them as among the 'most vulnerable groups in the United Kingdom' (Mollard, 2001: 12) and 'among the most vulnerable of vulnerable groups' (Burchardt, 2005: 210). Consequently there have been several major policy interventions which have attempted to address the problems associated with asylum in the United Kingdom (Sales, 2002; Roche 2004; Burchardt, 2005).

There is often conceptual confusion over the terms 'asylum seeker' and 'refugee'. Therefore the first part of this chapter will clarify what is meant when reference is made to these groups of people. It will then explore their vulnerabilities upon arrival in the United Kingdom and how life in this country can lead to an increase in their vulnerability and social exclusion. The extent to which existing policies have addressed the needs of asylum seekers and refugees in our society will be assessed and suggestions made about possible ways forward for future policy development. Child asylum seekers are also included in the discussions in order to reflect the concerns about their particular vulnerabilities.

ACTIVITY 8.1

What images of asylum seekers do the following newspaper headlines convey? See the 'Post-activity Comments' section for some suggestions.

Still at large, 126,000 asylum cheats
Asylum seekers get cash handouts
Creaming off the benefits system
Refugees cost tax payers more than £300 million each year
Send these scroungers home

One in five flock here; asylum: we're too dam' soft (*Daily Star*, 23 January 2004)

So called asylum seekers who, in reality, seek no more than access to our welfare system (*Sunday Express*, 2 May 2004)

Another influx of asylum seekers will be arriving in Scotland today

Asylum seekers overwhelming family doctors (*Daily Mail*, 15 March 2002)

There is far from a flood (of asylum seekers) in Britain ... North America has about twice the number of asylum seekers that Europe does

Britain the No.1 refugee magnet (*The Sun*, 14 September 2002)

Asylum chaos makes us the land of freeloaders (*Evening Standard*, 22 April 2003)

Bogus asylum seekers are draining millions from the NHS (*Daily Express*, 26 November 2002)

How immigrants fuel Britain's boom town (*Observer*, 6 April 2008)

(unless indicated otherwise, these quotes are taken from Mollard, 2001)

ACTIVITY 8.2

See what evidence you can find in the next two sections to refute or support such headlines. Some examples can be found in the 'Post-activity Comments' at the end of the chapter.

WHO ARE ASYLUM SEEKERS AND REFUGEES?

The terms 'asylum seekers' and 'refugees' are frequently used interchangeably even though they refer to different groups of vulnerable people; an asylum seeker is someone who has fled from their home country because of war, civil unrest or conflict, arrived in another country, made a formal application for asylum and is awaiting a decision about their status. The 1951 Refugee Convention gives *everybody* the right to apply for asylum, and to live in the country in which they have made their application until a decision on that application has been made. This includes those who are under 18 if they are separated from both parents or are not being cared for by an adult who by law or custom has responsibility to do so. A child who meets these criteria is defined as as an unaccompanied asylum-seeking child (UASC).

Currently, the most common countries of origin for asylum seekers are Turkey, Iraq, Iran, Afghanistan, Sri Lanka, Zimbabwe, China and Somalia. Once an individual has made an application for asylum, they are eligible for support from the National Asylum Support Service (NASS), a government-run agency established in 1999, while their application is being processed. Although NASS initially supplied asylum seekers with vouchers for purchases, these were phased out in 2002 and it now gives them a small amount of money for subsistence. It also provides access to free healthcare and education for children. In addition, under the dispersal programme, which means that since 1999 all newly arrived asylum seekers are compulsorily dispersed outside London and the Southeast, it allocates them accommodation in various local authority properties across the United Kingdom. Unaccompanied asylum seeking children are eligible for support services from local authorities in the form of an allocated social worker, a care plan, financial support and entitlement to leaving care services.

A refugee is someone whose asylum application has been successful and who has been granted permission to stay in the United Kingdom under the terms of the 1951 Refugee Convention because of a well-founded fear of persecution if they returned home due to race, religion, nationality, political opinion or membership of a social group. Refugee status brings entitlement to benefits, housing and services on the same basis as other United Kingdom citizens. Since 2005, those who are given refugee status are only initially given permission to stay in the United Kingdom for five years. If the situation in their home country has not improved after five years permanent refugee status is then granted. In recent years, around 70 per cent of asylum applicants have been rejected and those who are unsuccessful are referred to as **failed asylum seekers**. There are rights of appeal and, on average, a fifth of failed asylum seekers will be found to have been wrongly refused asylum. While some of those who are not granted asylum will return to their home country voluntarily, others will have to be forcibly returned. The nationalities with the highest numbers of those refused asylum in the United Kingdom who have returned to their country of origin are from Afghanistan, Iraq, Turkey, Pakistan, Iran, Albania, India and Sri Lanka. When someone cannot be granted asylum but it would be very dangerous for them to return home, they can be given Humanitarian Protection or Discretionary Leave, which allows them to stay in the United Kingdom for five and three further years respectively. After these periods their status is actively reviewed and they are expected to return to their country if the situation there improves (Sales, 2002; Burchardt, 2005; Refugee Council, 2007; UNHCR, 2007; National Statistics, 2008).

The information presented above shows that asylum decisions can take a long time to resolve and, despite measures introduced under the Nationality, Immigration and Asylum Act, 2002, asylum-seeker status may last for several years. Furthermore, under the Asylum and Immigration Act, 2004, at any point during the asylum application process, immigration detention can be used to detain asylum seekers. This usually takes place in a detention centre and occurs because there are, for example, reasons to suspect that their claim is not credible and/or they have outstanding legal issues in their cases. It is also used to effect the removal of people from the United Kingdom if their asylum claim is not successful (Refugee Council, 2007; Independent Asylum Commission, 2008).

Despite concerns about influxes of asylum seekers into this country, globally it is the poorer, developing countries that host most of the world's displaced and stateless people. Indeed, the United Kingdom is home to less than 3 per cent of the world's refugees; receives fewer than other European countries; and in 2006 ranked sixteenth in the league table of industrialised countries for the number of asylum applications per head. Furthermore, asylum seekers only make up a very small percentage of the population; in 2005, they represented just 0.025 per cent of the total entries to the United Kingdom and the government spends around 0.17 per cent of its total expenditure on supporting asylum seekers and their dependants. The number of asylum applications to this country has fallen quite dramatically over the past few years. For example, between 2001 and 2007 it fell by almost 75 per cent and in 2007 asylum applications were at their lowest level for 14 years (23,430) (National Statistics, 2008). However, this has in part been attributed to increased restrictions and requirements. Furthermore, numbers do fluctuate; as Figure 8.1 below shows, although the total number of asylum

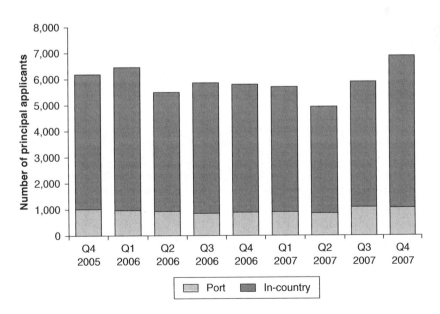

Figure 8.1   Asylum seeker applicants (excluding dependants) 2005–2007

Source: National Statistics, 2008

applicants for 2007 was lower than that for 2006, they did rise in the second half of 2007 (Mollard, 2001; Refugee Council, 2007; Home Office, 2008).

The main driver behind this group's decision to leave its own country is to reach a place of safety. While some have had to leave for environmental reasons, such as natural disasters, most are from nations gripped by serious conflict where there are grave abuses of human rights. Therefore, asylum seekers are generally escaping from persecution and intolerable situations and often have personal experience of violence. Examples are massacres, detentions, beatings, torture, rape, sexual assault, witnessing death squads and the torture of others, their own fake executions, and being held under siege or as hostages. They may also have experienced the destruction of their homes and property and forcible eviction. More persistent types of persecution include political repression, deprivation of human rights and harassment. If they have lived in refugee camps, they have often had to endure prolonged squalor, malnutrition and a lack of personal protection. Such personal experiences are usually accompanied by intentional damage to their 'social, economic and cultural institutions' (Burnett and Peel, 2001a: 486). (Burnett and Peel, 2001a; Robinson and Segrott, 2002; National Statistics, 2008).

Child asylum seekers will have experienced much physical and mental hardship; they will have lost their homes, schools, friends and members of their family, witnessed horrific events such as violence and torture, and maybe spent months in hiding. Some may have been tortured or abducted to become child soldiers and forced to commit violent acts themselves. Unaccompanied asylum-seeking children will have had the additional trauma of having lost, or been separated from, their parents (Burnett and Peel, 2001b; Coker, 2001).

Studies show that there are many constraints on asylum seekers' choice of destination country. Agents or traffickers play a key role in determining which country they will go to; in some cases agents give them no choice and, when they do furnish a priced 'menu' of destinations, their destination country is dependent on how much they can afford to pay. If they choose the United Kingdom, it is often on the advice of informal social networks or because they have relatives or friends here already and/or because of their perception of the United Kingdom as a free, democratic country, able to offer better life chances for them and their families. Factors identified as not being influential are asylum policies and procedures, housing, the availability of welfare benefits and the availability of work. Indeed, most do not want to depend on benefits and many hope that they will be able to return home once the situation in their country has improved (Robinson and Segrott, 2002; Koser and Pinkerton, 2002; Gilbert and Koser, 2004; Refugee Council, 2007).

Although worldwide most refugees are women, the majority of asylum seekers in Britain are single men under the age of 40. There is evidence that they are proportionately more highly qualified and skilled than Britain's native population. For example, 60 per cent have professional and/or academic qualifications (including a high proportion of medical and teaching qualifications);

around a third of the parents of refugee children have a first or postgraduate degree, most of them possess relevant work experience, and over 65 per cent speak two languages in addition to their mother tongue (Refugee Council, 2007). Consequently, many have also had a previously high standard of living (Burnett and Peel, 2001a; Mollard, 2001).

Upon arrival in the United Kingdom, they are often 'traumatised, penniless, alone and unable to speak the language' (Burchardt, 2005: 210). Many have health problems associated with the sorts of atrocities that they have endured, such as the psychological and physical effects of torture. Examples of the psychological effects of torture are sleep disturbances, nightmares, depression, headaches and intrusive images that affect concentration and memory. They may also be suffering from post-traumatic stress disorder, nutritional deficiencies and infections. Moreover, they will not necessarily have had access to healthcare in their own countries. One of the major consequences of this is that many of their conditions will have remained untreated and child asylum seekers will not have received immunisations. In addition, the nature of their journeys to the United Kingdom can lead to health problems; all will have travelled long distances, many will have experienced the stress of being smuggled and not knowing what will happen to them upon arrival, and some will have spent time in transit countries (Peel, 1996; Burnett and Peel, 2001b; Coker, 2001; Koser and Pinkerton, 2002; Gilbert and Koser, 2004).

Thus asylum seekers and refugees are not a homogeneous population; they come from many different countries, for a variety of reasons and have a wide range of experiences. Nonetheless, what they do have in common upon arrival in the United Kingdom is, as the above discussions have shown, their vulnerability. Indeed some, such as children and torture survivors, are very vulnerable. The effect of life in the United Kingdom on the nature and extent of this vulnerability is the subject of the second section in this chapter.

LIFE IN THE UNITED KINGDOM

Studies have shown that asylum seekers' and refugees' experiences when living in this country can compound their vulnerability and lead to social exclusion. The main contributory factors that have been identified are discussed below.

Poverty

Most asylum seekers and refugees live in poverty in the United Kingdom and they are one of the poorest groups in this country. As a result, 95 per cent are unable to buy essential items (such as clothes, shoes, bus tickets and nappies) and 85 per cent experience hunger (Burnett and Peel, 2001a; Mollard, 2001; Refugee Council, 2007).

One of the reasons for their poverty is that, although asylum seekers do want to support themselves by working, they are legally prevented from doing so unless they have waited over 12 months for an initial decision on their case. Consequently, most are forced to rely on NASS payments, which amount to only 70 per cent of income support. This means that they have to exist on an income that is 30 per cent below the poverty line. They are also denied some benefits, such as disability living allowance, and take-up of benefits for which they might qualify is low because, contrary to allegations that they come to this country to claim benefits, they know little about the benefit system and their entitlements. Many do voluntary work while their asylum application is being processed. Indeed provisions have recently been made to enable asylum seekers awaiting decisions on their applications for refugee status to undertake volunteering. This is seen as helping them to contribute to the community and to improve relationships with the local host communities in which they are living (Department for Work and Pensions, 2005b; Home Office, 2005, 2006b; Refugee Council, 2007).

Although a large proportion are more qualified and skilled than many other groups, once they are able to apply for paid work, they experience high levels of unemployment. Their levels of long-term unemployment are particularly high. Several recent cross-governmental initiatives have aimed to help them towards employment through the introduction of a mentoring scheme, which gives them intensive one-to-one support with a dedicated caseworker to help them find work using the services available and to update their specialist skills (Department for Work and Pensions, 2005b; Home Office, 2005).

However, several other barriers to their employment have been identified; those asylum seekers who apply for permission to work after the 12-month wait for a decision on their asylum claim are excluded from certain types of employment, such as becoming self-employed and engaging in business or professional activity. Furthermore, their application will only be considered if any delays in the decision process cannot be attributed to the applicant (Home Office, 2006b). These restrictions reduce the chances of employment for those whose asylum applications take a long time to process. Another barrier is that the skills and experience of those who are highly skilled (for example, the medically qualified or teachers) are not always recognised and they may not be able to obtain the training needed to practise in the United Kingdom. Language skills are also a problem and studies have shown that standards of good practice with regards to provision of language support are not being met in a number of areas. In addition, as community networks have been found to play an essential role in the search for employment, those who are not part of a significant, well-established community do not have the access to appropriate networks that may increase their chances of employment (Burnett and Peel, 2001a; Sales, 2002; Aspinall, 2006; Refugee Council, 2007; Phillimore and Goodson, 2008).

There have been criticisms of policies that restrict asylum seekers in terms of the paid work that they can undertake and of the measures addressing their high unemployment rates. The initiatives (described above) that help asylum seekers and refugees into voluntary and paid work have been introduced in the context of New Labour's push towards citizenship for individuals who seek to become British citizens. The aim is to ensure that asylum seekers and refugees play an active role in society and are active citizens. To this effect, the rights and responsibilities of their status are being set out; they are expected to use their skills or gain the skills necessary to give something back to the community. However, the emphasis on employment-based citizenship in New Labour's interpretation of citizenship means that policies preventing asylum seekers from undertaking paid employment thus exclude them from citizenship. Hence existing polices are contradictory; some encourage citizenship while others hinder the achievement of this status. Moreover, New Labour attaches great importance to paid work as a precondition for addressing the social exclusion of vulnerable groups. If this vulnerable group is either not allowed to undertake paid employment and/or continues to experience high levels of unemployment even when they can legally work, it is hard for them to escape their social exclusion (Sales, 2002; Spicer, 2008).

Housing

Dispersal polices (referred to above) under the National Asylum Support Service (NASS) have meant that asylum seekers are moved to accommodation across the country without necessarily taking into account their individual needs. They may also be moved several times during the application process. The areas to which they are dispersed are usually those where others do not want to live and which have high levels of deprivation and unemployment. The housing is also poor, frequently damp and infested and lacking privacy. The characteristics of these areas and the housing within them reinforce the exclusion of asylum seekers. The low success rate of appeals to NASS for rehousing has been seen as evidence of the increasingly restrictive nature of policies on asylum seekers' housing rights (Burnett and Peel, 2001a; Mollard, 2001; Burchardt, 2005; Spicer, 2008).

When asylum seekers are detained, as detention is indefinite, substantial amounts of time can be spent in detention centres where accommodation is unsuitable, cramped and facilities are shared. Asylum seekers can also be moved frequently between different centres, and such moves can involve a loss of belongings (Independent Asylum Commission, 2008).

Despite the existence of NASS, there are high levels of homelessness among asylum seekers. Moreover, even if they have been in NASS accommodation while their asylum application was being processed, although they are eligible for social housing on the same basis as United Kingdom nationals if their application is successful, they are paradoxically likely to find themselves homeless. This is because they are required to leave their NASS accommodation within 28 days once they have been granted refugee status. It is difficult to find accommodation in such a short period of time and delays in processing housing applications can mean that they end up homeless. In fact, refugees, (particularly those who are single and couples without children) are overrepresented in the street homeless population. When they are allocated housing, they do not get any preferential treatment on waiting lists and cannot choose where they live (Bradshaw and Mayhew 2005; Shelter, 2006; Firth, 2007; Refugee Council, 2007; Independent Asylum Commission, 2008).

Hostility and harassment

Research has shown that asylum seekers and refugees suffer from hostility and harassment in detention centres, the areas in which they live and within wider society. Women in particular are at risk of assault and sexual harassment (Refugee Council, 2007). Although most are law-abiding and there is no evidence of higher criminality rates among asylum seekers and refugees, they do feel that they are viewed as criminals. In fact, they are more likely to be the victims of crime but often feel unable to report incidents of racial harassment or violence. Such experiences make them feel vulnerable and unsafe (Bowes et al., 2008; Spicer, 2008).

There are those who argue that some of the responsibility for this lies with the government's negative approach to asylum seekers and refugees; various documents have indicated that there is a belief that welfare benefits are an incentive to those seeking asylum in the United Kingdom. The fact that NASS has the power to pay unannounced visits to asylum seekers to check if they have possessions to which they are not entitled is also used as further indication of governmental distrust. However, much of the blame has been apportioned to the media. Prior to 2003, negative, unbalanced and inaccurate coverage of asylum seekers and refugees in the media was blamed for causing a climate of fear among the general public, which in turn led to hostility and harassment. For instance, studies undertaken highlighted the frequency of headlines featuring words such as arrested, jailed, bogus, false and illegal. There were also stories of alleged influxes/floods of asylum seekers and/or suggestions of their antisocial criminality and how much they cost the taxpayer. These were often written by those with limited knowledge or experience of asylum seekers and refugees and/or those with a political interest in shaping the public's views on these issues. Scant space was afforded to the opinions of asylum seekers themselves, those who work with them and the organisations who support them. Thus the non-political, humanitarian aspects of asylum were ignored (Mollard, 2001; Sales, 2002; Spicer, 2008; Bowes et al., 2008).

In 2003 the Press Complaints Commission introduced guidance for journalists on reporting on asylum seekers and refugees. Recent research based on the systematic monitoring of United Kingdom newspapers reporting on asylum issues has shown that press coverage of asylum has improved since the introduction of these guidelines: inaccurate terminology only appeared in 1 per cent of articles and a small number breached the guidelines. Nonetheless, articles did still seem to emphasise that the asylum system was in 'chaos' as opposed to presenting more enlightened discussions about asylum (Smart et al., 2007).

Ill-informed, adverse attitudes represent considerable barriers to social inclusion and overlook the fact that many refugees make a significant contribution to the United Kingdom at many different levels, both culturally and economically. Indeed, they contribute more to the economy in taxes and national insurance than they consume in benefits and public services (Mollard, 2001; Refugee Council, 2007). Moreover, they could make an even greater contribution if their considerable skills and qualifications were fully utilised.

Isolation

Many different factors have led to the isolation and marginalisation of asylum seekers and refugees in the United Kingdom. These have been shown to exacerbate feelings of social exclusion.

One example was the voucher system. This excluded asylum seekers from the cash economy and prevented them from taking part in everyday activities for which cash is required. Another is dispersal: prior to 1999 most asylum seekers settled in London and hence they gradually developed support systems such as social networks based on ethnic and faith communities and **voluntary organisations**. Since dispersal was introduced, they are not necessarily located near these organisations and systems and consequently lack the invaluable and cohesive social support that they provide (Burchardt, 2005).

Established voluntary organisations, such as those referred to above, have been found to be particularly effective in supporting asylum seekers and refugees; in their work on migrant communities, Agar and Strang's (2004) work identified three dimensions to social networks: **social bonds**, **social bridges** and **social links**. Social bonds are those connections within ethnic and/or faith communities whereas social bridges are connections between members of migrant communities and communities that do not share the same ethnicity and/or faith. Social links refer to relationships between individuals and/or groups and institutions, agencies and services. Studies have indicated that voluntary organisations dealing with asylum issues play an important role in fostering asylum seekers' and refugees' social networks because they provide important social links and enable the development of social bonds (Zetter et al., 2005; Spicer, 2008).

Support systems in general are also recognised as playing an important role in the social inclusion of asylum seekers and refugees. This is because they offer practical support (such as help with accessing services, financial advice and interpretation) as well as emotional support, which helps them develop self-confidence and reduces feelings of isolation and vulnerability. Statutory and voluntary services in dispersal areas are not always able to provide much in the way of redress; they often have little experience of working with asylum seekers and refugees and/or find it difficult to respond effectively (Burchardt, 2005; Spicer, 2008; Independent Asylum Commission, 2008). Where there are innovative and responsive services, these have mainly been developed by the voluntary sector because it has greater flexibility than statutory services (Bowes et al., 2008).

Indeed, despite the expansion of some initiatives, there is a general lack of specialist services and they are unevenly spread throughout the country. Those that exist are often subject to short-term funding, are provided by voluntary organisations and tend to be overwhelmed by demand. In particular, English classes are often hard to access. This is of greater importance for the women in these groups as they are less likely to speak English (Sales, 2002; Spicer, 2008). As mentioned above, a lack of language skills also reduces chances of employment and, in combination with the fact that they are cut off from community and kin networks, they can easily experience more isolation than men in the same situation. However, there is some evidence that men suffer in other ways: they feel a loss of status more acutely because they can no longer fulfil their traditional 'breadwinner role' (Coker, 2001; Aspinall, 2006; Phillimore et al., 2007).

The isolation experienced by those in detention centres is particularly acute; as they can be frequently moved between different centres they are often a long way from family and friends. The fact that they can be detained alongside convicted foreign prisoners adds to their sense of alienation. They also have inadequate access to services essential to finding a way out of detention, such as legal advice and representation (Johnson, 2003; Independent Asylum Commission, 2008).

Health

The physical and mental health of asylum seekers and refugees is adversely affected by many aspects of their experiences, both before and upon arrival in the United Kingdom. The first section described how they have often experienced trauma and violence in their own countries, followed by a highly stressful departure and journey to an unknown country. The material presented about their lives in the United Kingdom shows that they experience poverty, poor housing, hostility, discrimination, isolation and a lack of support. In addition to these stresses, they have lost their identity and status, may be facing bereavement, have concerns about family and loved ones left behind, be anxious about the future, have to deal with the complex and uncertain process of application for asylum, fear being sent back to their own country and have to adapt to a new culture. Such tensions also increase the risk of marital breakdown and domestic violence. All of these factors affect their physical and mental health – 20 per cent have serious physical health problems and 66 per cent have psychological problems. The former include asthma, diabetes, hypertension, heart disease, TB, chronic hepatitis B and the physical effects of beatings and torture. Examples of psychological problems are insomnia, depression, anxiety, panic attacks and post-traumatic stress disorder. Women are more likely than men to have very poor health outcomes and maternal deaths are much higher than average (Burnett and Peel, 2001a, 2001b; Coker, 2001; Phillimore et al., 2007; Refugee Council, 2007).

As discussed above, unlike other overseas visitors, asylum seekers and refugees are entitled to NHS services, but studies have shown that many experience difficulties in accessing healthcare and the uptake of preventative services is low. While this is caused in part by the frequent moves some of them have to contend with, it is mainly due to language barriers, a lack of interpreters and a failure to understand the system. Furthermore, healthcare workers find it difficult to communicate with them because of language, pressure of time, a lack of understanding of cultural differences, and a lack of training about their distinct needs and the resources required to meet these. Misconceptions also occur: asylum seekers and refugees are perceived as being very demanding but in fact many are reluctant to make demands. Hence their healthcare needs may be not be adequately diagnosed and met within the NHS as the very small number of culturally appropriate services available for these groups are often outside the NHS (Bischoff et al., 2003; Hull and Boomla, 2006; O'Donnell et al., 2007; Phillimore et al., 2007).

Some groups of asylum seekers are even less likely to have their healthcare needs met than others: failed asylum seekers are entitled to free primary healthcare but are not eligible for free secondary care, except emergency (A and E) care (Refugee Council, 2007). This has damaging consequences in that people with potentially fatal conditions are being refused free treatment and cannot afford to pay. It has been argued that this is inhumane because it jeopardises their health and illegal because it violates international law. Asylum seekers in detention centres are vulnerable to high levels of mental illness, suicide and self-harm. However, they have poor access to medical care, medication and psychiatric care, and interpreters (Hall, 2006; Independent Asylum Commission, 2008).

Although there have been strategies to coordinate asylum seekers' health issues, it is clear from the above that those in the United Kingdom experience many negative influences on their health status but they may also not receive adequate healthcare. Indeed, there is evidence their physical and mental health deteriorates during their first two to three years in this country (British Medical Association, 2002; Johnson, 2003).

Child asylum seekers

The severe poverty suffered by most asylum seekers and refugees (as described above) means that children in asylum seekers' families are unable to enjoy basic living standards, and lack fundamental necessities like adequate food and clothing. Due to the length of time it can take to finalise asylum claims, they often have to endure years of living in poverty (Refugee Council, 2007; Reacroft, 2007). They also experience frequent changes of school, further interruptions to their education due to delays in getting into schools, and damp and unsafe housing, as well as suffer racial abuse. Research has shown that their parents are less likely to let them play outside due to fears of abuse and they are more likely to be bullied at school and have difficulties in making friendships than other children. The Home Office detains around 2,000 asylum-seeking children with their families each year and those that have to live in detention centres are even more excluded from the normal everyday activities in which children participate. A high rate of developmental difficulties among children in asylum-seekers' families has been identified and they have also been found to experience nightmares and to be anxious, withdrawn or hyperactive. Their parents may be unable to provide them with the necessary support because of their own vulnerable state. Furthermore many government initiatives aimed at improving the plight of children in the United Kingdom do not apply to children whose parents are asylum seekers (Burnett and Peel, 2001b; Coker, 2001; Bradshaw and Mayhew, 2005).

Nonetheless, there is some recent evidence that children in asylum-seeking families integrate more easily than their parents. While schools are important in the promotion of their integration, they flourish most in those schools where there are other children from black and ethnic minority groups. This is because it is easier to make friends in such schools as there are children with similar backgrounds who can support them, protect them from bullying, and help with schoolwork and integration into the local community. Children attending these sorts of schools are also more likely to contribute positively to school life, have raised career aspirations and to see their future in this country (Spicer, 2008).

As well as experiencing many of the above, unaccompanied asylum-seeking children have additional problems; the age of an asylum seeker determines the services that they are eligible for and how they will be accommodated. It prevents children being housed with adults and adults being accommodated with children. Both are scenarios which carry risks for the individual and others. However, it is often difficult to determine an unaccompanied asylum-seeking child's age and hence provide the appropriate services. This is because they may not have the relevant documents, such as birth certificates and passports, due to the fact that their country of origin has no system for producing these or because they had to leave in such a hurry that they were unable to obtain such documentation. Children and young people may also look and act older than their counterparts from other countries because of their experiences and lifestyles. Some children come from countries where birthdays are not marked or celebrated so may not know their age. Although an age assessment is carried out by childcare professionals when unaccompanied asylum-seeking children's ages cannot be established, this inevitably leads to a delay in service delivery. Such assessments have also been criticised for perpetuating the culture of disbelief about asylum issues. The Home Office is still seeking to improve the processes for dealing with the asylum claims of unaccompanied asylum-seeking children and to achieve better outcomes and support for them; other measures that have been introduced include the National Register for Unaccompanied Children (NRUC). This national database contains details about all unaccompanied asylum-seeking children in the United Kingdom. Its main purposes are to enable care and support services for this vulnerable group to be tracked, reduce the opportunity for the human trafficking and flag up individuals at risk of being retrafficked. However, the data on it need improving in order to broaden its capacity to assist its stakeholders. This fact has been identified (Crawley, 2006; Independent Asylum Commission, 2008).

The above evidence has shown how asylum seekers' and refugees' experiences of poverty, unemployment, poor accommodation, living in deprived areas, homelessness, hostility, harassment, isolation and poor health in the United Kingdom can combine and lead to an increase in their existing vulnerabilities. The ways in which this fosters their social exclusion have also been highlighted. While they share many of these experiences with ethnic minority groups (see Chapter 5), it has been argued that social exclusion is more acute among asylum seekers because they are not entitled to welfare benefits, have no choice as to where they live, are unable to work, have limited access to heath services and live with the uncertainty of whether their applications will be successful, which prevents them from feeling settled in the United Kingdom (Burchardt, 2005; Spicer, 2008).

Some policies and legislation have been mentioned during the discussions in this chapter. Although there have been positive developments, the criticisms of these clearly indicate that improvements are required in the United Kingdom's asylum policy. Indeed, asylum policy has been described as 'not an example of joined up government' (Burchardt, 2005: 226) and the treatment of asylum seekers and refugees has been the subject of a recent report by the Independent Asylum Commission (2008). This concludes that while the asylum system has improved, it is not yet 'fit for purpose' and the way it still treats this vulnerable group is inhumane and below the standards expected in a civilised society. Reference has already been made to some of the findings in this report in connection with other relevant research. The wealth of information that such reports and studies provide about the plight of asylum seekers and refugees also indicates ways in which future policies to address their vulnerability and social exclusion can be usefully developed. These are discussed in the next section.

ACTIVITY 8.3

From what you have read about the way in which asylum seekers' and refugees' vulnerability can increase in the United Kingdom what do you think can be done to effectively address this? List your ideas and compare them with those put forward below.

FUTURE DIRECTIONS FOR POLICIES

Improve employment prospects

Further steps that could be taken to reduce asylum seekers' and refugees' social exclusion would be to increase their chances of employment and hence reduce their poverty levels. Given that there is evidence that most of them want to work, an obvious strategy would be to remove legal impediments to their employment wherever possible. Other ways of enabling them to contribute economically, and simultaneously to be of benefit, to this country, include an expansion of the opportunities for developing language skills, especially for women. The provision of more retraining to enable those who are highly skilled, for example, doctors and teachers, to apply for jobs in their professions in the United Kingdom is another way forward. It also makes economic sense: it costs £10,000 to retrain a refugee doctor to practise in this country, compared to £250,000 to train a doctor from scratch (Burnett and Peel, 2001a; Refugee Council, 2007). With reference to young refugees, many have been found to be highly aspirational and view higher education as a way of realising their aspirations and a route out of their poverty. Studies have identified a need to ensure their parity with other ethnic groups in terms of the support available to them to access and participate in higher education (Stevenson and Willott, 2007).

Integration into community networks

Another factor highlighted in the second section that can be instrumental in improving employment prospects is belonging to a community network. The way that social networks based around ethnic and faith communities and specialist voluntary organisations operate as support systems and play a vital role in the social inclusion of asylum seekers and refugees was also described. Therefore future strategies need to ensure that asylum seekers and refugees are accommodated within or near appropriate community networks as these will have positive effects not only on their employment but on their social integration in general. In addition, regular moves from place to place should be avoided. Recent research provides additional guidance about the types of community networks that are more likely to be most effective in these respects. For instance, Spicer (2008) found that asylum seekers and refugees feel and are more socially included when they are integrated into social networks based on their own ethnicity, religion and culture rather than by establishing links with white and majority-ethnic communities. As discussed earlier, children in asylum-seeking families are more integrated when they attend schools with high levels of cultural diversity. These types of schools are usually found in such communities. This integration of the next generation strengthens the arguments for using these findings about ways of maximising the social inclusion of asylum seekers through the locations in which they are housed.

Given the value of voluntary organisations in supporting asylum seekers and refugees and fostering social networks, a further direction for future initiatives is to ensure that they have the resources to cope with the demands placed on them and to develop and strengthen their role.

Development of more specialist services

Specialist services can also help asylum seekers and refugees to integrate into mainstream society. Research indicates that building stronger partnerships between voluntary and statutory organisations working within asylum seekers' and refugees' communities helps to ensure that appropriate specialist support is delivered. Health services have been identified as being one of the most important services. Ways in which they can be improved include placing a greater focus on the specific needs of asylum seekers and refugees (especially their mental health care needs) and on helping them to understand the healthcare system in the United Kingdom, together with providing more interpreters and adopting culturally sensitive approaches to care. To achieve these sorts of change, training for healthcare professionals in both primary and secondary care, including training in the use of interpreters, is required (Burnett and Peel, 2001b; Coker, 2001; Bischoff et al., 2003; Gerrish et al., 2004; Hull and Boomla, 2006; O'Donnell et al., 2007; Phillimore et al., 2007; Bowes et al., 2008).

Reduction of hostility

Other impediments to the social inclusion of asylum seekers and refugees are the negative attitudes and hostility that continue to exist towards them. Several useful recommendations about addressing these more rigorously and reducing the social exclusion of these groups have emerged from studies. An example is further strengthening the guidelines for the press, with the emphasis being placed on developing knowledge about asylum from those with firsthand experience, such as asylum seekers and the organisations that support them (Mollard, 2001; Smart et al., 2007).

Improvements to the asylum process

Some of the factors that can heighten their sense of social exclusion also need to be addressed. An example is the way that the uncertainty of the outcome of their application leads to them being unable to feel a sense of belonging in this country. Improving the speed and standard of decision-making and providing better advice about asylum procedures would help to relieve some of the uncertainty experienced (Koser and Pinkerton, 2002; Gilbert and Koser, 2004; Refugee Council, 2007).

More generally, in addition to being informed by current and objective research, future policy-making needs to take account of what has gone wrong in the past and both learn from, and build on, successful initiatives. They also need to take into consideration that the social inclusion of vulnerable groups does not need to be totally prescribed through policy. For instance, not all asylum seekers and refugees passively accept the situation in which they find themselves and many play an active role in addressing their social exclusion by building relationships and integrating themselves into mainstream society. Indeed, the fact that they have successfully reached this country indicates that they are resourceful and resilient – qualities that indicate positive outcomes in terms of inclusion into a host society.

The approach to citizenship for asylum seekers and refugees reflected in policies needs careful consideration; there should be a balance between requirements for their cultural assimilation as a precondition for citizenship and affirming cultural diversity. As discussed in the chapter on ethnic minority groups (Chapter 5), too great an emphasis on cultural assimilation leads to questions about the equal status of citizens. Recent research has shown that shared symbols of citizenship between local people and asylum seekers can develop spontaneously when, for example, they have a sense of a common struggle against perceived injustices in their local area (Bowes et al., 2008). Hence, in addition to working towards multicultural citizenship (as argued in the aforementioned chapter), other examples of citizenship in relation to asylum seekers and refugees that are not shaped by policy interventions need to be identified and researched. This information can then inform policy and not only makes more effective use of existing elements of citizenship but also represents less of a top down approach. Finally, there needs to be a greater emphasis on developing a national approach to the social inclusion of asylum seekers and refugees as opposed to the more piecemeal initiatives that currently exist. This would also help to ensure consistency between the policies adopted that is required to achieve citizenship for this vulnerable group in society (Lister, 1997; British Medical Association, 2005; Aspinall, 2006).

CONCLUSIONS

This chapter has explored the needs of asylum seekers and refugees in the United Kingdom and the extent to which they have been addressed. During this exploration, some of the differences between this group and the other vulnerable groups in this book have emerged, for instance, the way that the government actually prevents some asylum seekers from working, as opposed to encouraging them into work, as it does so resolutely with other vulnerable groups. The most notable difference is that members of this vulnerable group have considerable pre-existing vulnerabilities over which the government has no control. However, the extent to which they are vulnerable and socially excluded when living in this country is within government control and ways in which policies have failed them have been highlighted. Asylum issues are unpredictable and shaped by global forces. Nonetheless, this country has an international responsibility to ensure humane treatment and equality for those who seek asylum within it. As this chapter has demonstrated, this requires a holistic and concerted approach focusing on the asylum process and the social inclusion of successful asylum applicants.

DISCUSSION POINTS

Who is most vulnerable – asylum seekers or refugees?

To what extent does living in the United Kingdom increase the vulnerability of asylum seekers and refugees?

How do asylum seekers or refugees differ from other vulnerable groups in the United Kingdom?

FURTHER STUDY

If you wish to examine the social inclusion of asylum seekers and refugees in more depth, it is worth looking at current research by Alison Bowes and Jenny Phillimore. Burchardt (2005) addresses the issue of social inclusion

(Continued)

too, and also provides a useful overview of the historical context of asylum. Chapter 4 in Lewis (2004) in association with the Open University will help with further explorations of the concept of citizenship in relation to asylum seekers and refugees.

Several websites carry up-to-date information, details of research projects and analysis of policy developments. These include the Information Centre about Asylum and Refugees in the United Kingdom (ICAR), the Refugee Council, the United Nations High Commissioner for Refugees (UNHCR) and the Home Office.

Key readings

Burchardt, T. (2005). "Selective inclusion: asylum seekers and other marginalized groups" in Hills, J. and Stewart, K. (eds) *A more equal society? New Labour, poverty, inequality and exclusion*. Bristol: Policy Press

Coker, N. (2001). *Asylum seekers' and refugees' health experience*. London: Kings Fund

Refugee Council (2007). *The truth about asylum*. London: British Refugee Council

Sales, R. (2002). "The deserving and the undeserving? Refugees, asylum seekers and welfare in Britain." *Critical Social Policy*, 22(3) 456–478.

POST-ACTIVITY COMMENTS

ACTIVITY 8.1

Some suggestions about the sort of images conveyed by the newspaper headlines in this activity are that asylum seekers:

- claim benefits and services that they are not entitled to;
- come here to abuse our benefit system;
- cost this country a fortune;
- are here because the asylum system is too lenient and in chaos;
- are more likely to come here than other countries which means that the United Kingdom has a very high number of asylum seekers;
- can contribute to life in this country.

Although most of the headlines convey negative messages, there is some recognition of the positive contribution made by people taking up residence in this country.

ACTIVITY 8.2

What did you find to support or refute the claims made in the newspaper headlines making up the activity at the beginning of the chapter? Some examples, based on the suggestions about the themes in the claims, are set out below:

- Asylum seekers claim benefits and services that they are not entitled to: *when in this country, they seem to have limited knowledge of the benefits system and are not applying for benefits for which they might be eligible. The type of benefits which they can apply for are tightly prescribed.*

- They come here to abuse our benefit system: *there is evidence that asylum policies and procedures, housing, the availability of welfare benefits or the availability of work do not influence choice of country for asylum. Most do not want to be dependent on benefits and want to work to support themselves.*

- They cost this country a fortune: *0.17 per cent of government expenditure.*

- They are here because the asylum system is too lenient and in chaos: *70 per cent of applications are rejected but 5 per cent of rejected applicants are accepted upon appeal.*

- There are more asylum seekers in the United Kingdom than other countries: *poorer, developing countries are far more likely to host the world's displaced and stateless people. Indeed the United Kingdom is home to less than 3 per cent of the world's refugees and receives fewer than many other European countries. Numbers have also declined considerably this century.*

- They can contribute to life in this country: *they are proportionately more highly skilled and qualified than the rest of the population of this country and want to work. Child asylum seekers can make positive contributions to their schools.*

It can therefore be concluded that most of the more negative claims in the newspaper headlines can be refuted and the more positive ones supported.

Chapter 9

Concluding Comments: The Future for Vulnerable Groups in Health and Social Care

OVERVIEW

- Vulnerability groups and social exclusion
- Vulnerable groups and citizenship
- Future policies to address the needs of vulnerable groups

INTRODUCTION

In the Introduction to this book, the way that vulnerable groups have been politically reframed across the Western world in terms of the concepts of inclusion and citizenship was emphasised. These concepts have therefore been a constant theme throughout the discussions. This concluding chapter essentially summarises the main arguments presented about vulnerable groups in health and social care in relation to vulnerability, social exclusion and citizenship. Suggestions are also made about directions for future policies.

VULNERABLE GROUPS IN HEALTH AND SOCIAL CARE TODAY

While acknowledging the heterogeneity of each group, the fact that the distinctions between them are not arbitrary and that individuals can belong to several vulnerable groups at any one time, the evidence in this book has clearly demonstrated the vulnerability of each group discussed. It has also shown how some members of each group are more vulnerable than others. For instance, teenage lone parents generally face more disadvantages than other lone parents. Among older people, it is those who are over 85 and those who live alone who tend to be the most vulnerable. Furthermore, some groups are perceived as being more vulnerable than others, such as those who are disabled and asylum seekers. There is also an intergenerational element in the vulnerability of some groups; examples are the homeless and those who suffer from mental illness.

The extent to which the experiences of these vulnerable groups constitute barriers to social inclusion and the relationship of their vulnerability to the social exclusion agenda have been explained. The discussions of the latter showed that reducing the social exclusion of these groups is highly complex: it not only involves addressing multidimensional disadvantages, which can interact in unpredictable ways, but also there is sometimes uncertainty about the direction of causality in social exclusion.

Critics have pointed to the fact that inclusion on this agenda indicates more of a political concern with the costs that some of these groups impose on society as opposed to their welfare (Burchardt, 2005). Examples from this book are lone parents, disabled people, older people, children and the mentally ill. Nonetheless, being targeted within this agenda means that policy-makers have at least aimed to improve their life chances and the profile of these groups has been raised. This is particularly so for groups, such as the homeless, who have been identified as requiring additional targeting. Surely it is better that the needs of these groups are addressed under the social exclusion agenda than not at all? Moreover several of the groups have experienced reductions in their social exclusion. For example, older people now experience lower poverty rates, an increased standard of living and higher employment rates and there are more positive representations of old age. There have also been some recent improvements in children's lives and in those of some ethnic minority groups.

However, as demonstrated, the success of initiatives introduced within this agenda can be questioned. In addition, there is evidence that some people within these groups still remain highly vulnerable to social exclusion. Those identified included asylum seekers' children, young carers and older homeless people who are also mentally ill. The sort of reasons for the lack of progress discussed are the complex, multidimensional and dynamic nature of many exclusionary processes and a lack of recognition regarding barriers to social inclusion such as self-perceptions, gender, language and age. Policies have been criticised for failing to deliver integrated and coordinated services that address the unique factors needing consideration when addressing social exclusion. Some elements of vulnerability are also beyond governmental control, particularly in the case of asylum seekers who have considerable pre-existing vulnerabilities.

The concept of citizenship has shaped approaches to the inclusion of vulnerable groups. As mentioned in the Introduction, there have been many criticisms of this concept and further evidence of these emerged during the discussions in the various chapters. The way that citizenship is exclusionary in relation to some vulnerable groups, such as the homeless and the mentally ill, has been demonstrated. In addition, criticisms of New Labour's interpretation of citizenship have been identified; its emphasis on paid work as a route out of social exclusion for vulnerable groups and the ensuing shift to employment-based citizenship is exclusionary. For instance, this disregards the other activities by which people achieve citizenship, such as voluntary work, unpaid participation in community life and the unpaid work that caring for children and elderly relatives involves. It also ignores structural and contextual obstacles to employment that people face, such as age, chronic illness, disability and lone parenting, and the fact that employment does not always benefit some vulnerable groups.

RECOMMENDATIONS FOR FUTURE POLICY DIRECTIONS FOR VULNERABLE GROUPS IN HEALTH AND SOCIAL CARE

Each chapter showed how ensuring a more secure future for vulnerable groups in health and social care is challenging for policy-makers and depends on further initiatives. Several general conclusions can be drawn from the evidence presented about the nature of future initiatives required to effectively address the social exclusion of vulnerable groups. These are as follows.

1 Although the most important requirement is adequate funding, its allocation needs to be based on rigorous research, both in this and other European countries. This research should both monitor and review policies, and take into consideration the dynamic nature of vulnerability and social exclusion. It also needs to include the tracking of individuals to ensure that those who have made progress do not slip back into vulnerability at different points in their lives.

2   It is essential to continue to work at breaking the 'cycle of disadvantage' faced by so many vulnerable people both to prevent them from experiencing social exclusion throughout their own lifetimes and to ensure that disadvantage does not persist across generations.

3   The heterogeneity of each group and the varying needs within groups should be acknowledged. Those who have remained the most vulnerable within each group require targeting, in particular in order to tackle the specific and more complex barriers to their social inclusion.

4   The adoption of a holistic approach, which addresses both the individual and structural causes of social exclusion, is required. Hence, as well as addressing structural causes, such as poverty and unemployment, individual factors such as personal constructions also need to be addressed. An integral part of this approach should be ascertaining the efforts made by vulnerable individuals to overcome their exclusion themselves. These should be built upon, and ways of encouraging those who are not taking responsibility for helping themselves must be identified. Policies should be flexible enough so that they can be adapted accordingly.

5   Coordination of services is pivotal in the successful delivery of policies aimed at reducing social exclusion. This applies to statutory, private and voluntary services as they all play a role in meeting the needs of vulnerable groups.

6   A move way from the existing focus on identified 'vulnerable' groups and mainstreaming social inclusion so that all policy proposals are subjected to a social exclusion audit would ensure that other potentially vulnerable groups are not overlooked.

7   There needs to be a a culture of inclusion. This means efforts to eliminate discrimination and negative attitudes towards vulnerable groups in our society must continue. Less of an emphasis on paid work as the route to citizenship and more on unpaid work would also help to create a more inclusive culture.

Even when the concept of vulnerability has lost political favour, it is vital that the needs of those who are vulnerable and excluded in our society should not be allowed to slip down the political agenda. Without a firm and ongoing commitment to an agenda tackling social exclusion in whatever guise or form, we cannot hope to achieve an inclusive society.

Glossary

absolute poverty Also known as subsistence poverty, this refers to the lack of basic resources such as food and shelter that are necessary to sustain a physically healthy existence. This concept is frequently used in the analysis of poverty worldwide.

acute illness Short-term illnesses, such as a chest infection or chicken pox.

ageism When a person is discriminated against on the grounds of age.

anti-psychiatry movement The work of a range of academics in the 1960s and 1970s from several different countries, which criticised traditional theory and practice in psychiatry.

asylum seeker Someone who has fled from their home country because of war, civil unrest and conflict, has arrived in another country, has made a formal application for asylum and is awaiting a decision about their status.

bed and breakfasts Temporary accommodation for homeless people that provides them with sleeping accommodation and one meal (breakfast) only. Bathrooms are often shared with other residents.

biomedicine This rests on an assumption that all causes of disease – mental disorders as well as physical disease – are understood in biological terms and it views disease and sickness as deviations from normal functioning, which medicine has the power to put right with its scientific knowledge and understanding of the human body.

chronic illness This is defined as a long-term health disorder that interferes with social interaction and role performance, for example, heart disease and asthma.

citizenship A concept that has re-emerged in political and academic discourses since the late twentieth century. The main dimensions of the contemporary approach to citizenship are that all those who are full members of society are conferred with the status of citizenship. This locates them in reciprocal relationships with other individuals and with the state, involving equal rights and obligations.

communitarianism: An ideology which has strong moral and ethical elements, is opposed to pure individualism, and stresses common interests and common values arising from communal bonds. While it does emphasise the responsibilities of the state and the rights of individuals, it also stresses the social responsibilities of individual citizens, families and communities.

competition for scarce resources: A Weberian concept that refers to the way that social groups compete with each other for advantages in society, such as economic rewards, status, and employment opportunities.

consumerism: The focus on consumption in capitalist societies, as opposed to production. Consumption is used in a very broad sense and refers to consumption in many areas of life, such as food, fashion, home improvements, leisure, healthcare and education.

day shelters: Places where homeless people who sleep on the streets can go during the day. The services on offer not only address their immediate needs but can also include activities to help prevent their continued homelessness, such as learning and skills development.

direct racism: Being subjected to verbal and/or physical abuse because of membership of an ethnic minority group.

discourse The set of ideas and conceptualisations that shape ways of thinking about a particular subject. Use of language is central to the construction of discourses. A variety of discourses can exist at any one time; some discourses are more powerful than others and often reflect the interests of dominant groups.

discrimination When members of a particular group in society are denied the resources, rewards and opportunities that are available to, and can be obtained by, others in society.

dominant ideology A term used to indicate the dominant or prevailing ideas, beliefs and assumptions in a society (ideology), which tend to be those which serve the interests of the dominant social groups or classes in society.

ethnicity A social concept applied to social groups, the members of which share common characteristics often perceived to be associated with 'race' and physical appearance but incorporating the broadly defined culture of the group, for example, family structures, music or literature. An ethnic group can also be defined in terms of its dominant cultural characteristics such as religion and language.

extended family   When a nuclear family (see below) is part of a larger kinship network of grandparents, brothers, sisters, aunts, uncles, nieces, nephews and so forth. The nuclear family either lives with or very near these close relatives and has a close and continuous relationship with them.

failed asylum seeker   Someone who has fled from their home country because of war, civil unrest or conflict, arrived in another country, and made a formal application that has been rejected. Some failed asylum seekers return to their home country voluntarily while others are forcibly returned.

feminism   A body of thought arguing that inequalities between the sexes are caused by patriarchal societies in which it is assumed that men should and can dominate and have most of the power because they are superior and that women should be subordinate to them. There are many different types of feminist theories (such as Marxist and liberal) but a central theme common to all of them is that it is *men* who have oppressed and excluded women from social, political and economic power.

functionalism   Views society as a biological organism, such as the body, made up of different integrated parts. In order for society to function properly and maintain its structure these parts or subsystems have to fulfil their role in accordance with cultural and social expectations.

globalisation   The set of global processes that are changing the nature of human interaction across a wide range of social spheres such as the economic, political and environmental. This has led to an increasing global cultural system and, because of the uneven impact of these processes, further inequalities.

hidden homeless   Those people without a home who do not appear in government statistics about homelessness. They are usually single people and couples without children who live in hostels, squats, bed and breakfasts or with family and friends.

hostels   These provide accommodation for those sleeping on the streets.

ideology   Ideas and beliefs reflecting the interests of a particular social group in society which may change over time.

indirect racism   The fear of being subjected to verbal and/or physical abuse because of membership of an ethnic minority group.

individualism   This stands for the rights of the individual and individual liberty against the power of the state or ruling elite.

individualist explanations   These emphasise the way that individuals themselves contribute to social problems. They maintain that individuals are autonomous and highlight the role of characteristics, such as personality and aptitudes, in shaping choices about their actions that individuals make. The impact of social factors are usually ignored in individualist explanations.

institutional racism   When a public or private body intentionally or unintentionally discriminates against people from ethnic minority groups.

labelling theory   Focuses on the reactions of others to perceived deviance and how that deviance is maintained by their reactions.

life-course perspective   Although there are different strands to this perspective, the predominant theme is that stages in life are not necessarily standardised, chronologically or biologically fixed, sequential or gendered but are subject to a variety of social, historical and cultural influences.

lone/one-parent family   A divorced, separated, single or widowed mother or a father living without a spouse (and not cohabiting) with his or her never-married dependent child or children.

Marxist theory   Approaches based on this theory maintain that the way the economy of a society is run determines the social relationships, such as inequalities, in that society. Marxists blame capitalism for these inequalities; they argue that in capitalist societies there is a minority who exploit the majority and it is this exploitation that leads to inequalities.

modernisation agenda   Introduced by New Labour across all sectors of the government. Its main themes were the promotion of parternerhips between government departments with the voluntary and private sector, consultation with service users, target setting, performance monitoring and greater valuing of public services.

night shelters   These provide overnight accommodation for the homeless.

nuclear family   Two adults living together in a household with their own or adopted children.

outreach teams   These are usually attached to day centres. They work on the street and advise people how to find accommodation and claim benefits.

postmodernism   A set of theories emphasising that it is impossible to uncover the 'truth' about society. This is because knowledge about the social world is socially constructed and therefore constantly changing.

power A contested concept concerning the capacity of individuals, groups, social classes or institutions to shape and mobilize action, achieve goals and protect their interests.

race Refers to physical differences between people such as skin pigmentation, hair texture and facial features.

racism The belief that biologically rooted racial characteristics determine social activities and abilities. The result is that those groups who believe themselves to be inherently 'superior' discriminate against those who belong to groups deemed to be 'inferior'. This can lead to discriminatory and aggressive behaviour towards members of ethnic groups believed to be 'inferior'.

reconstituted family A household unit including a step-parent as a consequence of divorce, separation and remarriage. This type of family is created when a new partnership is formed by a mother and/or father who already have dependent children. Since most children remain with their mother following divorce or separation, stepfamilies are more likely to have a stepfather than a stepmother.

refugee Someone whose asylum application has been successful and has been granted permission to stay in the United Kingdom under the terms of the 1951 Refugee Convention because of a well-founded fear of persecution due to race, religion, nationality, political opinion or membership of a social group if they returned home.

relative poverty Refers to poverty relative to standards in particular societies and reflects differences in living standards between societies and across time within the same society. It is used to indicate those groups who are excluded from full participation in their society because of a lack of resources.

reserve army of labour Composed of groups of workers or potential workers (for example, unemployed people) who are most vulnerable to irregular employment, being employed (often on only a part-time basis) or laid off as the demand for labour from employees rises and falls.

resettlement teams These are usually attached to hostels for the homeless. They can help people to find longer-term housing and may also help them to find work or enrol on a training scheme.

rough sleepers People who sleep in the open in unsuitable places deemed unfit for habitation. Examples of these are doorways, parks and disused buildings.

settled accommodation Accommodation in which residents have medium- to long-term security of tenure.

social bonds A dimension of social networks denoting the connections within ethnic and/or faith communities.

social bridges A dimension of social networks relating to connections between members of migrant communities and communities that do not share the same ethnicity and/or faith.

social capital The resources, trust and social networks within a community which, when accessed by individuals, are beneficial as they empower them and enable them to improve their lives.

social causation This refers to those perspectives that focus on how various social processes lead to particular social issues or problems.

social closure Practices whereby groups preserve their status by restricting entry into their ranks (for example, through setting various conditions for entry such as certain qualifications) and separate themselves from other groups.

social construction This refers to the way that aspects of society or behaviour are actively viewed or 'constructed' in a particular way as a result of social relations and human agency rather than being 'natural' or biological in origin. Social constructions vary historically, socially and culturally.

social divisions These are the substantial differences between people in society, which involve some people being in better positions than others. Examples are class, gender and race. Social divisions often interconnect and can reinforce inequalities. They are socially constructed and hence change over time.

social drift hypothesis This is based on Darwinist theories of natural selection and has been used to explain why those who are poor have higher rates of ill health. It hypothesises that those who are physically and mentally ill move down the social system and accumulate at the bottom.

social exclusion A contested concept that addresses the range of factors that constrain an individual's full participation in society. Examples of such factors are a lack of material resources, discrimination, chronic ill health, geographical location and cultural identification.

social inequalities Differences in people's share of resources in society. This can involve a wide range of such resources, such as wealth, education, health, housing, power, status and life chances.

social integration   This concept is about the relationships between individuals and societal institutions, such as the family, employment, and religious, political and voluntary groups. Integration into these societal institutions helps people to cope when facing stressful life events because they provide mutual moral support and access to resources.

social justice   This will be achieved when existing inequalities are eradicated and there are equal rights and equity for everyone in society.

social links   A dimension of social networks that refers to the relationships that individuals and/or groups have with institutions, agencies and services.

social networks   The patterns of individuals' social relationships and interactions with those to whom they are connected by ties such as kinship, friendship and work relationships.

social position   The social identity a person has in a given group or society.

social support   This is provided by positive involvement in social networks. It has been shown to act as a buffer to stress, particularly if intimate and confiding reelationships are involved.

statutory homeless   Those who do not have a home but are regarded as being legally homeless and entitled to help from their local authority.

statutory services   Services to which prescribed individuals and/or groups have a legal right, such as local authorities, social services and health services. They are paid for out of taxation, with their function prescribed by law, and have a large bureaucratic structure.

stigma   The social consequences of socially constructed negative characteristics that are associated with members of a particular social group.

street homelessness   Those who live on the streets in the day and have nowhere to sleep at night. Some end up sleeping in the sorts of places that are unfit for habitation (such as doorways, parks, disused buildings) while others sleep at friends' houses for short periods of time, in a squat, hostel, prison or hospital.

structuralist explanations   Focus on the way that macro-level political, economic and social factors which are beyond an individual's control cause social problems.

unaccompanied asylum-seeking child (UASC)   An individual under 18 who is applying for asylum in his or her own right and is *either* separated from both parents *or* is not being cared for by an adult who has responsibility to do so by law or custom.

underclass   Those groups who fall below the lowest occupational class because they are dependent on benefits, live in poor housing, do not have a job, and have a poor employment history and limited prospects of acquiring an occupation.

unpaid carer   Someone who cares for a dependant who cannot care for himself/herself and, excluding benefits, this is on an unpaid basis.

voluntary organisations   These are self-governing, non-profitmaking and not directly controlled by a private (for-profit) entity or by the state. There is usually a meaningful degree of voluntarism in terms of money or time through philanthropy or voluntary citizen involvement.

Weberian perspectives   These argue that class, status and authority determine the distribution of power in society. Each of these has an effect on life chances. With reference to class, scarce resources (such as educational and economic resources) give people the capacity to acquire income and assets. Where a particular category of individuals have similar resources and use these to secure certain advantages for themselves, a class relationship is formed. Class situation determines life chances, which are protected and enhanced by those individuals within the class through the exclusion of others.

welfare-to-work   These policies aim to reduce the numbers of those in receipt of out-of-work benefits by encouraging as many of them to take up paid employment as possible. They have been produced in response to concerns over the costs of benefits and as part of efforts to tackle poverty and social exclusion.

References

Abbas, T. (2007). 'Muslim minorities in Britain: integration, multiculturalism and radicalism in the post-7-7 period.' *Journal of Intercultural Studies*, **28** (3) 287–300

Action on Elder Abuse (2004). *Hidden voices: older people's experience of abuse*. London: Help the Aged

Action on Elder Abuse (2007). *The UK study of abuse and neglect of older people*. London: Kings Institute of Gerontology

Adamson, P. (2007). *Child poverty in perspective: an overview of child well-being in rich countries*. Florence: Innocenti Research Centre

Agar, A. and Strang, A. (2004). *Indicators of integration: the experience of integration final report*. London: Home Office

Ahmad, W. and Bradby, H. (2008). 'Ethnicity and health: key themes in a developing field.' *Current Sociology*, **56** (1) 47–56

Aitchison, C. (2003). 'From leisure and disability to disability leisure: developing data, definitions and discourses.' *Disability and Society*, **18** (7) 955–969

Albrecht, G.L. (2001). 'Rationing healthcare to disabled people.' *Sociology of Health and Illness*, **23** (5) 654–677

Aldridge, J. and Becker, S. (1999). 'Children as carers: the impact of parental illness and disability on children's caring roles.' *Journal of Family Therapy*, **21** (3) 303–320

Aldridge, J. and Becker, S. (2003). 'Children who care, Zero2Nineteen.' *Community Care*, 24–25

Allender, S., Cowburn, G. and Foster, C. (2006). 'Understanding participation in sport and physical activity amongst children and adults: a review of qualitative studies.' *Health Education Research, Theory and Practice*, **21** (6) 826–835

American Psychiatric Association (2004) *DSM-IV-TR Diagnostic and Statistical Manual of Mental Disorders*. Arlington, VA: American Psychiatric Publishing Inc.

Anthias, F. (2007). 'Ethnic ties and the question of mobilisation.' *Sociological Review*, **55** (4) 788–805

Arber, S. and Ginn, J. (1995). *Connecting gender and ageing: a sociological approach*. Buckingham: OUP

Arber, S., Davidson, S. and Ginn, J. (eds) (2003). *Gender and ageing: changing roles and relationships*. Buckingham: OUP

Aries, P. (1965). *Centuries of childhood*. London: Cape

Aspinall, P. (2006). *Enhancing the health promotion evidence base on minority ethnic groups, refugees/asylum seekers, and gypsy travellers*. Cardiff: Health ASERT Programme Wales

Aspinall, P. and Mitton, L. (2007). 'Are English local authorities' practices on housing and council tax benefit administration meeting race quality requirements?' *Critical Social Policy*, **27** (3) 381–414

Asthana, A. and McNeil, A. (2007). 'Official: obesity risk to half of all children'. *The Observer*, 2 September

Aubrey, C. and Dahl, S. (2006). 'Children's voices: the views of vulnerable children on their service providers and the relevance of services they receive.' *British Journal of Social Work*, **36**, 21–39

Baggott, R. (1998). *Health and health care in Britain*. London: Macmillan

Bailey, N. (2004). 'Does work pay? Employment, poverty and exclusion from social relations' in Pantazis, C., Gordon, D. and Levitas, R. (eds) *Poverty and social exclusion in Britain: the millennium survey*. Bristol: Policy Press

Bambra, C., Whitehead, M., and Hamilton, V. (2005). 'Does "welfare-to-work" work? A systematic review of the effectiveness of the UK's welfare-to-work programmes for people with a disability or chronic illness.' *Social Science and Medicine*, **60** (9) 1905–1918

Bandeira, D.R., Pawlowski, J., Goncalves, T.R., Hilgert, M.C., Bozzetti, M.C. and Hugo, F.N. (2007). 'Psychological distress in Brazilian caregivers of relatives with dementia.' *Aging and Mental Health*, **11** (1) 14–19

Barry, A. and Yuill, C. (2008). *Understanding health: a sociological introduction*. London: Sage

Barton, L. (2004). 'The disability movement: some observations' in Swain, J., French, S., Barnes, C. and Thomas, C. (eds) *Disabling barriers, enabling environments*. London: Sage in association with the Open University

Becker, S. (2000). 'Carers and indicators of social exclusion.' *Benefits*, **28**, 1–4

Beckett, A. E. (2005). 'Reconsidering citizenship in the light of the concerns of the UK disability movement.' *Citizenship Studies*, **9** (4) 405–421

Bell, A., Finch, N., La Valle, I., Sainsbury R. and Skinner, C. (2005). *A question of balance: lone parents, childcare and work*. Department for Work and Pensions Research Report 230. Leeds: Corporate Document Services

Beresford, B. (2002). 'Children's health' in Bradshaw, J. (ed.) *The well-being of children in the UK*. London: Save the Children Fund

Berkman, L.F. (1995). 'The role of social relations in health promotion'. *Psychosomatic Medicine*, **57**, 245–254

Berkman, L.F. and Syme, S.L. (1979). 'Social networks, host resistance, and mortality: a nine-year follow-up of Alameda County residents.' *American Journal of Epidemiology*, **109** (2) 186–204

Berkman, L.F., Glass, T., Brissette, I. and Sutman, T.E. (2000). 'From social integration to health: Durkheim in the new millennium.' *Social Science and Medicine*, **51**, 843–857

Bhopal, R.S. (2007). *Ethnicity, race and health in multicultural societies*. Oxford: Oxford University Press

Biggs, S. (2000). *Understanding ageing: images, attitudes and professional practice*. Buckingham: Open University Press

Bischoff, A., Bovier, P.A., Isah, I., Fran, G., Trkhk, L., Ariel, E. and Louis, L. et al. (2003). 'Language barriers between nurses and asylum seekers: their impact on symptom reporting and referral.' *Social Science and Medicine*, **57** (3) 5003–5012

Blair, T. (1998). *New ambitions for our country: a new contract for welfare*. London: Department of Social Security

Blakemore, K. (2001). *Social policy: an introduction*. Buckingham: Open University Press

Blanden, J. and Gibbons, S. (2006). *The persistence of poverty across generations*. London: Policy Press

Bond, M., Clark, M. and Davies, S. (2003). 'The quality of life of spouse dementia caregivers: changes associated with yielding to formal care and widowhood.' *Social Science and Medicine*, **57**: 2385–2395

Bond, R. (2006). 'Belonging and becoming: national identity and exclusion.' *Sociology*, **40** (4) 609–626

Borell, K. and Ghazanfareeon Karlsson, S. (2003). 'Reconceptualizing intimacy and ageing: living apart together' in Arber, S. et al. (eds) *Gender and ageing: changing roles and relationships*. Buckingham: OUP

Bowes, A. (2006). 'Mainstreaming equality: implications of the provision of support at home for majority and minority ethnic older people.' *Social Policy and Administration*, **40** (7) 739–757

Bowes, A., Ferguson, I. and Sim, D. (2008). 'Asylum policy and asylum experiences: interactions in a Scottish context.' *Ethnic and Racial Studies*, **31** (1) 1–21

Bradshaw, J. (ed.) (2002). *The well-being of children in the UK*. London: Save the Children Fund

Bradshaw, J. (2006). 'Child poverty and deprivation' in Bradshaw, J. and Mayhew, E. (eds.) (2005) *The well-being of children in the UK*, 2nd edn. London: Save the Children Fund

Bradshaw, J. and Mayhew, E. (eds) (2005). *The well-being of children in the UK*, 2nd edn. London: Save the Children Fund

Bradshaw, J., Hoelscher, P. and Richardson, D. (2006). *Comparing child Well-being in OECD countries: concepts and methods*. Florence: UNICEF

Breheny, M. and Stephens, C. (2007). 'Irreconcilable differences: health professionals' constructions of adolescence and moterhood.' *Social Science and Medicine*, **64** (1) 112–124

Brewer, M., Browne, J. and Sutherland, H. (2006). *What will it take to end child poverty?* York: Joseph Rowntree Foundation

British Medical Association (2002). *Asylum seekers: meeting their health care needs.* London: BMA

British Medical Association (2005). *Asylum seekers and their health.* London: BMA

Brown, G.W. and Harris, T. (1978). *Social Origins of Depression: A study of psychiatric disorder in women.* London: Tavistock.

Brown, M. and Stetz, K. (1999). 'The labor of caregiving: a theoretical model of caregiving during potentially fatal illness.' *Qualitative Health Research*, **9** (2): 182–197

Brown, N. and Hosie, A. (2005). *The education of pregant young women and young mothers in England.* Bristol: University of Bristol

Buchanen, A. (2007). 'Including the socially excluded: the impact of government policy on vulnerable families and children in need.' *British Journal of Social Work*, **37**, 187–207

Burchardt, T. (2005). 'Selective inclusion: asylum seekers and other marginalized groups' in Hills, J. and Stewart, K. (eds) *A more equal society? New Labour, poverty, inequality and exclusion.* Bristol: Policy Press

Burnett, A. (2002). *Older people and fear of crime.* London: Help the Aged

Burnett, A. and Peel, M. (2001a). 'Asylum seekers and refugees in Britain: What brings asylum seekers to the United Kingdom?' *British Medical Journal*, **322**, 485–488

Burnett, A. and Peel, M. (2001b). 'The health of survivors of torture and organised violence.' *British Medical Journal*, **322**, 606–609

Butterworth, P. (2004). 'Lone mothers' experience of physical and sexual violence: association with psychiatric disorders.' *The British Journal of Psychiatry*, **184**, 21–27

Bytheway, B. (2003). 'Visual representations of later life' in Faircloth, C. (ed.) *Ageing bodies: Images and everyday experience.* Walnut Creek, California: Altamira Press

Cabinet Office (2005). *Controlling our borders: making migration work for Britain. Five year strategy for asylum and immigration.* London: HMSO

Cabinet Office (2006). *Reaching out: an action plan on social exclusion.* London: HMSO

Cadwalladr, C. (2007). 'Albion Drive: a saga of modern Britain.' *The Observer,* 13 May, 6–9

Campbell, S. (2004). *A review of antisocial behaviour orders.* London: Home Office Research, Development and Statistics Directorate

Carabine, J. (2001). 'Constituting sexuality through social policy: the case of lone motherhood 1834 and today.' *Social and Legal Studies,* **10** (3) 291–314

Carter, J. (2003). *Ethnicity, exclusion and the workplace.* Basingstoke: Palgrave Macmillan

Carver, V. and Liddiard, P. (eds) (1978). *An ageing population: a reader and sourcebook.* Milton Keynes: Open University Press

Cawson, P., Wattam, C., Brooker, S. and Kelly, C. (2000). *Child maltreatment in the UK: a study of the prevalence of child abuse and neglect.* London: NSPCC

Chambaz, C. (2001). 'Lone parent families in Europe: a variety of economic and social circumstances.' *Social Policy and Administration,* **35** (6) 658–671

Chamberlayne, P. and King, A. (2000). *Cultures of care: biographies of carers in Britain and the two Germanies.* Bristol: Policy Press

Chittleborough, C.R., Grant, J.F., Phillips, P.J. and Taylor, A.W. (2007). 'The increasing prevalence of diabetes in South Australia: the relationship with population ageing and obesity.' *Public Health,* **121** (2) 92–99

Choi, N.G. and Wodarski, J.S. (1996). 'The relationship between social support and health status of elderly people: does social support slow down physical and functional deterioration?' *Social Work Research,* **20** (1) 52–63

Chun, M., Knight, B.G. and Youn, G. (2007). 'Differences in stress and coping models of emotional distress among Korean, Korean-American and White-American caregivers.' *Aging and Mental Health,* **11** (1) 20–29

Civitas (2002). *The lone parent trap: how the welfare system discourages marriage.* www.civitas.org.uk

Clark, K. and Drinkwater, S. (2007). *Ethnic minorities in the labour market: dynamics and diversity.* Abingdon: Policy Press

Cloke, P., Johnsen, S. and May, J. (2007). The periphery of care: emergency services for homeless people in rural areas.' *Journal of Rural Studies,* **23** (4) 387–401

Cohen, G. (ed.) (1987). *Social change and life course.* London: Tavistock Publications

Cohen, N. (2006). 'Poor Cathy still can't come home because there is no home to go to.' *The Observer,* 15 October, 11

Coker, N. (2001). *Asylum seekers' and refugees' health experience.* London: Kings Fund

Corrigan, P.W. (2007). 'How clinical diagnosis might exacerbate the stigma of mental illness.' *Social Work,* **52** (1) 31–39

Craig, G. (2004). 'Citizenship, exclusion and older people.' *Journal of Social Policy,* **33** (1) 95–114

Crane, M. and Warnes, A.M. (2005). 'Responding to the needs of older homeless people.' *Innovation: The European Journal of Social Science Research,* **18** (2) 137–152

Crawley, H. (2006). *Child first, migrant second: ensuring that every child matters.* London: Immigration Law Practitioners' Association

Crisis (2008). *What we do.* London: Crisis

Daguerre, A. and Nativel, C. (2006). *When children become parents: welfare responses to teenage pregnancy.* Bristol: Policy Press

Dale, A., Lindley, J. and Dex, J. (2006). 'A life-course perspective on ethnic differences in women's economic activity in Britain.' *European Sociological Review,* **22** (4) 459–476

Danieli, A. and Wheeler, P. (2006). 'Employment policy and disabled people: old wine in new glasses.' *Disability and Society,* **21** (5) 485–498

Dass-Braillsford, P. (2007). 'Racial identity amongst white graduate students.' *Journal of Transformative Education,* **5** (1) 59-78

Datta, J. and Hart, D. (2007). *A shared responsibility: safeguarding arrangements between hospitals and children's social services.* London: National Children's Bureau

Davis, J. (2002). 'Disenfranchising the disabled: the inaccessibility of internet-based health information.' *Journal of Health Communication,* **7** (4) 355–367

Davison, T.E., McCabe, M.P., Mellor, D., Ski, C., George, K. and Moore, K.A. (2007). 'The prevalence and recognition of major depression among low-level aged care residents with and without cognitive impairment.' *Ageing and Mental Health,* **11** (1) 82–88

Deacon, A. (2002). *Perspectives on welfare: ideas, ideologies and policy debates.* Buckingham OUP

Deal, M. (2007). 'Aversive disablism: subtle prejudice towards disabled people.' *Disability and Society,* **22** (1) 93–107

Degnen, C. (2007). 'Minding the gap: the construction of old age and oldness amongst peers.' *Journal of Aging Studies,* **21** (1) 69–80

Delsol, R. and Shiner, M. (2006). 'Regulating stop and search: a challenge for police and community relations in England and Wales.' *Critical Criminology,* **14** (3) 241–263

Dench, S. (2006). *Impact of care to learn: tracking the destinations of young parents funded in 2004/5.* Brighton: Institute of Employment Studies

Department for Children, Schools and Families (2007a). *The children's plan: building brighter futures.* Stationery Office

Department for Children, Schools and Families (2007b). *Sure Start children's centres: Phase 3 planning and delivery.* Nottingham: HMSO

Department for Children, Schools and Families (2007c). *Extended schools: building on experience.* Nottingham: HMSO

Department for Education and Skills (2003). *Every child matters.* London: DfES

Department for Education and Skills (2004). *Children Act 2004.* London: HMSO

Department for Education and Skills (2006). *Ethnicity and education – the evidence on minority ethnic pupils aged 5–16.* London: HMSO

Department for Work and Pensions (1999). *Opportunity for all.* London: Stationery Office

Department for Work and Pensions (2004). *Opportunity for all: Sixth Annual Report 2004.* London: Stationery Office

Department for Work and Pensions (2005a). *Opportunity age.* London: Stationery Office

Department for Work and Pensions (2005b). *Working to rebuild lives: a refugee employment strategy.* London: Stationery Office

Department for Work and Pensions (2006). *Work, saving and retirement among ethnic minorities: a qualitative study.* London: HMSO

Department for Work and Pensions (2007). *In work, better off.* London: Stationery Office

Department of Communities and Local Government (2006). *Homeless prevention – a guide to good practice. Policy Briefing* 15. London: HMSO

Department of Communities and Local Government (2007a). *Statutory homelessness: 3rd quarter 2007.* London: HMSO

Department of Communities and Local Government (2007b). *Evaluating homelessness prevention.* London: HMSO

Department of Health (1999). *National service framework for mental health.* London: HMSO

Department of Health (2000). *Health survey for England.* London: HMSO

Department of Health (2001). *National plan for safeguarding children from commercial sexual exploitation.* London: HMSO

Department of Health (2004a). *Community care statistics.* London: HMSO

Department of Health (2004b). *Better health in old age.* London: HMSO

Department of Health (2004c). *Choosing health: making healthy choices easier.* London: HMSO

Department of Health (2004d). *Action on stigma: promoting mental health, ending discrimination at work.* London: HMSO

Department of Health and Home Office (2000). *No secrets: guidance on developing and implementing multi-agency policies and procedures to protect vulnerable adults from abuse.* OH Circular HSC 2000/007

Desai, S. (2000). 'Maternal education and child health: A feminist dilemma.' *Feminst Studies,* **26** (2) 425–446

Disability Rights Commission (2006). *Disability briefing.* Disability Rights Commission Research Paper

DPI (1982). *Disabled People's International: proceedings of the First World Congress.* Singapore: Disabled People's International

Dixon-Woods, M. Kirk, D., Agarwal, S., Annandale, E., Arthur, T. and Harvey, J. (2005). *Vulnerable groups and access to health care: a critical interpretive review.* London: NCCSDO

Donnellan, C. (ed.) (2004). *Dealing with homelessness.* Cambridge: Independence

Doward, J. (2006). 'Freedom can sometimes mean that you have nowhere to stop.' *The Observer,* 19 November, 4

Dowler, E. and Calvert, C. (1995). *Nutrition and diet in lone parent families in London.* London: Family Policy Studies Centre (Social Policy Research 71–January 1995)

Doyal, L. (1995). *What makes women sick?* Basingstoke: Macmillan

Driver, S. and Martell, L. (2002). 'New Labour, work and the family.' *Social Policy and Administration,* **36** (1) 46–61

Durkheim, E. (1968). *Suicide: a study in sociology.* London: Routledge

Ensign, J. and Bell, M. (2004). 'Illness experiences of homeless youth.' *Qualitative Health Research,* **14** (9) 1239–1254

Ermisch, J. and Francesconi, M. (2000). 'The increasing complexity of family relationships: lifetime experience of lone motherhood and stepfamilies in Great Britain.' *European Journal of Population,* **16** (3) 235–249

European Commission (2007). *The European Uunion disability strategy.* http://ec.europa.eu

Evandrou, M. and Falkingham, J. (2005). A secure retirement for all? Older people, and New Labour' in Hills, J. and Stewart, K. (eds) *A more equal society for all? New Labour, poverty, inequality and exclusion.* Bristol: Policy Press

Evans, M. and Scarborough, J. (2006). *Can current policy end child poverty in Britain by 2020?* York: Joseph Rowntree Foundation

Fawcett, B. (2000). *Feminist perspectives on disablity.* Harlow: Pearson Education Limited

Finch, N. and Searle, B. (2005). 'Children's lifestyles' in Bradshaw, J. and Mayhew, E. (eds.) *The well-being of children in the UK*, 2nd edn. London: Save the Children Fund

Finkelstein, V. (1981). 'Disability and the helper/helped relationship: an historical view' in Brechin, A., Liddiard, P. and Swain, J. (eds) *Handicap in a social world*. London: Hodder and Stoughton

Firth, L. (2007a). *Teen pregnancy and lone parents*. Cambridge: Independence Educational Publishers

Firth, L. (ed.) (2007b). *Homelessness*. Cambridge: Independence

Fitzpatrick, S. and Jones, A. (2005). 'Pursuing social justice or social cohesion?: Coercion in street homelessness policies in England.' *Journal of Social Policy*, **34** (3) 389–406

Foresight (2007). *Trends and drivers of obesity: a literature review for the Foresight Project on Obesity*. London: Government Office for Science

Fortin, J. (2008). 'Children as rights holders: awareness and scepticism' in Invernizzi, A. and Williams, J. (eds) *Children and citizenship*. London: Sage

Foster, M., Harris, J., Jackson, K., Morgan, H. and Glendinning, C. (2006). Personalised social care for adults with disabilities: problematic concept for frontline practice.' *Health and Social Care in the Community*, **14** (2) 125–135

Foucault, M. (1961). *Madness and civilisation: a history of insanity in the age of reason*. New York: Vintage Books

Freund, P. and McGuire, M. (1995) *Health, illness and the social body: a critical sociology*. New Jersey: Prentice-Hall, Inc

Gannon, B. and Nolan, B. (2007). 'The impact of disability transitions on social inclusion.' *Social Science and Medicine*, **64** (7) 1425–1447

Garbarino, J., Dubrow, N., Kostelny, K. and Pardo, C. (1992). *Children in danger: coping with the consequences of community violence*. San Francisco: Jossey-Bass Publishers

Gardiner, K. and Millar, J. (2006). 'How low-paid employees avoid poverty: an analysis by family type and household structure.' *Journal of Social Policy*, **35** (3), 351–369

Garland, J. and Chakraborti, N. (2007). 'Protean times?: Exploring the relationships between policing, community and "race" in rural England.' *Criminology and Criminal Justice*, **7** (4) 347–365

Gerrish, K., Sobowale, A. and Birks, E. (2004). 'Bridging the language barrier: the use of interpreters in primary care nursing.' *Health and social care in the community*, **12** (5) 407–413

Gilbert, A. and Koser, K. (2004). *Information dissemination to potential asylum seekers in countries of origin and/or transit*. London: Home Office

Gill, T. (2007). *No fear: growing up in a risk averse society*. London: Calouste Gulbenkian Foundation

Goffman, E. (1963). *Stigma: some notes on the management of spoiled identity*. Harmondsworth: Penguin

Goldson, B. (2002). *Vulnerable inside: children in secure and penal settings*. London: Children's Society

Goodwin, A.M. and Kennedy, A. (2005). 'The psychosocial benefits of work for people with severe and enduring mental health problems.' *Community, Work and Family*, **8** (1) 23–35

Gott, M. (2005). *Sexuality, sexual health and ageing*. Buckingham: Open University Press

Gott, M. and Hinchliff, S. (2003). 'Sex and aging: a gendered Issue' in Arber, S., Davidson, S. and Ginn, J. (eds) *Gender and Ageing. Changing Roles and Relationships*. Buckingham: OUP

Grover, C. and Piggott, L. (2005). 'Disabled people, the reserve army of labour and welfare reform'. *Disability and Society,* **20** (7) 705–717

Grue, L. and Laerum, K.T. (2002). '"Doing motherhood": some experiences of mothers with physical disabilities.' *Disability and Society,* **17** (6) 671–683

Grundy, E. (2006). 'Ageing and vulnerable elderly people: European perspectives.' *Ageing and Society,* **26** (1) 105–134

Hall, P. (2006). 'Failed asylum seekers and health care.' *British Medical Journal,* **333** (7559) 109–110

Halpern, D. (2005). *Social capital.* London: Routledge

Hanratty, B., Drever, F., Jacoby, A. and Whitehead, M. (2007). 'Retirement age caregivers and deprivation of area of residence in England and Wales.' *European Journal of Ageing,* **4** (1) 35–43

Hareven, T.K. (1995). 'Changing images of aging and the social construction of the life course' in Featherstone, M. and Wernick, A. (eds) *Images of aging: cultural representations of later life.* London: Routledge

Heenan, D. (2002). '"It won't change the world but it turned my life around": participant's views on the Personal Advisor Scheme in the New Deal for disabled people.' *Disability and Society,* **17** (4) 383-401

Heywood, F. (2001). *Money well spent: the effectiveness and value of housing* adaptations. Bristol: Policy Press

Hill, A. (2006). 'Battered to desperation.' *The Observer,* 19 November, 4

Hill, A. (2007). 'Inside the violent chaotic world of our mental wards.' *The Observer,* 8 April, 24–25

Hirst, M. (1999). *Informal care-giving in the life course.* York: SPRU

Hockey, J. and James, A. (2003). *Social identities across the life course.* Basingstoke: Palgrave Macmillan

Hodgetts, D., Cullen, A. and Radley, A. (2005). 'Television characterizations of the homeless in the United Kingdom.' *Analyses of Social Issues and Public Policy,* **5** (1) 29–48

Hodgetts, D., Hodgetts, A. and Radley, A. (2006). Life in the shadow of the media: imaging street homelessness in London.' *European Journal of Cultural Studies,* **9** (4) 497–516

Holmes, J.D. (2007). *Liaison psychiatry services for older people project.* Leeds: NHS SDO (in progress)

Holstein, J.A. and Gubrium, J.F. (2000). *Constructing the life course.* New York: General Hall, Inc

Home Office (2003). *Home Office Citizenship Survey: people, families and communities.* London: HMSO

Home Office (2005). *Integration matters.* London: HMSO

Home Office (2006a). *A guide to anti-social behaviour orders.* London: HMSO

Home Office (2006b). *Policy bulletin 72: Employment and voluntary activity.* London: HMSO

Home Office (2007). *Guidance on the use of acceptable behaviour contracts and agreements.* London: HMSO

Home Office (2008). *Asylum Statistics: 4th quarter 2007 United Kingdom.* London: HMSO

Home Office, Department for Constitutional Affairs, Youth Justice Board (2004). *Parenting contracts and orders guidance.* London: HMSO

Hooper, C. (2002). 'Maltreatment of children' in Bradshaw, J. (ed.) *The well-being of children in the UK.* London: Save the Children Fund

Hooper, C. (2005). 'Child maltreatment' in Bradshaw, J. and Mayhew, E. (eds.) *The well-being of children in the UK*, 2nd edn. London: Save the Children Fund

House of Commons (2006). *Safeguarding Vulnerable Groups Bill (HL) (2006). Research Paper 06/35.* (http://www.parliament.uk/commons/lib/research/rp2006/rp06-035.pdf)

Howard, M. (1999). *Enabling government: joined up policies for a national disability strategy.* London: Fabian Society

Hughes, B., Russell, R. and Paterson, K. (2005). 'Nothing to be had "off the peg": consumption, identity and the immobilization of young disabled people.' *Disability and Society*, **20** (1) 3–17

Hughes, G. (1998). 'A suitable case for treatment? Constructions of disability' in Saraga, E. (ed.) *Embodying the social: constructions of difference.* London: Routledge

Hull, S.A. and Boomla, K. (2006). 'Primary care for refugees and asylum seekers.' *British Medical Journal*, **332**, 62–63

Humphrey, J.C. (2000). Researching disability politics, or, some problems with the social model in practice.' *Disability and Society*, **15** (1) 63–85

Humphries, S. and Gordon, P. (1992). *Out of sight: experiences of disability 1900–50.* Plymouth: Northcote

Hunt, S. (2005). *The life course: a sociological introduction.* Basingstoke: Palgrave Macmillan

Hutton, J. (2007). 'Lone parents move', *The Guardian*, 30 January

Hutton, W. (2007). You're never too old to rock and roll – or work. *The Observer*, 17 June

Huxley, P. and Thornicroft, G. (2003). 'Social inclusion, social quality and mental illness.' *British Journal of Psychiatry*, **182**, 289–290

Hyde, M. (2000a). 'Disability' in Payne, G. (ed.) *Social divisions.* Basingstoke: Macmillan

Hyde, M. (2000b). 'From welfare-to-work? Social policy for disabled people of working age in the United Kingdom in the 1990s.' *Disability and Society*, **15** (2) 327–341

Imrie, R. (2006). 'Independent lives and the relevance of lifetime homes.' *Disability and Society*, **21** (4) 359–374

Independent Asylum Commission (2008). *Fit for purpose yet? The Independent Asylum Commission's interim findings.* London: Independent Asylum Commission

Invernizzi, A. and Williams, J. (eds) (2008). *Children and citizenship.* London: Sage

Israeli, A. (2002). 'A preliminary investigation of the importance of site accessibility factors for disabled tourists.' *Journal of Travel Research*, **41** (1) 101–104

Jackson, S. and Scott, S. (2006). 'Childhood' in Payne, G. (ed.) *Social divisions.* Basingstoke: Macmillan

Johnson, M. (2003). *Asylum seekers in dispersal – healthcare issues.* London: Home Office

Johnson, M.J., Jackson, N.C., Arnette, J.K. and Koffman, S.D. (2005). 'Gay and lesbian perceptions of discrimination in retirement care facilities.' *Journal of Homosexuality*, **49** (2) 83–102

Johnson, N. (2000). 'The personal social services and community care' in Powell, M. (ed.) *New Labour, new welfare state?* Bristol: Policy Press

Jordan, B. (2005). 'New Labour: choice and values.' *Critical Social Policy*, **25** (4) 427–446

Kelly, B.D. (2006). 'The power gap: freedom, power and mental illness.' *Social Science and Medicine*, **63** (8) 2118–2128

Kemp, L. (2002). 'Why are some people's needs unmet?' *Disability and Society*, **17** (2) 205–218

Keogh, A.F., Halpenny, A.M. and Gilligan, R. (2006). 'Educational issues for children and young people in familes living in emergency accommodation – an Irish perspective.' *Children and Society*, **20** (5) 360–375

Kidger, J. (2004). 'Including young mothers: Limitations to New Labour's strategy for supporting teenage mothers.' *Critical Social Policy*, **24** (3) 291–311

Koser, K. and Pinkerton, C. (2002). *The social networks of asylum seekers and the dissemination of information about countries of asylum.* London: Home Office

Kyle, T. and Dunn, J.R. (2008). 'Effects of housing circumstances on health, quality of life and healthcare use for people with severe mental illness.' *Health and Social Care in the Community*, **16** (1) 1–15

Larsson, K., Thorslund, M. and Kareholt, I. (2006). 'Are public care and services and services for older people targeted according to need? Applying the behavioural model on longitudinal data of a Swedish urban older population.' *European Journal of Ageing*, **3** (1) 22–33

Lee, B.A., Farrell, C.R. and Link, B.G. (2004). 'Revisiting the contact hypothesis: the case of public exposure to homelessness.' *American Sociological Review*, **69** (1) 40–63

Leipessberger, T. (2007) 'An investigation of mental health care delivery from customers' perspectives.' *Journal of Human Behaviour in the Social Environment*, **15** (1) 1–22.

Lester, H. and Glasby, J. (2006). *Mental health policy and practice.* Basingstoke: Palgrave Macmillan

Leutz, W. and Capitman, J. (2007). 'Met and unmet needs, and satisfaction among social HMO members.' *Journal of Ageing and Social Policy*, **19** (1) 1–19

Levenson, R. (2003). *Auditing age discrimination: a practical guide to promoting age equality in health and social care.* London: Kings Fund

Levitas, R. (2006). 'The concept and measurement of social exclusion' in Pantazis, C., Gordon, D. and Levitas, R. (eds) *Poverty and social exclusion in Britain: the millennium survey.* Bristol: Policy Press

Levitas, R., Head, E. and Finch, N. (2006). 'Lone parents, poverty and social exclusion' in Pantazis, C., Gordon, D. and Levitas, R. (eds) *Poverty and social exclusion in Britain: the millennium survey.* Bristol: Policy Press

Levitas, R., Pantazis, C., Fahmy, E., Gordon, D., Lloyd., E. and Patsios, D. (2007). *The multidimensional analysis of social exclusion.* London: Cabinet Office

Lewis, D. and Gunn, R. (2007). 'Workplace bullying in the public sector: understanding the racial dimension.' *Public Administration*, **85** (3) 641–665

Lewis, G. (ed.) (2004). *Citizenship: personal lives and social policy.* Bristol: Policy Press in association with the Open University

Lewis, J. (ed.) (1997). *Lone mothers in European welfare regimes: shifting policy logics.* London: Jessica Kingsley

Lewis, J. and Meredith, B. (1988). *Daughters who care.* London: Routledge

Lister, R. (1997). 'Citizenship: towards a feminist synthesis.' *Feminist Review*, **57**, 28–48

Lister, R. (1998). 'Vocabularies of citizenship and gender: the UK.' *Critical Social Policy*, **18** (3) 309–331

Lister, R. (2002). 'The dilemmas of pendulum politics: balancing paid work, care and citizenship.' *Economy and Society*, **31** (4) 520–532

Lister, R. (2003). 'Investing in the citizen-workers of the future: transformation in citizenship and the state under New Labour.' *Social Policy and Administration*, **37** (5) 427-443

Lister, R. (2008). 'Unpacking children's citizenship' in Invernizzi, A. and Williams, J. (eds) *Children and citizenship.* London: Sage

Lloyd, E. (2006). 'Children, poverty and social exclusion' in Pantazis, C., Gordon, D. and Levitas, R. (eds) *Poverty and social exclusion in Britain: the millennium survey.* Bristol: Policy Press

Lunt, N. (2006). 'Employability and New Zealand welfare restructuring.' *Policy and Politics*, **34** (3) 473–494

Mabbett, D. (2005). 'Some are more equal than others: definitions of disability in social policy and discrimination law in Europe.' *Journal of Social Policy*, **34** (2) 215–233

McCarthy, H. and Thomas, G. (2004). *Home alone: combating isolation with older housebound people*. London: Demos

McCusker, J., Cole, M., Ciampi, A., Latimer, E., Winholz, S. and Belzile, E. (2006). 'Does depression in older medical inpatients predict mortality?' *Journals of Gerontology*, **61** (9) 975–981

McLaughlin, E. and Ritchie, J. (1994). 'Legacies of caring: the experiences and circumstances of ex-carers'. *Health and Social Care*, **2** (4) 241–253

Magadi, M. and Middleton, S. (2005). *Britain's poorest children revisited :Evidence from the BHPS (1994-2002)*. Loughborough University: Centre for Research in Social Policy

Manning, N. (2000). 'Psychiatric diagnosis under conditions of uncertainty: personality disorder, science and professional legitimacy.' *Sociology of Health and Illness*, **22** (5) 621–639

Markowitz, F.E. (2006). 'Psychiatric hospital capacity, homelessness and crime and arrest rates.' *Criminology*, **44** (1) 45–72

Marmot, M., Shipley, M., Brunner, E. and Hemingway, H. (2001). 'Relative contribution of early life and adult socio-economic factors to adult morbidity in the Whitehall II study.' *Journal of Epidemiology and Community Health*, **55** (5) 301–307

Marshall, T.H. (1992). 'Citizenship and social class' in Marshall, T.H. and Bottomore, T. (eds) *Citizenship and social class*. London: Pluto Press

Martin, L.G., Schoeni, R.F., Freedman, V.A. and Andreski, P. (2007). 'Feeling better? Trends in general health status.' *The Journals of Gerontology. Series B., psychological sciences and social sciences*, **62** (1) 11–21

Mason, D. (2006). 'Ethnicity' in Payne, G. (ed.) *Social divisions*. Basingstoke: Macmillan

Matthewman, S., West-Newman, C.L. and Curtis, B. (eds) (2007). *Being sociological*. Basingstoke: Palgrave Macmillan

Mawby, R. (2004). 'Reducing burglary and fear amongst older people: An evaluation of a Help the Aged and Homesafe initiative in Plymouth.' *Social Policy and Administration*, **38** (1) 1–20

May, J., Cloke, P. and Johnsen, S. (2006). 'Shelter at the margins: New Labour and the changing state of emergency accommodation for single homeless people in Britain.' *Policy and Politics*, **34** (4) 711–729

Mayhew, L. (2005). 'Active ageing in the UK – issues, barriers, policy, directions.' *Innovation: the European Journal of Social Science Research*, **18** (4) 455–477

Meadows, M. and Grant, D. (2005). 'Social and psychological exclusion: the value of community interventions for lone mothers.' *Community, Work and Family*, **8** (1) 5–21

Means, R. (2007). 'Safe as houses? Ageing in place and vulnerable older people in the UK.' *Social Policy and Administration*, **41** (1) 65–85

Meltzer, H., Singleton, N., Lee, A. and Bebbington, P. (2002). *The social and economic circumstances of adults with mental disorders*. London: Office for National Statistics

Melville, C. (2005). 'Discrimination and health inequalities experienced by disabled people.' *Medical Education*, **39** (2) 124–126

Merritt, S. (2008). 'A new plague facing women.' *The Observer*, 6 January 26–27

Millar, J. and Rowlingson, K. (eds) (2001). *Lone parents, employment and social policy.* Bristol: Policy Press

Miller, A. (2003). 'Link no longer missing.' *Community Care,* 4–10 December, 38

Modood, T. (1997). 'Culture and identity' in Modood, T., Berthoud, R., Lakey, J. and Nazroo, J. (eds) *Ethnic minorities in Britain.* London: Policy Studies Institute

Mogadi, M. and Middleton, S. (2005). *Britain's poorest children revisited: evidence from the BHPS (1994–2002).* Loughborough: Centre for Research in Social Policy

Mollard, C. (2001). *Asylum: the truth behind the headlines.* Oxford: Oxfam

Morris, J. (2004). Independent living and community care: a disempowering framework'. *Disability and Society,* **19** (5) 427–442

Morris, L. (1998). 'Legitimate membership of the welfare community' in Langan, M. (ed.) *Welfare: needs and rights.* London: Routledge

Morrow, V. (2008). 'Dilemmas in children's participation in England' in Invernizzi, A. and Williams, J. (eds) *Children and citizenship.* London: Sage

National Social Inclusion Programme (2007). *Third annual update.* London: Department of Health

National Statistics (2002) *Labour Market Trends.* London: Stationary Office.

National Statistics (2004). *Focus on social inequalities.* London: Stationery Office

National Statistics (2005). *Focus on older people.* London: Stationery Office

National Statistics (2006a). *Population estimates.* National Statistics website: www.statistics. gov.uk

National Statistics (2006b). *Focus on health.* National Statistics website: www.statistics. gov.uk

National Statistics (2006c). *Focus on ethnicity and identity.* National Statistics website: www.statistics.gov.uk

National Statistics (2007a). *Focus on families.* Basingstoke: Palgrave Macmillan

National Statistics (2007b). *Social trends 37.* Basingstoke: Palgrave Macmillan

National Statistics (2008). *Population trends 131.* Basingstoke: Palgrave Macmillan

Neal, S. and Agyeman, J. (2006). *The new countryside? Ethnicity, nation and exclusion in contemporary rural Britain.* Bristol: Policy Press

Neale, J. (2005). Children, crime and illegal drug use' in Bradshaw, J. and Mayhew, E. (eds) (2005) *The well-being of children in the UK,* 2nd edn. London: Save the Children Fund

New Policy Institute (2007). *About homelessness.* London: Crisis

Nozal, A., Lindeboom, M. and Portrait, F. (2004). 'The effect of work on mental health: does occupation matter?' *Health Economics,* **12** (10) 1045–1062

O'Donnell, C., Higgins, M., Chauhan, R. and Mullen, K. (2007). '"They think they're ok and we know they're not." A qualitative study of asylum seekers' access, knowledge and views to healthcare in the UK.' BMC *Health Services Research,* **7** (75) 1–11

O'Grady, A., Pleasence, P., Balmer, N.J., Buck, A. and Genn, H. (2004). 'Disability, social exclusion and the consequential experience of justiciable problems.' *Disability and Society,* **19** (4) 259–271

Office for National Statistics (2000). *Psychiatric morbidity survey.* London: HMSO

Office for National Statistics (2003). *General household survey 2003.* London: HMSO

Office for National Statistics (2004). *Focus on social inequalities.* London: HMSO

Office for National Statistics (2007). *Labour force survey*. London: HMSO

Office of the Deputy Prime Minister (2005). *Sustainable communities: settled homes; changing lives*. London: HMSO

Oliver, M. (1990). *The politics of disablement*: Basingstoke: Macmillan

Oliver, M. (1996). *Understanding disability: from theory to practice*. Basingstoke: Macmillan

Oliver, M. (1998). *Disabled people and social policy: from exclusion to inclusion*. London: Longman

Oliver, M. (2004). 'If I had a hammer; the social model in action' in Swain, J., French, S., Barnes, C. and Thomas, C. (eds) *Disabling barriers, enabling environments*. London: Sage in association with the Open University

O'Neill, T., Jinks, C. and Squire, A. (2006). '"Heating is more important than food": older women's perceptions of fuel poverty.' *Journal of Housing for the Elderly*, **20** (3) 95–108

Ozawa, M.M. and Lum, T.Y. (2005). 'Men who work at 70 and over.' *Journal of Gerontological Social Work*, **45** (4) 41–63

Palmer, G. and Kenway, P. (2007). *Poverty rates amongst ethnic groups in Great Britain*. York: Joseph Rowntree Foundation

Pandiani, J.A., Boyd, M.M., Banks, S.M. and Johnson, A.T. (2006). 'Elevated cancer incidence among adults with serious mental illness.' *Psychiatric Services*, **57** (7) 1032–1034

Parker, J. (1998). *Citizenship, work and welfare*. Basingstoke: Macmillan (cited in Lister, 2002)

Parliamentary Office of Science and Technology (2007). *Ethnicity and health*. London: HMSO

Pascall, G. (1997). 'Women and the family in the British welfare state: the Thatcher/Major legacy.' *Social Policy and Administration*, **31** (3) 290–305

Patsios, D. (2006). 'Pensioners, poverty and social exclusion' in Pantazis, C., Gordon, D. and Levitas, R. (eds) *Poverty and social exclusion in Britain: the millennium survey*. Bristol: Policy Press

Payne, G. (ed.) (2006) *Social divisions*. Basingstoke: Macmillan

Payne, S. (2006). Mental health, poverty and social exclusion' in Pantazis, C., Gordon, D. and Levitas, R. (eds) *Poverty and social exclusion in Britain: the millennium survey*. Bristol: Policy Press

Peel, M.R. (1996). 'Effects on asylum seekers of illtreatment in Zaire.' *British Medical Journal*, 312, 293–294.

Perry, B.L. and Wright, E.R. (2006). 'The sexual partnerships of people with serious mental illness.' *Journal of Sex Research*, **43** (2) 174–181

Phelan, E. and Norris, M. (2008). 'Neo-corporatist governance of homeless services in Dublin: reconceptualization, incorporation and exclusion.' *Critical Social Policy*, **28** (1) 51–73

Phillimore, J. and Goodson, L. (2008). *New migrants in the UK: education, training, employment, policy and practice*. Stoke-on-Trent: Trentham

Phillimore, J., Ergun, E., Goodson, L. and Hennessy, D. (2007). *They do not understand the problem I have: refugee well being and mental health*. York: Joseph Rowntree Foundation

Phillipson, C. (1998). *Reconstructing old age: new agendas in social theory and practice*. London: Sage

Pilgrim, D. (2007). *Key concepts in mental health*. London: Sage

Platt, L. (2007a). *Poverty and ethnicity in the UK*. Abingdon: Policy Press

Platt, L. (2007b). 'Child poverty, employment and ethnicity in the UK: the role and limitations of policy.' *European Societies*, **9** (2) 175–199

Popay, J. and Jones, G. (1990) 'Patterns of Health and Illness Among Lone Parents', *Journal of Social Policy*, 19(4) 499–534.

Postman, N. (1983). *The disappearance of childhood.* London: W.H. Allen.

Powell, M. (ed.) (2000). *New Labour, new welfare state?* Bristol: Policy Press

Price, D. (2006). "The poverty of older people in the UK.' *Journal of Social Work Practice*, **20** (3) 251–266

Pritchard, J. (2001). *Good practice with vulnerable adults.* London: Jessica Kingsley

Pritchard, J. (2006). *Putting a stop to the abuse of older people.* London: Help the Aged

Putman, R. (2000). *Bowling alone: the collapse and revival of American community.* New York: Simon and Schuster

Rajkonen, O., Laaksonen, M. and Karvonen, S. (2005). 'The contribution of lone parenthood and economic difficulties to smoking.' *Social Science and Medicine*, **61** (1) 211–216

Ram, B. and Hou, F. (2003). 'Changes in family structure and child outcomes: the roles of economic and familial resources.' Policy Studies Journal, **31** (3) 309–330

Reacroft, J. (2007). *Like any other child? Children and families in the asylum process.* London: Barnardos

Refugee Council (2007). The truth about asylum. London: British Refugee Council

Revill, J. (2007). 'No one is left without care if they are poor'. *The Observer*, 24 June, 16

Riddell, M. (2006). '40 years after Cathy Come Home.' *The Observer*, 10 November, 1

Riddell, M. (2007). 'But not everyone can grow old gracefully.' *The Observer*, 10 June, 35

Roberts, E. (2000). *Age discrimination in health and social care.* London: Kings Fund

Robinson, V. and Segrott, J. (2002). *Understanding the decision making of asylum seekers.* London: Home Office

Roche, M. (2004). 'Complicated problems, complicated solutions? Homelessness and joined-up policy responses.' *Social Policy and Administration*, **38** (7) 758–774

Rogers, A. (1997). 'Vulnerability, health and healthcare.' *Journal of Advanced Nursing*, **26**, 65–72

Rogers, A. and Pilgrim, D. (2003). *Mental health and inequality.* Basingstoke: Palgrave Macmillan

Rogers, A. and Pilgrim, D. (2005). *A sociology of mental health and illness*, 3rd edn. Maidenhead: Open University Press

Rokach, A. (2004). 'The lonely and homeless causes and consequences.' *Social Indicators Research*, **69** (1) 37–50

Rokach, A. (2005). 'Private lives in public places: loneliness of the homeless.' *Social Indicators Research*, **72** (2) 99–114

Rowe, M., Kloos, B., Chinman, M., Davidson, L. and Boyle Cross, A. (2001). 'Homelessness, mental illness and citizenship.' *Social Policy and Administration*, **35** (10) 14–31

Rummery, K. (2006). 'Disabled citizens and social exclusion: the role of direct payments.' *Policy and Politics*, **34** (4) 633–650

Sales, R. (2002). 'The deserving and the undeserving? Refugees, asylum seekers and welfare in Britain.' *Critical Social Policy*, **22** (3) 456–478

Sanatana, P. (2002). 'Poverty, social exclusion and health in Portugal.' *Social Science and Medicine*, **55** (1) 33–35

Sapey, B. (2004). 'Disability and social exclusion in the information society' in Swain, J., French, S., Barnes, C. and Thomas, C. (eds) *Disabling barriers, enabling environments.* London: Sage in association with the Open University

Schulman, G. and Hammer, J. (1988). 'Social characteristics, the diagnosis of mental disorders and the change from DSMII to DSMIII'. *Sociology of Health and Illness*, **10**, (4) 543–560

Shelter (2006). *Street homelessness*. London: Shelter

Shelter (2007a). *Vulnerable groups*. London: Shelter

Shelter (2007b). *Older people and housing*. London: Shelter

Shelter (2008). *About us*. London: Shelter

Shinn, M. (2007). 'International homelessness: policy, socio-cultural and individual perspectives.' *Journal of Social Issues*, **63** (3) 657–677

Simm, C., Aston, J., Williams, C., Hill, D., Bellis, A. and Meager, N. (2007). Organisations' responses to the Disability Discrimination Act. DWP Research Report DWPRR 210

Simpson, A. (2006). 'Promoting the health of looked-after children.' *Community Practitioner*, **79** (7) 217–220

Sloboda, Z. (1999). 'Problems of the future? Drug use amongst vulnerable groups of young people.' Drugs: *Education, Prevention and Policy*, **6** (2) 195–210

Sloper, P. and Quilgars, D. (2002). 'Mortality' in Bradshaw, J. (ed.) *The well-being of children in the UK*. London: Save the Children Fund

Smart, C., Grimshaw, R., McDowell, C. and Crosland, B. (2007). *Reporting asylum: The UK press and the effectiveness of PCC guidelines*. London: Information Centre about Asylum and Refugees in the UK

Smith, A. and Twomey, B. (2002). 'Labour market experiences of people with disabilities.' *Labour Market Trends*, 415–427

Smith, R. (2007). *Youth justice: ideas, policy and practice*, 2nd edn. Devon: Willan Publishing

Social Exclusion Taskforce (2007). *Reaching out: an action plan on social exclusion*. London: Cabinet Office

Social Exclusion Unit (1999). *Teenage pregnancy*. London: SEU

Social Exclusion Unit (2002). (www.socialexclusionunit.gov.uk) accessed 3/03/03

Social Exclusion Unit (2004a). *Breaking the cycle: taking stock of progress and priorities for the future*. London: Office of the Deputy Prime Minister

Social Exclusion Unit (2004b). Tackling social exclusion: taking stock and looking to the future – emerging findings. London: Office of the Deputy Prime Minister

Social Exclusion Unit (2004c). *Mental health and social exclusion*. London: Office of the Deputy Prime Minister

Social Exclusion Unit (2004d). *Action on mental health*. London: Office of the Deputy Prime Minister

Social Exclusion Unit (2005). *Excluded older people: Social Exclusion Unit interim report*. London: Office of the Deputy Prime Minister

Social Exclusion Unit (2006). *A sure start to later life: ending inequalities for older people*. London: Office of the Deputy Prime Minister

Spicer, N. (2008). 'Places of exclusion and inclusion: asylum-seeker and refugee experience of neighbourhoods in the UK.' *Journal of Ethnic and Migration Studies*, **34** (3) 491–510

Spieker, B. and Stetal, J. (2002). 'Sex between people with "mental retardation": an ethical evaluation.' *Journal of Moral Education*, **31** (2) 155–169

Spiers, J. (2000). 'New perspectives on vulnerability using emic and etic approaches.' *Journal of Advanced Nursing*, **31** (3) 715–721

Steeman, E., Godderis, J., Grypdonck, M., De Bal, N. and Dierckx de Casterle, B. (2007). 'Living with dementia from the perspective of older people: is it a positive story?' *Aging and Mental Health,* **11** (2) 119–130

Stephens, S. (1995). 'Children and the politics of culture in "Late Capitalism"' in Stephens S. (ed.) *Children and the politics of culture. Princeton,* N.J: Princeton University Press

Stevens, A. (2004). 'Closer to home: a critique of British Government policy towards accommodating learning disabled people in their own homes.' *Critical Social Policy,* **24**, (2) 233–254

Stevens, A., Berto, D., Frick, U., Kerschl, V., McSweeney, T., Schaaf, S., Tartari, M. and Werdenich, W. (2007). 'The victimization of dependent drug users; findings from a European study, UK.' *European Journal of Criminology,* **4** (4) 385–408

Stevenson, J. and Willott, J. (2007). 'The aspiration and access to higher education of teenage refugees in the UK.' *Compare,* **37** (5) 671–687

Stewart, I. and Vaitilingham, R. (2004). *Seven ages of man and woman: a look at life in Britain in the second Elizabethan era*: Swindon: ERSC

Sutton, L., Smith, N., Dearden, C. and Middleton, S. (2007). *A child's-eye view of social difference.* York: Joseph Rowntree Foundation.

Swain, J., French, S., Barnes, C. and Thomas, C. (eds) (2004). *Disabling barriers, enabling environments.* London: Sage in association with the Open University

Szasz, T. (1961). *The myth of mental illness: Foundations of a theory of person conduct.* New York: Harper and Row

Taylor-Gooby, P. (2005). 'Uncertainty, trust and pensions: the case of the current UK reforms.' *Social Policy and Administration,* **39** (3) 217–232

Temko, N. and Campbell, D. (2006). 'Parents "powerless to bring up their own children"'. *The Observer,* 12 November, 4

Thomas, P. (2004). 'The experience of disabled people as customers in the owner occupation market.' *Housing Studies,* **19** (5) 781–794

Tikly, L., Osler, A. and Hill, J. (2005). 'The ethnic minority achievement grant: a critical analysis.' *Journal of Education Policy,* **20** (3) 283–312

Timimi, S. (2004). 'Rethinking childhood depression.' *British Medical Journal,* **329** 1394–1396

Tinklin, T., Ridell, S. and Wilson, A. (2004). 'Policy provision for disabled students in higher education in Scotland and England: the current state of play.' *Studies in Higher Education,* **29** (5) 637–657

Tomassini, C., Glaser, K., Broese van Groenou, M.I. and Grundy, E. (2004). 'Living arrangements amongst older people: an overview of older people in Europe and the USA.' *Population Trends,* **115** 24–34

Tregakis, C. (2002). 'Social model theory: the story so far...' *Disability and Society,* **17** (4) 457–470

Twigg, J. (2006). *The body in health and social care.* Basingstoke: Palgrave Macmillan

UNHCR (2007). *Protection, emergencies, returning home, building a new life.* London: UN Refugee Agency

Union of Physically Impaired against Segregation (1976). *Fundamental principles of disability.* London: Union of Physically Impaired against Segregation van de Ven, L., Post, M., de Witte, L. and van den Heuvel, W. (2005). 'It takes two to tango: the inegration of people with disabilities into society.' *Disability and Society*, **20** (3) 311–329

van der Laan Boumadoff, W. (2007). 'Involuntary isolation: ethnic preferences and residential segregation.' *Journal of Urban Affairs*, **29** (3) 289–309

Van Hoten, D. and Bellemakers, C. (2002). 'Equal citizenship for all. disability policies in the Netherlands: empowerment of marginals.' *Disability and Society*, **17** (2) 171–185

Vera-Sanso, P. (2006). 'Experiences in old age: a South Indian example of how functional age is socially structured.' *Oxford Development Studies*, **34** (4) 457–472

Vincent, J.A. (2006). 'Age and old age ' in Payne, G. (ed.) *Social divisions*. Basingstoke: Macmillan

Walker, A. (1992). 'The social construction of dependency in old age' in Loney, M., Bocock, R., Clarker, J., Cochrane, A., Graham, P. and Wilson, M. (eds) *The state of the market*. London:Sage/Open University

Wanless, D. (2006). *Securing good care for older people: taking a long-term view*. London: Kings Fund

Wates, M. (2004). 'Righting the family picture: disability and family life' in Swain, J., French, S., Barnes, C. and Thomas, C. (eds) *Disabling barriers, enabling environments*. London: Sage in association with the Open University

Watson, K. (2007). 'Language, education and ethnicity: whose rights will prevail in an age of globalisation?' *International Journal of Educational Development*, **27** (3) 252–265

Watson, N. (2002). 'Well, I know this is going to sound very strange to you, but I don't see myself as a disabled person: identity and disability.' *Disability and Society*, **17** (5) 509–527

Weitoft, G.R., Burstrom, B. and Rosen, M. (2004). 'Premature mortality among lone fathers and childless men.' *Social Science and Medicine*, **59** (7) 1449–1459

White, K. (2002). *An introduction to the sociology of health and illness*. London: Sage

Whitehead, M., Burstrom, B. and Diderichsen, F. (2000). 'Social policies and the pathways to inequalities in health: a comparative analysis of lone mothers in Britain and Sweden.' *Social Science and Medicine*, **50** (2) 255–270

Wickrama, K.A.S., Lorenz, F.O., Conger, R.D., Elder Jr, G.H., Todd Abraham, W. and Fang, S.A. (2006). 'Changes in family financial circumstances and the physical health of married and recently divorced mothers.' *Social Science and Medicine*, **63** (1) 123–136

Williams, A., Ylanne, V. and Wadleigh, P.M. (2007). 'Selling the "Elixir of Life': images of the elderly in an Olivio advertising campaign.' *Journal of Aging Studies*, **21** (1) 1–21

Wistow, R. and Schneider, J. (2007). 'Employment support agencies in the UK: current operation and future development needs.' *Health and Social Care in the Community*, **15** (2) 128–135

Wolf, D.A., Mendes de Leon, C.F. and Glass, T.A. (2007). 'Trends in rates of onset of and recovery from disability at older ages: 1982-1994.' *Journal of Gerontology. Series B., psychological sciences and social sciences,* **62** (1) 3–10

Wong, Y-L. I., Metzendor, D. and Min, S-Y. (2006). 'Neighborhood experiences and community integration: perspectives from mental health providers and consumers.' *Social Work in Mental Health*, **4** (3) 45–59

World Health Organization (2001). *Declaration on young people and alcohol*. Geneva: WHO

Wright, E.R., Wright, D.E., Perry, B.L. and Foote-Ardah, C.E. (2007). 'Stigma and the sexual isolation of people with serious mental illness.' *Social Problems*, **54** (1) 78–98

www.socialexclusionunit.gov.uk

www.cabinetoffice.gov.uk/social_exclusion_task_force/

Zaidi, A. and Gustafsson, B. (2007). 'Income mobility among the elderly in Sweden during the 1990s.' International Journal of Social Welfare, **16** (1) 84–93

Zetter, R., Griffiths, D. and Sigona, N. (2005). 'Social capital or social inclusion? The impact of asylum seeker dispersal on UK refugee community organisations.' *Community Development Journal*, **40** (2) 169–181

Index

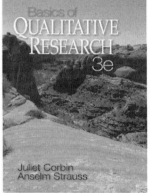

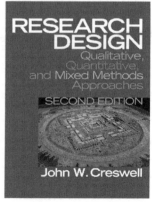

Supporting researchers for more than forty years

Research methods have always been at the core of SAGE's publishing. Sara Miller McCune founded SAGE in 1965 and soon after, she published SAGE's first methods book, Public Policy Evaluation. A few years later, she launched the Quantitative Applications in the Social Sciences series – affectionately known as the "little green books".

Always at the forefront of developing and supporting new approaches in methods, SAGE published early groundbreaking texts and journals in the fields of qualitative methods and evaluation.

Today, more than forty years and two million little green books later, SAGE continues to push the boundaries with a growing list of more than 1,200 research methods books, journals, and reference works across the social, behavioral, and health sciences.

From qualitative, quantitative, mixed methods to evaluation, SAGE is the essential resource for academics and practitioners looking for the latest methods by leading scholars.

www.sagepublications.com

The Qualitative Research Kit

Edited by Uwe Flick

Read sample chapters online now!

Doing Ethnographic and Observational Research — Michael Angrosino

Using Visual Data in Qualitative Research — Marcus Banks

Doing Focus Groups — Rosaline Barbour

Designing Qualitative Research — Uwe Flick

Managing Quality in Qualitative Research — Uwe Flick

Analyzing Qualitative Data — Graham Gibbs

Doing Interviews — Steinar Kvale

Doing Conversation, Discourse and Document Analysis — Tim Rapley

The SAGE Qualitative Research Kit

www.sagepub.co.uk